Praise for the "Kids Love" Guide

On-Air Personality Comments (Television Interviews)

"The great thing about these books is that your whole family actually lives these adventures" – **(WKRC-TV**, Cincinnati)

"Very helpful to lots of families when the kids say, I'm bored...and I don't want to go to same places again!" – **(WISH-TV**, Indianapolis)

"Dividing the state into many sections, the book has something for everyone...everywhere." – **(WLVT-TV**, Pennsylvania)

"These authors know first-hand that it's important to find hands-on activities that engage your children..." **(WBNS-TV**, Columbus)

"You spent more than 1000 hours doing this research for us, that's really great – we just have to pick up the book and it's done..."
(WTVR-TV, Richmond)

"A family that's a great source for travel ideas..."
(WBRA-TV, Roanoke)

"What a great idea...this book needed to be done a long time ago!"
(WKYT-TV, Lexington)

"A fabulous idea...places to travel that your kids will enjoy"
(WOOD-TV, Grand Rapids)

"The Zavatskys call it a dream come true, running their own business while keeping the family together. Their goal, encourage other parents to create special family travel memories." - **(WLVT-TV,** Pennsylvania)

"It's a wonderful book, and as someone who has been to a lot of these places...you hit it right on the money!" – **(WKRC-TV**, Cincinnati)

Praise for the "Kids Love" Guidebook travel series
Customer Comments (actual letters on file)

"I wanted to tell you how helpful all your books have been to my family of 6. I rarely find books that cater to families with kids. I have your Indiana, Ohio, Kentucky, Michigan, and Pennsylvania books. I don't want to miss any of the new books that come out. Keep up the great ideas. The books are fantastic. I have shown them to tons of my friends. They love them, too." – H.M.

"I bought the Ohio and Indiana books yesterday and what a blessing these are for us!!! We love taking our grandsons on Grammie & Papaw trips thru the year and these books are making it soooo much easier to plan. The info is complete and full of ideas. Even the layout of the book is easy to follow...I just wanted to thank you for all your work in developing these books for us..." – G.K

"I have purchased your book. My grandchildren and I have gone to many of the places listed in your book. They mark them off as we visit them. We are looking forward to seeing many more. It is their favorite thing to look at book when they come over and find new places to explore. Thank you for publishing this book!" - B.A.

"At a retail price of under $15.00, any of the books would be well worth buying even for a one-time only vacation trip. Until now, when the opportunity arose for a day or weekend trip with the kids I was often at a loss to pick a destination that I could be sure was convenient, educational, child-friendly, and above all, fun. Now I have a new problem: How in the world will we ever be able to see and do all the great ideas listed in this book? I'd better get started planning our next trip right away. At least I won't have to worry about where we're going or what to do when we get there!" – VA Homeschool Newsletter

"My family and I used this book this summer to explore Ohio! We lived here nearly our entire life and yet over half the book we never knew existed. These people really know what kids love! Highly recommended for all parents, grandparents, etc." – Barnes and Noble website reviewer

KIDS ♥ LOVE OHIO

A Family Travel Guide to Exploring "Kid-Tested" Places in Ohio...Year Round!

George & Michele Zavatsky

Dedicated to the Families of Ohio

For the latest major updates corresponding to the pages in this book visit our website:

www.KidsLoveTravel.com

Although the authors have exhaustively researched all sources to ensure accuracy and completeness of the information contained in this book, we assume no responsibility for errors, inaccuracies, omissions or any other inconsistency herein. Any slights against any entries or organizations are unintentional.

❑ *REMEMBER: Museum exhibits change frequently. Check the site's website before you visit to note any changes. Also, HOURS and ADMISSIONS are subject to change at the owner's discretion. If you are tight on time or money, check the attraction's website or call before you visit.*

❑ *INTERNET PRECAUTION: All websites mentioned in KIDS LOVE OHIO have been checked for appropriate content. However, due to the fast-changing nature of the Internet, we strongly urge parents to preview any recommended sites and to always supervise their children when on-line.*

ISBN-13: 978-0-9726854-7-4
ISBN-10: 0-9726854-7-2

KIDS ♥ OHIO ™   Kids Love Publications

TABLE OF CONTENTS

General Information...Preface
(Here you'll find "How to Use This Book", maps, tour ideas, city listings, etc.)

Chapter 1 – CENTRAL AREA (C).......................................1

Chapter 2 – CENTRAL EAST AREA (CE)............................29

Chapter 3 – CENTRAL WEST AREA (CW).........................63

Chapter 4 – NORTH CENTRAL (NC)...............................89

Chapter 5 – NORTH EAST AREA (NE)............................119

Chapter 6 – NORTH WEST AREA (NW)..........................155

Chapter 7 – SOUTH AREA (S).......................................169

Chapter 8 – SOUTH WEST AREA (SW)..........................193

Chapter 9 – SEASONAL & SPECIAL EVENTS..................217

Master Index...245

Activity Index...255
(Amusements, Animals & Farms, Museums, Outdoors, State History, Tours, etc.)

State Map

(With Major Routes and Cities Marked)

Chapter Area Map

CITY INDEX (Listed by City & Area)

Akron, NE
Alliance, CE
Amelia, SW
Amherst, NE
Andover, NE
Archbold, NW
Ashtabula, NE
Ashland, NC
Ashville, C
Athens, S
Aurora, NE
Bainbridge, S
Barnesville, CE
Bath, NE
Beavercreek, CW
Bellefontaine, CW
Bellevue, NC
Belmont, CE
Belpre, S
Berea, NE
Berlin, CE
Berlin Center, NE
Big Prairie, CE
Blue Rock, CE
Bluffton, NW
Bolivar, CE
Bowling Green, NW
Brecksville, NE
Brookpark, NE
Brunswick, NE
Bucyrus, NC
Burton, NE
Butler, NC
Cadiz, CE
Cambridge, CE
Canal Fulton, CE
Canal Winchester, C
Canfield, NE
Canton, CE
Canton, North, CE
Carrollton, CE

Catawba, NC
Centerburg, C
Centerville, CW
Chardon, NE
Chillicothe, S
Cincinnati, SW
Coshocton, CE
Columbiana, CE
Circleville, C
Cleveland, NE
Clifton, CW
College Corner, SW
Columbus, C
Cortland, NE
Corwin, SW
Coshocton, CE
Covington, KY, SW
Cumberland, CE
Dayton, CW
Defiance, NW
Delaware, C
Dellroy, CE
Delphos, NW
Dennison, CE
Dover, CE
Dublin, C
East Liverpool, CE
Eaton, CW
Edenton, SW
Elmore, NC
Fairborn, CW
Fairfield,   SW
Fairport Harbor, NE
Fayette, NW
Findlay, NW
Flat Rock, NC
Fort Recovery, CW
Fostoria, NW
Frazeysburg, CE
Fremont, NC
Gallipolis, S

Geneva / Lake, NE
Georgetown, SW
Glenford, C
Glouster, S
Gnadenhutten, CE
Grand Rapids, NW
Grandview, C
Greenville, CW
Grove City, C
Groveport, C
Hamilton, SW
Hartville, CE
Harveysburg, SW
Heath, C
Hebron, C
Hilliard, C
Hillsboro, SW
Hinckley, NE
Huber Heights, CW
Jackson, S
Jefferson, NE
Kent, NE
Kettering, CW
Kings Mills, SW
Kirtland, NE
Lake Milton, NE
Lakeside, NC
Lakeview, CW
Lancaster, C
Latham, S
Laurelville, S
Lebanon, SW
Lexington, NC
Lima, NW
Lisbon, CE
Litchfield, NE
Lithopolis, C
Lockington, CW
Logan, S
London, C
Lorain, NC

CITY INDEX (Listed by City & Area)

Loudonville, NC
Loveland, SW
Lucas, NC
Ludlow Falls, CW
Magnolia , CE
Mansfield, NC
Marblehead, NC
Marietta, S
Marion, C
Mason, SW
Maumee, NW
McArthur, S
Medina, NE
Mentor, NE
Miamisburg, CW
Middlefield, NE
Milan, NC
Milford, SW
Milford Center, C
Millersburg, CE
Millersport, C
Minster, CW
Morrow, SW
Mount Vernon, C
Mt. Gilead, C
Mt. Sterling, C
Mt. Vernon, C
Murray City, S
Nashport, CE
Nelsonville, S
New Bremen, CW
New Concord, CE
New Lexington, C
New Philadelphia, CE
Newark, C
Newbury, NE
Niles, NE
Norwich, CE
Oak Hill, S
Oberlin, NC
Obetz, C

Okeana, SW
Oregon, NW
Oregonia, SW
Orrville, CE
Oxford, SW
Painesville, NE
Pataskala, C
Pedro, S
Peebles, S
Peninsula, NE
Perrysburg, NW
Perrysville, NC
Pickerington, C
Piqua, CW
Point Pleasant, SW
Port Clinton, NC
Portage, NE
Portsmouth, S
Powell, C
Powhatan Point, CE
Put-in-Bay, NC
Ravenna, NE
Reedsville, S
Rio Grande, S
Ripley, SW
Rittman, NC
Rockbridge, S
Sagamore Hills, NE
Sandusky, NC
Sharonville, SW
Springfield, CW
St. Mary's, CW
St. Paris, CW
Steubenville, CE
Stockport, S
Sugarcreek, CE
Sugar Grove, C
Swanton, NW
Tiffen, NC
Toledo, NW
Trenton, SW

Trotwood, CW
Troy, CW
Twinsburg, NE
Upper Sandusky, NC
Urbana, CW
Utica, C
Van Buren, NW
Vandalia, CW
Vermillion, NC
Vienna, NE
Vincent, S
Walnut Creek, CE
Wapakoneta, CW
Warren, NE
Washington CH, SW
Waterville, NW
Waverly, S
Waynesville, SW
Wellington, NC
Wellston, S
West Liberty, CW
West Portsmouth, S
Westerville, C
Wilberforce, CW
Willard, NC
Wilmington, SW
Wilmot, CE
Winesburg, CE
Worthington, C
Wooster, CE
Xenia, CW
Yellow Springs, CW
Youngstown, NE
Zaleski, S
Zanesfield, CW
Zanesville, CE
Zoar, CE

Cities appearing in *italics* occur
only in the Seasonal Chapter

Acknowledgements

We are most thankful to be blessed with our parents, Barbara (Darrall) Callahan & George and Catherine Zavatsky who help us every way they can – researching, proofing and babysitting. More importantly, they are great sounding boards and offer unconditional support. So many places around Ohio remind us of family vacations years ago…

We also want to express our thanks to the many Convention & Visitor Bureaus' staff for providing the attention to detail that helps to complete a project. We felt very welcome during our travels in Ohio and are proud to call it home!

Our own kids, Jenny and Daniel, were delightful and fun children during our trips across the state. What a joy it is to be their parents…we couldn't do it without them as our "kid-testers"!

We both sincerely thank each other – our partnership has created an even greater business/personal "marriage" with lots of exciting moments, laughs, and new adventures in life woven throughout. Above all, we praise the Lord for His so many blessings through the last few years.

We think Ohio is a wonderful, friendly area of the country with more activities than you could imagine. Our sincere wish is that this book will help everyone "fall in love" with Ohio.

In a Hundred Years…
It will not matter, The size of my bank account…
The kind of house that I lived in, the kind of car that I drove…
But what will matter is…
That the world may be different
Because I was important in the life of a child.

- *author unknown*

HOW TO USE THIS BOOK

If you are excited about discovering Ohio, this is the book for you and your family! We've spent over a thousand hours doing all the scouting, collecting and compiling (*and most often visiting!*) so that you could spend less time searching and more time having fun.

Here are a few hints to make your adventures run smoothly:

❑ Consider the **child's age** before deciding to take a visit.

❑ Know **directions** and parking. Call ahead (or visit the company's website) if you have questions *and* bring this book. Also, don't forget your camera! *(please honor rules regarding use).*

❑ **Estimate the duration** of the trip. Bring small surprises (favorite juice boxes) travel books, and toys.

❑ Call ahead for **reservations** or details, if necessary.

❑ Most listings are **closed major holidays** unless noted.

❑ Make a **family "treasure chest"**. Decorate a big box or use an old popcorn tin. Store memorabilia from a fun outing, journals, pictures, brochures and souvenirs. Once a year, look through the "treasure chest" and reminisce. "Kids Love Travel Memories!" is an excellent travel journal & scrapbook that your family can create. *(See the order form in back of this book).*

❑ Plan **picnics** along the way. Many state history sites and state parks are scattered throughout Ohio. Allow time for a rural /scenic route to take advantage of these free picnic facilities.

❑ Some activities, especially tours, require **groups** of 10 or more. To participate, you may either ask to be part of another tour group or get a group together yourself (neighbors, friends, organizations). If you arrange a group outing, most places offer discounts.

❑ For the latest **updates** corresponding to the pages in this book, visit our website: **www.KidsLoveTravel.com.**

❑ Each chapter represents an area of the state. Each listing is further identified by city, zip code, and place/event name. Our popular **Activity Index** in the back of the book **lists places by Activity Heading** (i.e. State History, Tours, Outdoors, Museums, etc.).

MISSION STATEMENT

At first glance, you may think that this is a book that just lists hundreds of places to travel. While it is true that we've invested thousands of hours of exhaustive research (*and drove over 4000 miles in Ohio*) to prepare this travel resource…just listing places to travel is not the mission statement of these projects.

As children, Michele and I were able to travel extensively throughout the United States. We consider these family times some of the greatest memories we cherish today. We, quite frankly, felt that most children had this opportunity to travel with their family as we did. However, as we became adults and started our own family, we found that this wasn't necessarily the case. We continually heard friends express several concerns when deciding how to spend "quality" and "quantity" family time. 1) What to do? 2) Where to do it? 3) How much will it cost? 4) How do I know that my kids will enjoy it?

Interestingly enough, as we compare our experiences with our families when we were kids, many of our fondest memories were not made at an expensive attraction, but rather when it was least expected.

It is our belief and mission statement that if you as a family will study and use the contained information to create family memories, these memories will grow a stronger, tighter family. Our ultimate mission statement is, that your children will develop a love and a passion for quality family experiences that they can pass to another generation of family travelers.

We thank you for purchasing this book, and we hope to see you on the road (*and hear your travel stories!*)   God bless your journeys and happy exploring!

George, Michele, Jenny and Daniel

General State Agency & Recreation Information

Call *(or visit the websites)* for the services of interest. Request to be added to their mailing lists.

- ❑ **ArtsinOhio.com**
- ❑ Ohio Division of Travel & Tourism (800) BUCKEYE or **www.ohiotourism.com**
- ❑ **C** - Columbus Metro Parks (614) 508-8000
- ❑ **C** - Columbus Recreation & Parks (614) 645-3300
- ❑ **C** - Greater Columbus CVB (800) 345-4FUN or **www.visitcolumbus.org**
- ❑ **C** - Licking County Parks (740) 587-2535 or **www.msmisp.com/lpd**
- ❑ **CE** - Canton Park District (330) 489-3015
- ❑ **CE** - Carroll County CVB (877) 727-0103 or **www.carrollcountyohio.com**
- ❑ **CE** - Tuscarawas County CVB (800) 527-3387 or **www.neohiotravel.com**
- ❑ **CW** - Dayton Metroparks (937) 275-PARK
- ❑ **CW** - Greene County CVB (800) 733-9109 or **www.greenecountyohio.org**
- ❑ **CW** - Greene County Parks (937) 562-7440 or **www.co.greene.oh.us/parks.htm**
- ❑ **NC** - Lorain County Metroparks (440) 45805121 or **www.loraincountymetroparks.com**
- ❑ **NC** - Ottawa County Visitors Bureau (800) 441-1271 or **www.lake-erie.com**
- ❑ **NC** - Port Clinton Park & Rec (419) 732-2206
- ❑ **NC** - Sandusky County Parks (419) 334-4495
- ❑ **NC** - Sandusky/Erie County VCB (800) 255-ERIE or **www.buckeyenorth.com**
- ❑ **NE** - Akron Rec Bureau (330) 375-2804 or **www.ci.akron.oh.us/rec.html**
- ❑ **NE** - Ashtabula County Metroparks (800) 3 DROP-IN

- **NE** - Convention & Visitors Bureau of Greater Cleveland (800) 321-1001 or **www.travelcleveland.com**
- **NE** - Cleveland Metroparks (216) 351-6300
- **NE** - Lake Metroparks (800) 669-9226
- **NE** - Medina County Parks (330) 722-9364
- **NE** - Summit County Metroparks (330) 867-5511
- **NW** - Lima City Parks & Rec (419) 221-5195
- **NW** - Lima/Johnny Appleseed Metroparks (419) 221-1232
- **NW** - Toledo Area Metroparks (419) 535-3050
- **SC** - Ross County-Chillicothe CVB (800) 413-4118
- **SW** - Butler County Metroparks (513) 867-5835
- **SW** - Cincinnati Parks Department (513) 352-4080
- **SW** - Cincinnati Recreation Department (513) 352-4001
- **SW** - Cincinnati CVB (800) CINCYUSA or **www.cincyusa.com**
- **SW** - Hamilton County Park District (513) 521-PARK
- Ohio Department of Natural Resources, (877) 4BOATER, (800) WILDLIFE, or **www.dnr.state.oh.us/odnr**
- Ohio Campground Owner's Association (614) 764-0279
- Ohio State Parks (614) 466-0652 or **www.dnr.state.oh.us/parks**
- Ohio Camping (800) 376-4847
- National Camping Information **www.gocampingamerica.com**
- Muskingum Watershed Conservancy District (877) 363-8500 or **www.mwcdlakes.com**. Well-maintained boating, swimming and fishing lakes in CE Ohio.
- State Park Lodges & Resorts (800) 282-7275 or **www.ohiostateparks.org**.

RENT-A-CAMP STATE PARK PROGRAMS

The State Parks offer camping, horseback riding, boating, fishing, golfing, hiking, winter sports, and vacation planning assistance. The camping facilities can be lodges, cabins, or tents. The ODNR offers Rent-A-Camp. It is a unique program for beginning or infrequent campers to enjoy the experience of camping without purchasing the equipment. The cost begins at $20 per night ($45.00 per night for new Camper Cabins). You will arrive at your campsite to find a 10 x 12-foot sleeping tent already set up complete with a dining canopy. Inside are two cots, sleeping pads, cooler, propane stove, lantern, broom, dustpan and welcome mat. Outside, you will find a fire ring and picnic table. This way of camping allows you to pick up and go without packing up a lot of gear. LOG CABIN STYLE CAMPER CABINS sleep up to four adults. Amenities vary by location and may include A/C or a ceiling fan, gas fireplace, TV, compact frig and a microwave oven. The campsites are limited, so make your plans early and call to make your reservation (866) OHIOPARKS.

SKIING/TOBOGGANING

Usually December – early March. Ski Conditions, (800) BUCKEYE. Or contact local MetroParks or Ohio Department of Natural Resources for cross-country skiing.

- **C** - Clearfork – (800) 237-5673, Butler. **www.skiclearfork.com**.
- **C** - Snow Trails – (800) DEC-SNOW or (800) OHIO-SKI, Mansfield. **www.snowtrails.com**.
- **CW** - Mad River Mountain – (937) 599-1015 or (800) 231-7669, Bellefontaine. **www.skimadriver.com**
- **NE** - Alpine Valley - (440) 729-9775, Chesterland. **www.alpinevalleyohio.com**.
- **NE** - Boston Mills/Brandywine – (800) USKI241, Peninsula or Northfield. **www.bmbw.com**. (snowboarding capital of Ohio)
- **SC** - Spicy Run - (740) 493-2599, Latham. **www.spicyrun.com**

Skiing/Tobogganing (cont.)

- **CE** - Bear Creek Resort Ranch KOA, 3232 Downing St. SW, East Sparta. (330) 484-3901. Ohio's longest, fastest, and safest way to toboggan. Newly rebuilt twin half-mile-long refrigerated toboggan chutes operate 40 degrees or colder, snow or no snow. A bus takes riders and toboggans back to the top so there's no walking and hauling the toboggan back up the hill.
- **NE** – Cleveland Metroparks Chalet in Mill Stream Run Reservation, Strongsville. (440) 572-9990. Toboggan chutes 1000 feet long and 42 feet tall.

COLLEGE ATHLETICS

- **SW** - University of Cincinnati - (513) 556-CATS or **www.ucbearcats.com**. 18 sports. Fall, Winter, Spring.
- **SW** - Xavier University, Cintas Center - (513) 745-3900 or **www.xu.edu**. Volleyball, basketball.

CANOEING

SW - Morgan's Canoe - SR 350, Oregonia (Cincy) - (800) WE-CANOE. **www.morgancanoe.com**.

Check out these businesses / services in your area for tour ideas:

AIRPORTS

All children love to visit the airport! Why not take a tour and understand all the jobs it takes to run an airport? Tour the terminal, baggage claim, gates and security / currency exchange. Maybe you'll even get to board a plane.

ANIMAL SHELTERS

Great for the would-be pet owner. Not only will you see many cats and dogs available for adoption, but a guide will show you the clinic and explain the needs of a pet. Be prepared to have the children "fall in love" with one of the animals while they are there!

BANKS

Take a "behind the scenes" look at automated teller machines, bank vaults and drive-thru window chutes. You may want to take this tour and then open a savings account for your child.

CITY HALLS

Halls of Fame, City Council Chambers & Meeting Room, Mayor's Office and famous statues.

ELECTRIC COMPANY / POWER PLANTS

Modern science has created many ways to generate electricity today, but what really goes on with the "flip of a switch". Because coal can be dirty, wear old, comfortable clothes. Coal furnaces heat water, which produces steam, that propels turbines, that drives generators, that make electricity.

FIRE STATIONS

Many Open Houses in October, Fire Prevention Month. Take a look into the life of the firefighters servicing your area and try on their gear. See where they hang out, sleep and eat. Hop aboard a real-life fire engine truck and learn fire safety too.

HOSPITALS

Some Children's Hospitals offer pre-surgery and general tours.

NEWSPAPERS

You'll be amazed at all the new technology. See monster printers and robotics. See samples in the layout department and maybe try to put together your own page. After seeing a newspaper made, most companies give you a free copy (dated that day) as your souvenir. National Newspaper Week is in October.

PIZZA HUT & PAPA JOHN'S
❑ Participating locations

Telephone the store manager. Best days are Monday, Tuesday and Wednesday mid-afternoon. Minimum of 10 people. Small charge per person. All children love pizza – especially when they can create their own! As the children tour the kitchen, they learn how to make a pizza, bake it, and then eat it. The admission charge generally includes lots of creatively made pizzas, beverage and coloring book.

KRISPY KREME DONUTS
❑ Participating locations

Get an "inside look" and learn the techniques that make these donuts some of our favorites! Watch the dough being made in "giant" mixers, being formed into donuts & taking a "trip" through the fryer. Seeing them being iced and topped with colorful sprinkles is always a favorite with the kids. Contact your local store manager. They prefer Monday or Tuesday. Free.

SUPERMARKETS

Kids are fascinated to go behind the scenes of the same store where Mom and Dad shop. Usually you will see them grind meat, walk into large freezer rooms, watch cakes and bread bake and receive free samples along the way. Maybe you'll even get to pet a live lobster!

TV / RADIO STATIONS

Studios, newsrooms, Fox kids clubs. Why do weathermen never wear blue clothes on TV? What makes a "DJ's" voice sound so deep & smooth?

WATER TREATMENT PLANTS

A giant science experiment! You can watch seven stages of water treatment. The favorite is usually the wall of bright buttons flashing as workers monitor the different processes.

U.S. MAIN POST OFFICES

Did you know Ben Franklin was the first Postmaster General (over 200 years ago)? Most interesting is the high-speed automated mail processing equipment. Learn how to address envelopes so they will be sent quicker (there are secrets). To make your tour more interesting, have your children write a letter to themselves and address it with colorful markers. Mail it earlier that day and they will stay interested trying to locate their letter in all the high-speed machinery.

Chapter 1
Central Area

Our Favorites...

* Al's Delicious Popcorn - Columbus
* Anthony Thomas Candy Co. - Columbus
* COSI - Columbus
* Graeter's Ice Cream Factory - Columbus
* Ohio Historical Center - Columbus
* Santa Maria - Columbus
* American Whistle - Columbus (Worthington)
* Deer Creek State Park - Mt. Sterling
* Velvet Ice Cream & Olde Mill - Utica

SLATE RUN HISTORICAL FARM

1375 SR 674 North (in Slate Run Park on SR 674), **Ashville** 43103

❑   Phone: (614) 508-8000 or (614) 833-1880
❑   Hours: Tuesday, Wednesday, Thursday 9:00am-4:00pm, Friday and Saturday 9:00am-6:00pm, Sunday 11:00am-6:00pm (June-August). Wednesday-Saturday 9:00am-4:00 pm, Sunday 11:00 am-4:00 pm (September-May). Memorial and Labor Day, Noon – 6:00 pm
❑   Admission: FREE to browse around. Small admission for special programs.
❑   Tours: Available by appointment (special prices). Metro Park open 6:30am-dusk.

This historic farm depicts life on a working family farm of the 1880's. Visitors may join in with the barnyard and household chores. All the work is done using equipment and methods of the time (some horse-powered machinery). Some of the specially scheduled programs may be: maple syrup demonstrations and production, toy making, fishing, ice cream socials, making root beer, rope making and pretend old-fashioned school. Kids love getting involved and doing chores at Slate Run. They offer nature trails, picnic grounds, and children's play facilities at the adjoining Slate Run Metro Park.

MID-OHIO HISTORICAL DOLL & TOY MUSEUM

Canal Winchester - *700 Winchester Pike (off US 33 at Gender Road, east side of Columbus), 43110. Phone: (614) 837-5573. Web: http://home.att.net/~dollmuseum/ Hours: Wednesday-Saturday 11:00am-5:00pm. (Spring - Mid December). Miscellaneous: Gift Shop, Old and New Collectibles.* As you step in the door, you will see a train display in the lobby. To your left, you will go through a door into the magical world of dolls. The collection includes rare antique dolls and toys dating from the 1700's to contemporary. Barbie fans of all ages will love the extensive Barbie collection. Boys will love the GI Joe, Disney and Lionel trains. Admission $3.00 (6 and over).

A.W. MARION STATE PARK

Circleville - *(5 miles East of Circleville off SR 23 to SR 22), 43113.* **Web:** *www.dnr.state.oh.us/parks/parks/awmarion.htm.* Phone: (740) 869-3124. 454 acres of camping, hiking trails, boating and rentals, fishing, and winter sports. The nearby floodplains of the Scioto River are adorned with a variety of wildflowers. Wildlife indigenous to the area includes fox squirrel, ring-necked pheasant, a variety of songbirds, red fox and white-tailed deer.

COLUMBUS SPORTS

COLUMBUS CREW SOCCER - Major League Soccer (Mid April – Late September). (614) 221-CREW or **www.thecrew.com.** Crew stadium (near Ohio State Fairgrounds).

COLUMBUS BLUE JACKETS HOCKEY - (614) 246-PUCK or (800) NHL-COLS or **www.bluejackets.com.** Nationwide Arena. NHL Hockey in Ohio. Look for their mascot, Stinger here and at special events. Season runs October-early April.

COLUMBUS CLIPPERS BASEBALL - (614) 462-5250 or **www.clippersbaseball.com.** Cooper Stadium. Semi-professional farm team for the New York Yankees. LouSeal is the official mascot for the Columbus Clippers. Krash is the crazy parrot who has taken the position as LouSeal's First Mate. Many post game concerts and occasional fireworks. Tickets: $3.00-$9.00. (April – Labor Day weekend)

OHIO STATE UNIVERSITY BUCKEYES - (614) 292-2524 or **www.ohiostatebuckeyes.com.** Big 10 College sports: Football, Basketball (Men's & Women's), Hockey, OSU Ice Skating, Golf, Swimming, Tennis & Volleyball.

OHIO STATE UNIVERSITY MUSEUMS

Woody Hayes Dr. & High Street (most facilities between High St. & Olentangy River - off SR 315), **Columbus** 43201

❑   Phone: (614) 292-3030
❑   Miscellaneous: The Buckeye Hall of Fame Café (casual restaurant & gameroom) is down the road 1412 Olentangy River Road. Call (614) 291-2233.

The Student Visitors Center (Room 132 Enarson Hall) provides a packet to chaperones. The self-guided tour (with tour brochure for kids) includes information about ten specific locations on campus, is interactive and suggests activities that the kids can do as they move through campus. It asks questions at each stop geared towards kids in order to get them more acquainted with the university. A completed tour should take about 1 - 1½ hours.

Many other "add-on" Tour Options are available:

ATHLETIC FACILITY TOURS – Value City Arena, Monday-Friday on non-event days between. 9:00am-3:30pm. 60 minutes. (614) 292-3231. Ohio Stadium, Monday-Friday between 8:00am-5:00pm. (614) 292-9748. Athletic Facility Tours are for groups of students ages 12+.

JACK NICKLAUS MUSEUM - 2355 Olentangy River Road. Monday-Saturday   9:00am-5:00pm,   Sunday   1:00-5:00pm. Admission: $6.00-$9.00. Shows the long history of the game, Mr. Nicklaus' place in that history, famous OSU golfers and a prototype of the Nicklaus family's den with personal stories narrated by his wife.

WEXNER CENTER FOR THE ARTS – Family days and guided tours. www.wexarts.org/ctr/gen/overview.shtml or (614) 292-3535.

ASTRONOMY – (614) 292-1773 or www.astronomy. mps.ohio-state.edu/events/star.html. Perkins Observatory Lectures or monthly Star Talks.

BIOLOGICAL SCIENCES GREENHOUSE FACILITY – Insectary, a quarantine facility, two research labs, a growth chamber area and prep room. Monday - Friday 8:30am-4:30pm, except holidays. www.biosci.ohio-state.edu/~plantbio/greenhouse/index.html

FOOD SCIENCE BUILDING – tours of miniature pilot plant, OSU Dairy Store (ice cream treats, breakfast, lunch items), Parker Building, 2015 Fyffe Road (off Woody Hayes Dr) (614) 292-6281.

ORTON GEOLOGICAL MUSEUM – skeleton of a giant sloth, fossils, fluorescent minerals, and rocks. 9:00am-5:00pm. On the oval, open free to the public.

Ohio State University Museums (*cont.*)

HISTORIC COSTUME & TEXTILES COLLECTION – (614) 292-3090. Historic textiles from the 15th century to 20th century in costume pieces including men's, women's, and children's garments and accessories. **www.hec.ohio-state.edu/cts/collect/bucket/geninfo.htm.**

OHIO STATEHOUSE

Columbus - *Broad and High Streets (10 acre square in downtown), 43201. Phone: (614) 728-6350 or (888) OHIO-123 Web: www.statehouse.state.oh.us/welcome. Hours: Weekdays 7:00am-7:00pm, Weekends 11:00am-5:00pm. Admission: FREE. Tours: Walk-in tours begin at 10:00am, 11:30am, 1:00pm and 3:00pm on weekdays. Weekends: 11:15am, 12:30pm, 2:00pm and 3:00pm. Miscellaneous: Museum shop has clever and unique Ohio gifts and souvenirs.* Learn about Ohio's Statehouse history, its architecture and the legislative process. Visit the place where Abraham Lincoln made speeches in 1859 and 1861. Inside you'll see the rotunda with the state seal and historic paintings and documents. If the Ohio House or Senate is in session, you'll be able to listen to the debates. Outside is home to several war memorials and statues including the new Veterans Plaza where visitors read the letters sent home from enlisted men and women. Educational displays and touch-screen kiosks (ex. Pass through all 88 counties in the Map Room) along with a great Museum shop are found in the basement. The basement is all white painted brick and stone. Why are the formal walls painted light shades of pink or peach? The Atrium used to be called Pigeon Alley - why?

COLUMBUS CHILDREN'S THEATRE

Columbus - *775 East Long Street, 43203. Phone: (614) 224-6672. Web: http://colschildrenstheatre.org.* Theatre activities for youth of all ages, backgrounds and cultures. Do you remember your first magical theatrical moment? That moment when your heart flew into your mouth, you caught your breath and you were transferred to a new magical world? One of the greatest joys of theatre is witnessing a child's Wide-Eyed-Wonder when they really connect to a play. Many lessons to be learned watching plays like Oliver, Emperors New Clothes or the seasonal the Best

Christmas Pageant Ever. Tickets run $10.00-$20.00 per person, per show. Children's theatre classes are held at three different campuses (downtown, Dublin and Pickerington). (July-May)

FRANKLIN PARK CONSERVATORY AND BOTANICAL GARDENS

Columbus - *1777 East Broad Street (off I-71), 43203. Phone: (614) 645-TREE or (800) 214-PARK Web: www.fpconservatory.org. Hours: Tuesday-Sunday & Holiday Mondays 10:00am-5:00pm. Wednesday evenings 5:00-8:00 pm. Admission: $6.50 adult, $5.00 senior/student, $3.50 child (2-12).* A place where you can learn where coffee comes from or watch the careful pruning of Bonsai trees. The kid-friendly ants, iguanas, and lories are becoming permanent enhancements to the conservatory. The large 1895 glass structure resembles the style of London's Crystal Palace. The Conservatory is the only public botanical garden in the world to own a signature collection of Chihuly's artworks, which represents more than 3,000 pieces of glass. Flowers and mushrooms and vines - all made from glass - this color and art really engages the imagination. Walk through a simulated tropical rain forest, a desert, a tree fern forest, a Pacific Island water garden and then on to the Himalayan Mountains. Outside is a sculpture garden.

COLUMBUS MOTOR SPEEDWAY

Columbus - *1845 Williams Road, 43207. Phone: (614) 491-1047. Web: www.columbusspeedway.com.* Stock car racing. Kids Day (late August or September). Climb into a real race car! 7:00 pm race starts Saturdays.

OHIO HISTORICAL CENTER

1982 Velma Avenue (I-71 to 17th Avenue Exit), **Columbus** 43211

- ❑ Phone: (614) 297-2300 or (800) 646-5184
  Web: www.ohiohistory.org/places/ohc
- ❑ Hours: Tuesday-Saturday 9:00am-5:00pm, Sunday and Holidays Noon-5:00pm. Closed Christmastime, Thanksgiving & New Years.
- ❑ Admission: $7.00 adult, $3.00 student. Parking fee $4.00 per vehicle. Includes Ohio Village entrance (if open).

Ohio Historical Center (*cont.*)

- ❑ Tours: Summer Kids Kamps and Discovery Days bring out the hands-on fun. Pick up Educational Resource scavenger hunt game flyers near many area entrances. School groups can reserve a tour of the Center and the adjoining Ohio Village.
- ❑ Miscellaneous: Gift Shop, food and picnic tables. The adjacent Ohio Village is now open to the public for signature events only. Ohio Village is designed to recreate the appearance of a typical county-seat town in Ohio during the mid 19th century, about the time of the Civil War.

This is a museum and a whole lot more. There are exhibits and artifacts covering the history of Ohio from archaeology to natural history and the history of Ohio. There are many historical collections from early fossils and Indian tribes (large dioramas and artifact study of prehistoric Indians), original accounts from early explorers, and papers from political leaders such as General Meigs and Thomas Worthington. The newly renovated Battelle Discovery Park and Theater provide modern audiovisual technology, and an interactive science park for children makes learning about Ohio's natural history fun. The Center's permanent natural history exhibit features Ohio's plants, animals, geology, geography, and climate and weather. "The Nature of Ohio" exhibit is guarded by a huge mastodon found in a swamp in Clark County. See the quirky 2-headed calf and Egyptian mummy, too. Continuous early 1900s newsreels, an operating 1880s carriage shop, and vintage automobiles, Adena Pipe and Hopewell mica cutouts are here, too.

BALLETMET

Columbus - *322 Mt. Vernon Avenue, 43215. Phone: (614) 229-4860. Web: www.balletmet.org.* Classic to contemporary ballet including the famous Nutcracker. Step-by-Step program - spend time with dancers or Morning at the Ballet (mini programs like Cinderella) seem to engage the younger kids the most.

CENTRAL OHIO FIRE MUSEUM & LEARNING CENTER

240 N. 4th Street, Columbus 43215

❑ Phone: (614) 464-4099 **Web: www.fire.ci.columbus.oh.us**
❑ Hours: Tuesday-Saturday, 10:00am-4:00pm. Group tours by appt.
❑ Admission: $4.00 adult, $2.00 student, Under 6 FREE.

Visually, the hand-drawn, horse-drawn, & motorized fire vehicles will initially interest the kids. Curiosity will have them asking firefighters about the day-to-day lives in an engine house. Then, kids can climb on board a fire engine and video drive through a smoke-filled bedroom. Walk through a kitchen to see what dangers may lurk. A child paramedic can sit in the back of an ambulance, access a patient and listen to the radio calls coming in. On a group tour? Look for Boots the Fire Mouse as your escort.

COLUMBUS MUSEUM OF ART

Columbus - *480 East Broad Street (four blocks east of the Capitol), 43215. Web: www.columbusmuseum.org. Phone: (614) 221-4848 info line. Hours: Tuesday-Sunday 10:00am-5:30pm. Thursday until 8:30pm. Admission: $6.00 adult, $4.00 senior and student (age 6+). FREE on Sunday. Parking $3.00.* American and European art from 1850-1950. See the life-size horse of welded steel or the works of Columbus realist George Bellows and folk artist Elijah Pierce (go inside a barber shop with radio broadcast of the times). Doodles and Wow Art! Are weekly programs for families. Its My Museum Gallery/Sculpture Guide, Art Speaks audio tour $3.00- where art talks. EYE SPY adventure in art-interactive docent-led creative, colorful weekday mornings where kids learn how works of art are created and preserved. Maybe dress up like figures in a 17th century Dutch painting. Café & gift shop.

COLUMBUS SYMPHONY ORCHESTRA

Columbus - *55 East State Street (most performances at Ohio Theatre), 43215. Web: www.columbussymphony.org. Phone: (614) 228-8600.* Lollipop Concerts, Sunday Funday concerts and Youth Orchestra performances usually have pre-concert activities for families. Average $10.00+ for tickets.

COSI

333 West Broad Street (I-71 exit Broad or Front St. or I-70 exit Broad or Fourth St. to downtown riverfront), **Columbus** 43215

❏   Phone: (614) 228-COSI or (888) 819-COSI, **Web: www.cosi.org**

❏   Hours: Wednesday-Saturday 10:00am-5:00pm. Sunday Noon-6:00pm. Closed most major winter holidays.

❏   Admission: $12.50 adult, $10.50 senior, (60+), $7.50 child (2-12). Significant discounts for military and teaching personnel.

❏   Miscellaneous: Science 2 Go Store, AtomiCafé. Extreme Screen, Planetarium and Motion Simulators $5-$7.00 additional fee (reserve spot at admissions desk).

Explore hands-on exhibits focusing on science, technology, health and history. Take your preschool-aged children to Kid-Space. They pretend they are a doctor or nurse, paint their faces, do a puppet show, water play, ride in a boat, and just have a good active time there. Other favorite areas are Big Science Park (outdoor), where older kids conquer their fears and ride the high wire cycle. Ocean Learning World features a simulated shipwreck with dive tanks and a yellow submarine you can climb inside. Progress is where you travel through time and interact with people in a small Midwestern town. Gadgets is a giant "erector set". The Life area has an Echo Free room, Hot/Cold Coils and Rat Basketball (plus some mature displays that make this area PG). In Space, you get dizzy in a tunnel and see a great space 3D movie. The idea of learning worlds really makes visitors feel like they are someplace else.

DAVIS DISCOVERY CENTER

Columbus - *549 Franklin Avenue, 43215. Phone: (614) 645-SHOW. http://recparks.columbus.gov/arts/Davis_Performing_ Arts_ Program.asp.* The Children's Drama Company for 9 to 12-year-olds are held at the center. At the Davis Youth Complex, classes for children ages 4 through 19 include magic, piano, ballet, acting, puppetry and more. Children who are home-schooled may take advantage of theater and dance classes offered in the daytime at both locations. Shows like Treasure Island and Scrooge are performed during the school year.

SANTA MARIA

Battelle Riverfront Park Scioto River (Downtown – Northeast of
Broad Street Bridge at Marconi), **Columbus** 43215

❑   Phone: (614) 645-8760, **Web: www.santamaria.org**

❑   Hours: Wednesday-Friday 10:00am-3:00pm. Weekends & Holidays
Noon-5:00pm. (April-October). Early evenings in Summer.

❑   Admission: $3.50 adult, $3.00 senior (60+), $2.00 student (5-17).

The Columbus Santa Maria is the world's most authentic, museum
quality representation of Christopher Columbus' flagship. Climb
aboard and return to 1492 as costumed guides share facts about the
ship and the famous voyage. Feel the challenges and hardships
faced by Columbus and his crew. Hear the wood structure creek as
you hear stories about what they ate (no wonder they got sick a
lot!) or how they managed through rough waters. Most everything
is touchable - something we like in historical tours. You better be
on your best behavior or you'll have to "walk the gang plank"!
Sleeping quarters available for campouts.

THURBER HOUSE

Columbus - *77 Jefferson Avenue (Downtown) (I-71 exit Broad Street,
head west one block and turn north on Jefferson), 43215. Phone:
(614) 464-1032. Web: www.thurberhouse.org. Hours: Daily Noon-
4:00pm except major holidays. Tours: Self-guided tours are free
Monday through Saturday. Visitors have the option of taking a guided
tour every Sunday for a small fee of $2.50 for adults and $2.00 for
students and seniors. Group tours by reservation.* James Thurber, the
well-known humorist and cartoonist, grew up in Columbus. The
restored home is where James lived during his college years. Thurber
House is a living museum. They allow visitors to experience Thurber's
life by becoming a guest of the Thurber family. While in the house
museum, visitors are invited to sit on the chairs, play a tune on the
downstairs piano, or, touch the typewriter that was Thurber's while he
was at the New Yorker. The house is featured in several of Thurber's
stories. (Stories about the time Thurber lived in this house are included
in his My Life and Hard Times and The Thurber Carnival.) Be sure to
read some of Thurber's works before you visit or purchase some of his
books at the bookstore in Thurber House.

TOPIARY GARDEN

Columbus - *480 East Town Street (Old Deaf School Park, NW corner of E. Town & Washington, downtown, east of the Main Library), 43215. Web: www.topiarygarden.org.* Phone: (614) 645-0197. The topiary (greenery shaped like people, boats, animals, etc.) garden and pond depicts the theme "A Sunday Afternoon on the Island of La Grande Jaffe". FREE (open daily dawn to dusk).

GRAETER'S ICE CREAM FACTORY

2555 Bethel Rd. (near intersection of Sawmill Rd.), **Columbus** 43220

❑   Phone: (614) 442-0622, **Web: www.graeters.com**
❑   Tours: Group tours by appointment.

You can be guided through the factory by an experienced tour leader who can answer your questions or just look through the observation windows. You'll enjoy an informative video and see their unique French Pot process that makes only two gallons of ice cream at a time. Gourmet ice cream is made in small batches in French Pots (old-fashioned, no air whipped in as in modern, commercial brands). The tour lasts about 20 minutes and is appropriate for all ages. Guided Tours can be scheduled on any week day when they are making ice cream (minimum of 10 people). Self-guided tours are available anytime. There is no charge for the tour, only for whatever ice cream you choose to buy! The Soft Play Area may be just the place (indoors) to let the kids expend some of their sugar energy.

AL'S DELICIOUS POPCORN

1500 Bethel Rd. (SR 315 to Bethel Road exit west – Bethel Center)

Columbus 43220

❑   Phone: (614) 451-7677 or (800) 396-7010
     Web: www.thepopcornoutlet.com
❑   Hours: Monday-Saturday 11:00am-7:00pm.
❑   Admission: FREE
❑   Tours: By Appointment, Approximately 20-30 minutes. No minimum or maximum number of people.

This wonderfully enthusiastic staff will answer every question you've ever had about popcorn. Kids love watching the 2-minute video tour of the large poppers and closely watch the popped corn flow out. They have a tremendous assortment of 60 spicy and sweet flavors to coat the popcorn. They have a challenge presented with the Bubble Gum flavor: If you can blow a bubble from it (it tastes that real!), you get loads of free popcorn. You won't leave without trying lots of favorite flavors like Pizza, Columbus Mix or Jelly Bean. Kids and parents will want to bring their allowance to spend on these treats! Their huge selection of colorful tins will fill many of your gift needs.

SHRUM MOUND

Columbus - *Campbell Park, McKinley Avenue (5 miles northwest of downtown), 43222. Phone: (614) 297-2630. Web: www.ohiohistory.org/places/shrum*. Shrum Mound is one of the last remaining conical burial mounds in the city of Columbus. Conical 2000 year old Adena Indian burial mound - 2 feet high and 100 feet in diameter. Grass covered, it has steps leading to the summit. Open daylight hours.

ANTHONY THOMAS CANDY COMPANY

1777 Arlingate Lane (I-270W to Roberts Road Exit)

Columbus 43228

❑   Phone: (614) 274-8405 or (877) CANDY-21
    Web: www.anthony-thomas.com
❑   Admission: FREE
❑   Tours: Tuesdays and Thursdays from 9:30am to 2:30pm. You don't need to make an appointment and there is no size limit on the group. Free sample at end of tours. Approximately 60 minutes.
❑   Miscellaneous: Gift shop open during tour times. You finish your tour in the retail store.

Have you seen "Willy Wonka's Chocolate Factory?" This tour will remind you of that movie, especially when you first see the clean, bright white equipment, near spotless floors and dozens of silver insulated pipes running to several production lines. View chocolate and fillings being prepared and molded in rooms remaining at a constant 90 degrees F. with 0% humidity (so workers and chocolate don't sweat!) Walk along the comfortable, glass-enclosed suspended "Cat-Walk" and observe eight lines producing 25,000 pounds of chocolates per shift. A couple of wrapping machines are exclusively for fundraisers and airline chocolates, but most of the production line packers can be seen hand packing chocolates for stores. A giant physics and chemistry cooking lesson!

GLASS AXIS

Columbus (Grandview) - *1341B Norton Avenue (near SR 315, between Third and Fifth Streets), 43212. Phone: (614) 291-4250.* **Web:** *www.glassaxis.org.* Glass Axis is a non-profit glass art facility. It was founded by twelve 1987 OSU Glass program graduates, who shared a common goal: to enhance the vision of contemporary art by enabling people to experience glass art and glass making. Visit a working glassblowing studio with a step-by-step explanation of the process. Tour lasts about 1 hour and must be scheduled in advance. $3.00 per person, minimum 20 people for tour. (September–June)

MOTTS MILITARY MUSEUM

Columbus (Groveport) - *5075 South Hamilton Road, 43125.* **Web:** *www.mottsmilitarymuseum.org. Phone: (614) 836-1500. Hours: Tuesday-Saturday 9:00am-5:00pm, Sunday 1:00-5:00pm. Admission: $5.00 adult, $4.00 senior, $3.00 student.* Its purpose is to bring military history into perspective by collecting and preserving memorabilia. Secondly, it educates the public on the importance of past, present and new military events that impact our lives (good way to "tie-in" current events). Best on a group tour with a specific theme in mind.

MOTORCYCLE HERITAGE MUSEUM

Columbus (Pickerington) - *13515 Yarmouth Drive (I-70 east exit 112A, left on SR 204), 43147. Phone: (614) 856-2222.* **Web:** *www.motorcyclemuseum.org.   Hours: Daily 9:00am-5:00pm. Closed winter holidays. Open summer holidays Noon-4:00pm. Admission: $10.00 adult, $5.00 AMA members, $8.00 senior, $3.00* *student (12-17). FREE child (under 12).* The Museum is more than just a wide range of motorcycles on display. Its goal is to tell the stories and history of motorcycling. A self-guided tour features a wall mural, the history of motorcycles, and the Glory Days. Themed "sets" add to the presentation. Kids are most attracted to the 50 motorcycles on display. Motocross, BMW, and Harley abound here.

COLUMBUS ZOO AND AQUARIUM

9990 Riverside Drive (Route 257, I-270 to Sawmill Road exit, follow signs), **Columbus (Powell)** 43065

❏ Phone: (614) 645-3550, **Web: www.colszoo.org**
❏ Hours: Daily 9:00am-6:00pm (Summer), Daily 9:00am-5:00pm (September-May), 9:00am-8:00pm (Wednesday Family Night, mid-June to mid-August). Open 365 days a year.
❏ Admission: $9.00 adult, $7.00 senior (60+),$5.00 child (2-11). Tuesday is Senior Day and Wednesday is half off admission for Franklin County residents. Family Membership available. Parking fee. Discount winter admission.
❏ Miscellaneous: Gift Shops and Concessions. Food Court similar to a mall. Pony, boat, train and carousel rides (small additional fee). Play gym. Picnic facilities.

The famous Director Emeritus of the zoo, Jack Hanna, is a regular on national talk shows. Highlights of the naturally landscaped zoo include cheetahs, black rhinos, lowland gorillas, Habitat Hollow (what makes human/animal habitats home- play & pet area), and North American Bald Eagles (named George and Barbara). A 100,000-gallon coral reef exhibit and one of the largest reptile collections in the United States are also featured. The habitat "Manatee Coast" is modeled after the famous Island Refuge in Florida with a 190,000 gallon pool and floor to ceiling glass viewing walls! The expanded African Forest exhibit offers a walk-through rainforest-themed area with incredible interaction with all kinds of monkeys. Newer exhibits include the Islands of Southeast Asia (primitive ruins, Indonesian buildings and music, komodo dragons, orangutans and otters) and an Australia area. A waterway allows narrated boat rides through the exhibit to give visitors a different view while still providing more room for the animals to roam freely. It just keeps getting better!

WYANDOT LAKE ADVENTURE PARK

10101 Riverside Drive (I-270 to Sawmill Road Exit, follow signs)

Columbus (Powell) 43065

❑ Phone: (614) 889-9283 or (800) 328-9283
   Web: www.sixflags.com/wyandotlake

❑ Hours: Daily 10:00am-7:00pm, 8:00pm or 9:00pm (Memorial Day-Labor Day). Weekends only (mid-May to Memorial Day).

❑ Admission: $20.00-$27.00. $14.99 senior (55+). After 4:00pm, $14.99. FREE child (age 2 and under). Season Pass and Combo Packs with Columbus Zoo available.

❑ Miscellaneous: Concessions, Kiddie rides, and Gift Shops.

This is great fun for a summer day. Wyandot offers a huge wave pool, numerous thrilling water slides and a Tadpool water fun area for the little ones. Then, put on your shoes and get on the roller coaster or one of the amusement rides available. All this for one admission charge. Life vests and rafts are available, free, first come. Christopher Island Water Play Area – Tree house, lagoons, abandoned ships, heated water guns and sprayers, jet steams, and dark speed tunnels.

HANBY HOUSE

Columbus (Westerville) - *160 West Main Street (across from Otterbein College), 43081. Phone: (614) 891-6289. Web: www.ohiohistory.org/places/hanby. Hours: Saturday and Sunday 1:00-4:00pm (May-September). Groups by appointment.* Benjamin Hanby was the composer of over 80 folk songs and hymns including "Sweet Nelly Gray" and "Up On the Rooftop". Children will enjoy seeing Ben's original instruments and musical scores. This home was part of the Underground Railroad. Be sure to notice and ask about the roses in a vase by the front window. The tour also includes viewing a short introduction movie.

OHIO RAILWAY MUSEUM

Columbus (Worthington) - *990 Proprietors Road (Off State Route 161, just past railroad tracks, head north), 43085.* **Web:** *www.ohiorailwaymuseum.org.* *Phone: (614) 885-7345.* *Hours: Sunday 1:00-5:00 pm (Memorial Day-Labor Day).* They have displayed approximately 30 pieces of Ohio Railway History dating from 1897 – 1950. The guide explains that steam engines have their own personality. Get close to one under steam and hear it talk! Try a hand truck or catch a one mile trolley. Special seasonal train excursions take you on a steam train day-trip. See website for details. Small admission for museum.

ORANGE JOHNSON HOUSE

Columbus (Worthington) - *956 North High Street (just north of State Route 161), 43085.* *Phone: (614) 885-1247.* **Web:** *www.worthington.org.* *Hours: (Open House) Sunday 2:00-5:00pm (April-December).* *Closed holidays.* *Admission: $2.00-$3.00.* The Orange Johnson House is a restored early 1800's home. Part of it is Federal style, the back part is pioneer. There are many authentic objects and toys that children can pick up and pretend to use. The guide will describe chores children were given in those days (your own children will think they have it made!). A good time to visit is when they have cooking demonstrations. The smell in the air engages everyone to explore early settler's kitchen tools and techniques. The Old Rectory in downtown Worthington has a doll museum with changing exhibits.

AMERICAN WHISTLE CORPORATION

6540 Huntley Road (I-71 to Route 161 west, turn right on Huntley-look for small sign), **Columbus (Worthington)** 43229

❑ Phone: (877)876-2380 **Web: www.americanwhistle.com**
❑ Admission: $4.00 per person (15 person minimum) (whistle included).
❑ Tours: Monday-Friday 10:00am-4:00pm. One hour long, 15-40 people, appointment necessary.
❑ Miscellaneous: Gift shop where you'll want to buy a lanyard to go with your new whistle or a gold plated whistle!

American Whistle Corporation (*cont.*)

Do you know what a lanyard is? Do you know what makes a whistle louder? See and hear the only metal whistle manufactured in the United States (used by police, referees, coaches, etc.). These "American Classics" are the loudest whistles in the world - 4 decibels higher pitch than the competitors! You'll learn everything you ever wanted to know about whistles and really get to see a small manufacturing operation up close. See mechanical engineering at work - in one-of-a-kind machines designed to perform specific tasks. Learn how a whistle works - and how sciences like aerodynamics and chemistry contribute. Learn how a whistle can be an effective safety tool for people of all ages. These people know how to give great tours! Each person gets to take home a whistle they just watched being made!

ALUM CREEK STATE PARK

Delaware - *3615 South Old State Road (7 miles Southeast of Delaware off State Route 36/37, 1 mile West of I-71), 43015.* **Web:** *www.dnr.state.oh.us/parks/parks/alum.htm.* Phone: (740) 548-4631. 8,600 acres with a great beach with life guarded swimming and food service available. Camping, hiking trails, lots of good boating and rentals, fishing and winter sports. Over forty miles of trail wind along the lakeshore through mature beech-maple forests and across deep ravines. Large-flowered trillium, wild geranium, bloodroot, and spring beauties carpet the forest floor. The forest is home to the fox squirrel, woodchuck, rabbit, white-tail deer and many other species of wildlife.

DELAWARE STATE PARK

Delaware - *(6 miles North of Delaware on US 23), 43015.* **Web:** *www.dnr.state.oh.us/parks/parks/delaware.htm.* Phone: (740) 369-2761. Dense woodlands, expansive meadows and a reservoir blend to create Delaware State Park. Once home to the Delaware Indians, this recreational area offers 3,145 acres of camping, hiking trails, boating and rentals, fishing, swimming, and winter sports. The trails connect the lakeshore with each of the four camping areas, transecting meadows, woodlands and wetlands. Eat at the nearby Hamburger Inn, (740) 369-3850, 16 N. Sandusky St, 50's theme.

OLENTANGY INDIAN CAVERNS

1779 Home Road (US 23 North to Home Road, follow signs, 6 miles north of I-270), **Delaware** 43015

❑ Phone: (740) 548-7917
   Web: www.olentangyindiancaverns.com
❑ Hours: Daily 9:30am-5:00pm (April-October).
❑ Admission: $8.50 adult, $5.00 child (7-15).
❑ Miscellaneous: Large picnic facilities. Frontierland (cute western village) with gem mining, rock climbing wall & mini-golf $3.50. Gift shop, playground. Caverns are not wheelchair/stroller accessible.

Wyandot Indians used these underground caves until 1810 for protection from the weather and their enemies. The caves were formed by an underground river that flows to the Olentangy River hundreds of feet below the surface. The caves were originally discovered during a search for oxen that broke loose from a wagon train. Their owner, J. M. Adam's name and date can be seen on the entrance wall. The tour lasts 30 minutes and takes you through winding passages and coves underground. Then, you visit the museum where Indian artifacts found in the caves are displayed. If you're still in an adventurous mood, play a game of miniature golf, climb a rock wall, mine for gems or go on a nature hike past teepees and longhouses. Something for every size adventurer here.

PERKINS OBSERVATORY

Delaware - *State Route 23 (2 miles south of Delaware, 1 miles south of US 23/SR 315), 43015. Phone: (740) 363-1257* **Web:** *www.perkins-observatory.org. Hours: Friday or Saturday nights. Call for schedule. Admission: $6.00 adult, $4.00 senior/child. $1.00 more if purchased day of program. Highly recommended to order in advance, by phone or mail-in order form.* Children who have studied astronomy will especially enjoy this. The stars naturally fascinate them at night so this is a real treat to see them this close. The program includes a tour of the observatory, an amusing talk on astronomy, and then telescope observation if it is a clear night (otherwise, maybe a planetarium show). There's also Mind & Space games in the Kids Zone area. Occasional lawn telescope observation and rocket launches.

FLINT RIDGE STATE MEMORIAL MUSEUM

7091 Brownsville Road SE (SR 16 east to SR 668 south)

Glenford 43739

❑   Phone: (740) 787-2476 or (800) 283-8707
     Web: www.ohiohistory.org/places/flint
❑   Hours: Wednesday-Saturday 9:30am-5:00pm, Sunday Noon-
     5:00pm (Memorial Day-Labor Day).
❑   Admission: $3.00-$4.00 per person (student to adult)
❑   Miscellaneous: Flint Preserve open April - October, 9:30am-Dusk.

Because of this flint's features, it has been respected throughout the ages as the tools, weapons, and ceremonial objects of native cultures and in modern times in the production of jewelry. Indians came to see this stretch of hills for flint stone (official gemstone of the State of Ohio). Displays show how flint is formed from silica and what objects can be made today with flint (like sparks that start flames when flint is rubbed against steel). Outdoors you can explore the trails past ancient quarry pits. How else can we use flint?

JURASSIC JOURNEY

Heath - *4600 Ridgely Tract Road (Burning Tree Golf Course, off SR 79 south of Heath), 43056. Phone: (740) 522-3464 or (888) 37-DINOS. Web: www.jurassicjourney.com. Hours: Daily 7:00am-9:00pm (when the course is open). Closed when golf course is closed due to weather. Admission: $2.00-$3.00.* About 40 individual, full-size cast replicas of dinosaurs are made and on display here. Also, an Ice Age exhibit featuring the Burning Tree Mastodon, which was discovered on the golf course in 1989 while forming the back 9 holes.

BUCKEYE CENTRAL SCENIC RAILROAD

US 40 (3 miles East of Hebron – I-70 to Route 79 North Exit to US 40), **Hebron** 43025

❑   Phone: (740) 928-3827 or (800) 579-7521
     Web: www.buckeyecentralrailroad.org

❑   Hours: About two Weekends and Holidays/ month 1:00 & 3:00 pm Departures (Memorial Day-October). Seasonal rides also available. Call or visit website for details.

❑   Admission: $7.00 adult, $5.00 child (3-11). Extra $2.00 to ride in caboose.

Take a trip through Ohio farmland for a 90 minute ride on the same route the train traveled in the mid-1800's on the Shawnee line (important line for pioneers heading west). They offer a scenic, 1½ hour round trip excursion through the rolling countryside of central Ohio on historic rail in vintage passenger coaches powered by a classic diesel locomotive.

GEORGIAN / SHERMAN HOUSE MUSEUM

Lancaster - *105 East Wheeling and Broad Street and 137 East Main Street, 43130. Phone: (740) 654-9923. Web: www.fairfieldheritage.org. Hours: Tuesday-Sunday 1:00-4:00pm (April - mid-December). Guided tours last 45 minutes for each home.* 19th Century homes with period furnishings. War mementos of Civil War General William Tecumseh Sherman (his birthplace). Imagine how life must have been in the "Little Brown House on the Hill," the Sherman House, with eleven children and four adults as you visit the wooden structure in which one of the most famous / infamous Civil War Generals was born.

WAHKEENA NATURE PRESERVE

Lancaster - *2200 Pump Station Road (US 33 to County Road 86 west, follow signs), 43155. www.ohiohistory.org/places/wahkeena. Phone: (740) 746-8695 or (800) 297-1883. Hours: Wednesday-Sunday 8:00am-4:30pm (April-October). Admission: $7.00 per vehicle.* Wahkeena, named with an Indian word meaning "most beautiful" is a located on the edge of the Hocking Hills. Trees, ferns, mountain laurels, wildflowers, orchids, and sandstone cliffs.

All that beauty plus 70 species of birds and 15 species of mammals including woodpeckers and white-tailed deer. At the lodge, tour groups may view nature study exhibits. There are two trails available for hiking.

LITHOPOLIS FINE ARTS/WAGNALLS MEMORIAL LIBRARY

Lithopolis - *150 East Columbus Street, 43136. Phone: (614) 837-7003. Web: http://cwda.net/LAFAA.* Series of musical concerts and dramatic events in Wagnalls Memorial (Adam Wagnall was the co-founder of the Funk and Wagnalls Publishing Co.). The series programs and workshops have included light and serious drama, dance groups, mime, a puppeteer and a wide variety of musical events ranging from the classical to bluegrass. Tickets $8.00-$12.00. Tours of the library are available by appointment and include a description of the unusual architectural features and history of the Memorial and Wagnalls family.

MADISON LAKE STATE PARK

London - *(3 miles East of London off State Route 665), 43140. Web: www.dnr.state.oh.us/parks/parks/madison.htm. Phone: (740) 869-3124.* One of the best examples of existing prairie in Ohio is within the Darby Plains of Madison County. Bigelow Cemetery State Nature Preserve near Chuckery contains prairie plants including big bluestem, Indian grass and purple coneflower. Smith Cemetery Prairie contains stiff goldenrod, gray willow and wild petunia. The 106-acre lake is ideal for sailboats, row boats and canoes. A 300-foot sand beach provides enjoyment for swimmers and sunbathers. Changing booths and latrines are provided. A scenic ½-mile hiking trail takes visitors through woodlands and along the lakeshore.

HARDING MEMORIAL AND HOME

380 Mount Vernon Avenue (2 miles west of State Route 23 on State Route 95), **Marion** 43302

❑   Phone: (740) 387-9630 or (800) 600-6894
   Web: www.ohiohistory.org/places/harding

❑   Hours: Wednesday-Saturday 9:30am-5:00pm, Sunday and
     Holidays Noon-5:00pm (Summer). Weekends Only (April, May,
     September and October). By appointment in Spring.

❑   Admission: $6.00 adult, $3.00 student (all ages).

❑   Miscellaneous: Memorial is a circular monument (with columns
     of white marble) containing the tombs of Mr. and Mrs. Harding
     on Delaware Avenue.

A great way to learn Presidential history without a fuss from the
kids. Do you know what the fancy pot is in the guestroom - the
one lying on the floor? They have displayed a podium used at
Harding's inauguration in 1920 as our 29th President. See the
porch where Harding campaigned what was later called the "Front
Porch Campaign", speaking to over 600,000 people overall. The
original porch collapsed and a new one had to be built during the
campaign. A special small house was built behind the main house
for the press associates visiting the area to cover the campaign.
Look for the ornate collar worn by their dog "Laddie Boy".

MYSTERIOUS REVOLVING BALL

Marion - *Marion Cemetery, 43302. Hours: Dawn-Dusk.* Can you
scientifically solve the "Marion Unsolved Mystery"? Here's the
scoop! The ball is a grave monument for the Merchant family
(located in the northeast corner of the cemetery) erected in 1896.
The 5200-pound granite ball (located in the eastern section of the
cemetary) turns mysteriously with continuous movement. There
has been no scientific explanation for this revolution and the
phenomenon is featured in many newspapers including "Ripley's
Believe It or Not"!

WYANDOT POPCORN MUSEUM

Marion - *169 East Church Street (Heritage Hall – Marion County
Museum of History), 43302. Phone: (740) 387-HALL or (800)
WYANDOT.* **Web:** *www.wyandotpopcornmus.com. Hours:
Wednesday-Sunday 1:00-4:00pm (May-October). Weekends Only
(November-April). Closed most holidays. Admission: $1.00-$3.00
(age 6+).* Before you enter the Popcorn Museum, see the hand-made
miniature, working carousel and Prince Imperial (a stuffed 25 year
old horse from France). You won't believe how they braided his

mane! As you enter the large, colorful tent, you'll be enchanted by the antique popcorn poppers and concession wagons. See the first automated popper and the first all electric popper – all in pristine condition. It's the only museum like it in the world. Free popcorn is served daily - the smell wafting in the air adds to the atmosphere.

BUCKEYE LAKE STATE PARK

Millersport - *2905 Liebs Island Road (9 miles South of Newark off State Route 13), 43046. Phone: (740) 467-2690 Web: www.dnr.state.oh.us/parks/parks/buckeye.htm.* 3,557 acres of boating, fishing, swimming and winter sports. Public swimming areas with parking facilities, change booths and latrines are located at Fairfield Beach and at Brooks Park on the south side of the lake. Permanent & rental properties are available around the lake.

KNOX COUNTY HISTORICAL SOCIETY MUSEUM

Mount Vernon - *875 Harcourt Road (routes 3 and 36), 43050. Web: www.knoxhistory.org. Phone: (740) 393-KCHS. Hours: Thursday-Sunday 2:00-4:00pm, Wednesday 6:00-8:00pm (February-mid December).* Exhibits portray the life and travels of Johnny Appleseed, the story of educational institutions, the postal service and radio stations history, toys and dolls, business and industry collections (Cooper Heritage Collection 19th century steam farm engines- became Rolls Royce), Bridge Company exhibit and the musical heritage of the county (Dan Emmett-composer, musician "Turkey in the Straw" and "Old Dan Tucker" - festival in town mid-August).

MOUNT GILEAD STATE PARK

Mt. Gilead - *4119 State Route 95 (1 mile East of Mt. Gilead on State Route 95), 43338. Phone: (419) 946-1961. Web: www.dnr.state.oh.us/parks/parks/mtgilead.htm.* Mt. Gilead State Park is a quiet, small park centrally located in the state of Ohio. Picnicking, fishing and hiking can be enjoyed year-round. Six and a half miles of trails, including a two-mile multipurpose trail for hikers and horseback riders, traverse Mt. Gilead State Park. 172 acres of camping, hiking trails, boating, fishing & some winter sports.

For updates & travel games, visit: **www.KidsLoveTravel.com**

DEER CREEK STATE PARK

20635 Waterloo Road (I-71 to SR 56 to SR 207, 7 miles
south of town), **Mt. Sterling** 43143

❑   Phone: (740) 869-3124 Park or (740) 869-2020 Lodge or (877)
678-3337 Reservations **Web: www.visitdeercreek.com**

❑   Admission: FREE

A collage of meadows and woodlands surround the scenic reservoir. This resort park features a modern lodge, cottages, campground, golf course, swimming beach and boating for outdoor enthusiasts. Nature Programs, bike rentals, hiking trails, boating and rentals, fishing, golf, and winter sports are available throughout park. The Resort has over 100 guest rooms (some with bunk beds, some with lofts), 25 fully furnished two-bedroom cottages (screened porch, many with gas fireplaces, fire ring and grills), indoor/outdoor pools, whirlpool/sauna, gamerooms, sport courts, fitness center, full service restaurant and plenty of activities. Great to plan a group/family get-together here as there are things to do and places everywhere to gather for games (cards, board games) or crafts (Shrinky Dink, buttons, sand art, etc) or evening family videos or hayrides or campfires. They have short hiking trails that are "kid-friendly" (we loved "tracking" the paw prints on the trails early morning) and their Holiday or Theme Weekends are well-planned with entertainment and special guests (i.e. astronauts). Be careful, this place could be habit forming!

PERRY STATE FOREST

New Lexington - *(off of SR-345, 4 miles north of New Lexington), 43764. Phone: (740) 674-4035 (Blue Rock office). www.dnr.state.oh.us/forestry/Forests/stateforests/perry.htm*4,567 acres in Perry County. Area was formerly strip mined for coal. All purpose vehicle trails (16 miles), bridle trails (8 miles). Open daily 6:00am-11:00pm.

GREAT CIRCLE EARTHWORKS

Newark - *99 Cooper Avenue (I-70 to SR 79 north, between Parkview Drive and Cooper), 43055. Phone: (740) 344-1920,* **Web:** **www.ohiohistory.org/places/newarkearthworks/greatcircle.cfm** *or (800) 600-7174. Hours: Park open daylight hours (April-Labor Day weekend). Miscellaneous: Octagon State Memorial - Small mounds, Wright Earthworks State Memorial. Park open daylight hours.* The Moundbuilders is a circular mound 1200 feet in diameter with walls 8 to 14 feet high. As you walk outside, you walk right into the mouth opening of a circular mound. Once inside, just imagine the Hopewell Indian ceremonies that occurred many years ago. Research has concluded that the central Eagle shaped mound was the site of a grand ceremonial site. Admission is free.

DAWES ARBORETUM

Newark - *7770 Jacksontown Road (SR 13, I-70 exit 132), 43056.* **Web:** **www.dawesarb.org**. *Phone: (740) 323-2355 or (800) 44-DAWES. Hours: Grounds open daily dawn to dusk. Visitors Center open: Monday-Saturday, 8:00am-5:00pm, Sundays & holidays, 1:00pm-5:00pm. Closed Thanksgiving, Christmas and New Years. Admission: FREE.* The Dawes Arboretum features plants tolerant of central Ohio's climate. Azaleas, crab apples, hollies, oaks and conifers are a few of the collections accessible from the 4.5 mile Auto Tour and more than 8 miles of hiking trails. There's also meadows, woods, gardens, cypress swamp, holly, and Bird-Watching garden.

WORKS, (THE) - OHIO CENTER OF HISTORY, ART & TECHNOLOGY

Newark - *55 South First Street (I-70 to SR 13 north to between 1st & 2nd streets), 43058.* **Web:** **www.attheworks.org**. *Phone: (740) 349-9277. Hours: Monday-Friday 9:00am-5:00pm, Saturday 11:00am-4:00pm. Some Labs only open when staffed from 11:00am-2:00pm. Admission: $6.00 adult, $4.00 senior, $2.00 child (4-16).* "The Works" is a reoccurring theme. The art gallery and studio have the name, "Art Works." Pottery and ceramics are the central theme of the studio; you decide how you want to experience them, whether creating your own Bisque Studio (once fired pottery), or throwing on the wheel in the mud room. The newly refurbished glass studio has become "Glass Works". Watch workshop glass blowers demonstrate their craft as they create artistic pieces of glassware, including intricate vases, bowls, paperweights and seasonal items. Also found in the complex is the Digital Works (web design and TV studio). The original 1880s machine shop complex houses The Works (traces the development of industry in central Ohio from prehistoric Indians to the 21st century). Learn methods of transportation thru the years or which products were made here (Mason jars and engines for farm machines). See where local raw materials are used in manufacturing, farming and fuel production. Interactive touch displays educate kids on what, where, and how materials are extracted (raw and finished forms). INVENT Lab and TYKE Lab are new theme areas to check out.

VELVET ICE CREAM: YE OLDE MILL ICE CREAM MUSEUM

Velvet Ice Cream (State Route 13)

Utica 43080

❑   Phone: (740) 892-3921 or (800) 589-5000
    Web: www.velveticecream.com
❑   Hours: Daily 11:00am-8:00pm (May-October).
❑   Admission: FREE
❑   Tours: Public Tours, Monday-Thursday 11:00am-3:00pm only.

Did you know that the ice cream cone originated by mistake at the St. Louis World's Fair when a waffle vendor rolled waffles into cones for an ice cream vendor who ran out of serving cups? Learn all sorts of ice cream trivia at the Ice Cream Museum located in the restored 1817 mill and water wheel which is surrounded by 20 acres of wooded parklands with ducks and picnic areas. While you are at the mill, stop by the viewing gallery to watch ice cream being made and packaged. Then, come into the 18th century ice cream counter and try Velvet's newest creations such as Raspberry Fudge Cordial or an old favorite like Mint Chocolate Chip. Lunch menu also.

Chapter 2
Central East Area

Our Favorites...

* Amish Farms & Cheese Factories
* Wendell August Forge - Berlin
* Glass Factory Tours - Cambridge
* Salt Fork State Park Resort - Cambridge
* Bluebird Farm - Carrollton
* Roscoe Village - Coshocton
* Warther Carving Museum - Dover
* Longaberger Factory/Homestead - Frazeysburg
* Harry London Chocolate Factory - N. Canton
* Creegon Co. Animation Factory - Steubenville

Warther Carving Museum - He carved the entire collection instead of watching T.V. - Wow!

GLAMORGAN CASTLE

Alliance - *200 Glamorgan Street, 44601. Phone: (330) 821-2100. Web: www.aviators.stark.k12.oh.us/history.html. Tours: By Appointment. Generally weekdays at 2:00 pm. Small admission fee.* Home of the City School District's Administration office and once the early 1900's home of the late Col. William Henry Morgan (inventor/businessman). The building measures 185 feet in overall front elevation, with 13" thick walls, and truly looks like a giant castle. A quick walk through will give you the flavor of each room open.

DICKSON LONGHORN CATTLE COMPANY

Barnesville - *35000 Muskrat Road (I-70 exit 202 south, then west), 43713. Web: www.texaslonghorn.com. Phone: (740) 758-5050. Hours: Monday-Saturday 10:00am-5:00pm, Sunday 1:00-6:00pm (June-Labor Day). Tours: One hour. Tours for adults are $10.00 with special rates for youth.* Large, family-owned ranch offers narrated tours on an adorable purple with white polka-dotted cow bus. See up to 1000 Texas Longhorns grazing the fields, hand-feed the cattle and clear water fish. Gizmo is an International Champion Sire that is on the tour route. What shape do they use for branding?

BARKCAMP STATE PARK

Belmont - *65330 Barkcamp Park Road (I-70 exit 208, off SR 149), 43718. www.dnr.state.oh.us/odnr/parks/parks/barkcamp.htm. Phone: (740) 484-4064.* Belmont County's rugged hills provide the backdrop for picturesque Barkcamp State Park. Miles of hiking trails invite visitors to enjoy the solitude of the forest. The Lakeview Trail, Woodchuck Nature Trail, Hawthorn Trail and Hawk Trail lead to natural treasures and provide opportunities for nature study, bird watching and wildlife observation. Barkcamp's bridle trail meanders along the entire lakeshore affording a pleasant day's ride. A special paved trail winds through the pioneer village, enters the adjoining mature woodlands and provides access to the Antique Barn. Interpretive signs are placed along the route explaining the cultural and natural history of the park. 1,232 acres of camping, hiking trails through rolling hills and woodlands, boating, fishing, swimming and winter sports.

BEHALT

5798 County Road 77 (north of State Route 39), **Berlin** 44610

❑ Phone: (330) 893-3192, **Web: www.behalt.com**
❑ Hours: Monday-Saturday 9:00am-5:00pm. Friday-Saturday 9:00am-8:00pm (May-October).
❑ Admission: $6.50 adult, $3.00 child (6-12).
❑ Tours: 30min. guided or video (15min. background to Amish area).
❑ Miscellaneous: Pioneer Barn will house original Conestoga Wagon that brought early settlers to Holmes County. Restored one-room school, dating from 1856 used to tell story of Amish education.

Behalt means "to keep or remember". Behalt offers fascinating and enjoyable way to learn about the Amish and Mennonite people. Besides a free 15-minute video presentation, visitors may take a 30-minute interpretive tour (paid admission) of a colorful, stunning 265-ft x 10-ft original oil painting depicting Amish and Mennonite history. This 10' x 265' cyclorama mural by artist Heinz Gaugel clearly explains the heritage of Amish and Mennonite people from the beginnings of their faith to the present day. The circular mural took four years to paint using superimposing layers of oil paint to create a sense of many events occurring in a small space and time. This makes the mural almost 3D when viewing. The exterior of the building is painted with an old technique called "sgraffito" which means scratched. Mr. Gaugel applied five layers of plaster to the wall (green, dark red, dark yellow, white and black). The artist starts scratching through the layers to expose the colors he wants. The tour is narrated with stories so vivid that you feel as if you are a part of the scene. We were fortunate to meet Heinz Gaugel in the gift shop and it was amazing to meet such a humble man with such apparent, unique artistic talent.

SCHROCK'S AMISH FARM AND HOME

4363 State Route 39 (1 mile East of Downtown)

Berlin 44610

❑ Phone: (330) 893-3232, **Web: www.amish-r-us.com**
❑ Hours: Monday-Friday 10:00am-5:00pm, Saturday 10:00am-6:00pm (April-October).

- ❏ Tours and Admission: Buggy Ride - $2.00-$3.00 (age 3+). Home Tour and Slides - $2.00-$3.00 (age 3+). Farm Only - $1.50 (age 3+). Train Ride $2.00-$3.00. Discount combo prices. $7.00-$9.75
- ❏ Miscellaneous: Gifts shops (many). Enjoy a 1.2 mile train ride through the farm grounds. This 16 gauge train ride is great for the entire family.

We started with a buggy ride driven by an Amish man and his horse named "Leroy". After our ride, we were given a sticker to wear that says, "I rode my first Amish buggy ride with Leroy". We then stopped at the farm to pet animals and then watched a slide show about Amish lifestyles. The guide then shows you through the home. Kids, even adults, were surprised to see that all appliances were gas fueled including the lamps (the gas generated light source was hidden in the table under the lamp). We learned why there are no faces on Amish dolls and why only pins and occasional buttons are used in clothing.

WENDALL AUGUST FORGED GIFT TOUR

7007 Dutch Country Lane (3 miles West of Berlin - Route 62)

Berlin 44610

- ❏ Phone: (330) 893-3713 or (866) 354-5192
  Web: www.wendell.com
- ❏ Tours: Tuesday-Saturday 9:00am-4:00pm.

Free tour of the production workshop as metal giftware is taken through a fascinating eleven step process. The gift metal is hammered over a pre-designed template with random hand, or machine operated hammer motions. It was interesting to think someone close to the craft had to design the machine operated hammer for this specific purpose – probably a craftsman who's hands got tired! The impression is now set in one side and the signature hammer marks will stay on the other side. The artist stamps his seal and then the item is forged (put in a log fire) to get smoke marks that bring out the detail of the design. After the item cools, it is cleaned to remove most of the dark smoke color and the metal object is then thinned by hand hammering. The facility also features a video highlighting the company's history and the showroom has the World's Largest Amish Buggy – over 1200 pounds, and each wheel is over 5 feet tall!

BLUE ROCK STATE FOREST

Blue Rock - *6665 Cutler Lake Road (located 12 miles SE of Zanesville off SR 60), 43720. Phone: (740) 674-4035. www.dnr.state.oh.us/forestry/Forests/stateforests/bluerock.htm Hours: Daily 6:00am - 11:00pm.* 4,579 acres in Muskinghum County. 26 miles of bridle trails and fishing are offered. Former fire lookout tower. Blue Rock State Park is adjacent. Several miles of hiking trails begin near the campground and picnic areas of the park. Additional hiking trails are in the adjacent forest lands. Horsemen can enjoy more than 26 miles of bridle trails through the Blue Rock State Forest. No overnight facilities are available. You must provide your own horse as no rentals are available.

FORT LAURENS STATE MEMORIAL AND MUSEUM

Bolivar - *11067 Fort Laurens Rd. NW (I-77 and State Route 212 - Follow Signs), 44612. Phone: (800) 283-8914 or (330) 874-2059. Web: www.ohiohistory.org/places/ftlauren. Hours: Wednesday-Saturday 9:30am-5:00pm, Sunday and Holidays Noon-5:00 pm (Summer). Admission: $3.00-$4.00 per student or adult.* Visit the site of the only U.S. Military fort in Ohio during the American Revolution. Built in 1778 in an ill-fated campaign to attack the British at Detroit. Supplying this wilderness outpost was its downfall, as its starving garrison survived on boiled moccasins and withstood a month-long siege by British-led Indians. The fort was abandoned in 1779. Today, only the outline of the fort remains, but a small museum commemorates the frontier soldier, houses a video giving the fort's history and action packed audiovisual displays from the fort's excavation. Re-enactment weekends are the best time to visit to help visualize the horrible conditions of the short-lived fort.

HARRISON STATE FOREST

Cadiz - *(3 miles north of Cadiz, east of SR-9), 43907. Phone: Web: www.dnr.state.oh.us/forestry/Forests/stateforests/harrison.htm. (330) 339-2205 (New Philadelphia office)* 1,345 acres in Harrison County. Area formerly strip mined for coal. Bridle and hiking trails (24 miles), family and horse camping (no fee), fishing ponds. Open daily 6:00 am-11:00 pm.

BOYD'S CRYSTAL ART GLASS COMPANY

Cambridge - *1203 Morton Avenue (off State Route 209 North), 43725. Web: www.boydglass.com/aboutus.htm. Phone: (740) 439-2077. Tours: Monday – Friday 8:00am – 11:00am and Noon – 3:30pm, 15 minutes. (September – May).* The Cambridge area became popular for glass manufacturing because of good sand and abundant wells of natural gas. Boyd Glass still manufactures collectibles the old-fashioned way, to the delight of visitors and collectors, with a man and a mould and not with an automated machine. Typical shapes made are trains, airplanes, cars, small animals and Teddy the Tugboat. Watch molten glass being poured into one of 300 molds and put in a furnace. When they cool, they are hand-painted.

LIVING WORD PASSION PLAY

Cambridge - *6010 College Hill Road (2 miles west of State Route 209), 43725. Web: http://visitguernseycounty.com/outdoor.html. Phone: (740) 439-2761. Hours: Thursday – Saturday 8:00 pm (Mid-June – Labor Day). Saturday Only 7:00 pm (September). Admission: $13.00 adult, $11.00 senior (60+), $6.00 child (under 12). Free Set Tours 7:15pm. Miscellaneous: Concessions, Gift Shop, Rain Checks, Free Parking.* Bible stories come to life before your eyes. Experience an evening back in the Holy Land, in 30 AD with an authentic representation of Old Jerusalem. Beginning with the Sermon on the Mount, The Living Word reflects on the last three years of the life of Christ, with dramatic depictions of Palm Sunday, the last supper, Gethsemane, Pilate's court, the crucifixion and the resurrection. The play is full of biblical animals and costumes, even chariots.

MOSSER GLASS

9279 Cadiz Road (I-77 exit 47. US 22 West)

Cambridge 43725

❑   Phone: (740) 439-1827. **Web: www.mosserglass.com**
❑   Tours: Monday-Friday 8:30am-10:00am and 11:00am-2:30pm.
No tours first 2 weeks in July and last 2 weeks in December. Best
not to tour if it's hot outside as the plant is not air conditioned. FREE

Mosser makes glass pitchers, goblets, lamps, figurines, auto parts
(headlights), and paper weights. Your guide starts the tour
explaining the glassmaking process from the beginning when glass
powder (sand and cullet-broken glass) are heated to 2000 degrees
F. in a furnace. Once melted, the molten glass is pulled on a stick
and then iron molded or pressed, fire glazed and finally cooled in a
Lehr which uniformly reduces the temperature of the object to
prevent shattering. We saw them make old Ford car headlight
covers and red heart shaped paperweights. They add selenium to
make red glass. A little toothpick holder or doll's glass is typical
of the free souvenir of this great tour!

SALT FORK STATE PARK RESORT

14755 Cadiz Road (7 miles Northeast of Cambridge on US 22)

Cambridge 43755

❑   Phone: (740) 439-2751 lodge or (740) 439-3521 park or (800)
282-7275 reservations **Web: www.saltforkresort.com** or
www.dnr.state.oh.us/parks/parks/saltfork.htm
❑   Admission: FREE

What a great, family-friendly outdoor resort with many hotel
comforts! As Ohio's largest state park, Salt Fork boasts
recreational facilities to suit nearly every taste. Everyone seems to
spend at least a couple of hours each day at the Lodge area with
overnight rooms, gift shops, indoor and outdoor pools & spa,
fitness center, volleyball, basketball and tennis. The dining room
serves breakfast, lunch and dinner in a rustic overlook setting (also,
seasonal snack bars are available). The gameroom with multiple
ping-pong and air hockey tables is downstairs. Fun family

activities are planned seasonally (i.e. crafts, pool games, kid's bingo, family movies, bonfires, plus Parent's Night Out (once or twice a week). The cabins are where memories are made! Best for grade-schoolers and up (bunk beds) because they're right in the woods. The Nature Center is open with planned activities (seasonally, Wednesday-Sunday) and explorations. Bring your own boat to this beautiful lake (or rent one at Sugartree Marina (740) 439-5833 - Kids love the pontoon or speed/ski boats). Lots of camping, fishing, golfing, and well marked hiking trails too. A great place to kick back and create family memories!

ST HELENA III

Canal Fulton - *103 Tuscarawas Village Park (I-77 to Exit 111 Portage Street West, follow signs), 44614. Phone: (330) 854-3808 or (800) HELENA-3. Hours: Daily 1:00 – 3:00pm (Summer). Weekends 1:00 – 3:00pm (May, September, October). Admission: $4.50-$6.50 (age 3+).* A one-hour horse drawn canal boat freighter ride with a narrative history of the canal system and the local area. Appearing as it did in the 1800's, the view also includes Lock IV, one of the few remaining working locks on old canal routes. Included in the tour is a Canal Museum with pictorial stories of colorful local history and canal memorabilia including tools used to build and repair canal boats.

CANTON CLASSIC CAR MUSEUM

Canton - *Market Avenue at 6th Street entrance, 44702. Phone: (330) 455-3603. Web: www.cantonclassiccar.org. Hours: Daily 10:00am-5:00pm. Admission: $5.00-$7.50 (age 6+).* Housed in Ohio's earliest Ford-Lincoln dealership, this museum offers over 45 antique, classic and special interest cars displayed in the motif of flapper era Roaring 20's. Favorite exhibits are the Rolls Royce, the Bullet Proof Police Car, the Amphicar (car and boat) and famous movie cars or Amelia Earhart's 1916 Pierce Arrow.

CANTON SYMPHONY ORCHESTRA

Canton - *2323 17th Street NW, 44702. Phone: (330) 452-2094. Web: www.cantonsymphony.org* Presents classical, holiday, pops, family and youth concerts/symphony.

PLAYERS GUILD THEATRE

Canton - *1001 North Market Avenue, 44702. Phone: (330) 453-7619. Web: www.playersguildtheatre.com.* Family series presents plays based on award winning children's stories like The Hobbit and a Christmas Carol. Performances Thursday-Sunday. Tickets run $8.00-$10.00 per seat.

MCKINLEY MUSEUM & DISCOVER WORLD

800 McKinley Monument Drive, NW (I-77 south exit 106, I-77 north exit 105, follow signs), **Canton** 44708

- ❑   Phone: (330) 455-7043 **Web: www.mckinleymuseum.org**
- ❑   Hours: Monday-Saturday 9:00am-5:00pm, Sunday Noon-5:00 pm. Closed major holidays.
- ❑   Admission: $7.00 adult, $6.00 senior, $5.00 child (3-18).
- ❑   Miscellaneous: Planetarium. Museum Shop.

After you park, take the 108 steps leading up to the bronze doors of the stunning McKinley Memorial where President William McKinley and his wife and children were laid to rest. A few steps away is the McKinley Museum where you can visit McKinley Hall, Historical Hall and the Street of Shops. Walk along the 19th Century Street of homes, general store, print shop, and doctor's office – all indoors on exhibit. Kid's eyes sparkle at the model trains and pioneer toys such as paper dolls and or mini cast-iron kitchen appliances. Last, but even more exciting for kids, is Discover World. A large dinosaur robot named "Alice" greets you and a real Stark County mastodon Bondo Betty is around the corner. Find hidden fossil drawers, make a fossil, look for the queen bee in a living beehive, touch a chinchilla, play a tune on tone pipes, visit Space Station Earth or be a weather forecaster – All in one afternoon!

PRO FOOTBALL HALL OF FAME

2121 George Halas Drive NW (I-77 and US 62), **Canton** 44708

- ❑ Phone: (330) 456-8207, **Web: www.profootballhof.com**
- ❑ Hours: Daily 9:00am-8:00pm (Memorial Day-Labor Day).
  Daily 9:00am-5:00pm (Rest of Year). Closed Christmas Only.
- ❑ Admission: $15.00 adult , $12.00 senior (62+), $8.00 youth (14
  & under), $45.00 family. Discount coupon on their website.
- ❑ Miscellaneous: Tailgating Snack Bar – over the counter /
  vending with Top Twenty Tele-trivia and QBI Call-the-Play
  Game. Special video presentations in the center of each room.

If you're an NFL Football Fan, the anticipation builds as you enter the grounds of the sprawling Hall of Fame. At the top of the curving ramp upstairs you view the first 100 years of football with Pro Football's Birth Certificate and the oldest football (1895) available for display. Then, hit some Astroturf and browse through Pro Football today and Photo Art Gallery (award winning, some amazing, photographs of football heroes in action). Older children look forward to the Enshrinement Galleries and Super Bowl Room. A newer addition to the Hall is Game Day Stadium. A 100-Yard film is shown in a two-sided rotating theater. Start at the Locker Room Show. Then the entire seating area rotates 180 degrees to the Stadium Show where you become part of a NFL game with a 2 story Cinemascope presentation. You see, hear and almost make contact with the players! What a rush!

HOOVER HISTORICAL CENTER

Canton - *1875 Easton Street NW (I-77 Portage Street/North Canton Exit to Walsh University campus), 44720. Phone: (330) 499-0287. Web: www.hoover.com. Tours: Wednesday- Saturday at 1:00, 2:00, 3:00 and 4:00pm (March-December). Closed holidays. Admission: $3.00 (age 13+). Miscellaneous: Only known vacuum cleaner museum in the world.* See the Hoover Industry beginnings as a leather tannery. When automobiles came on the scene, W. H. Hoover searched for a new product. He bought the rights to inventor Murray Spangler's upright vacuum player cleaner and introduced it in 1908 - The Hoover Suction Sweeper Model O (On display). A short video details the history of the company. Guided tours of the farmhouse with include a display of antique vacuums. A favorite is the Kotten Suction Cleaner (1910) that requires a person to rock a bellows with their feet to create suction. An early 1900's electric vacuum weighed 100 pounds (and they advertised it as a portable!).

HARRY LONDON CHOCOLATE FACTORY

5353 Lauby Road (I-77 Exit 113 Airport),

Canton (North) 44720

- ❑   Phone: (330) 494-0833 or (800) 321-0444. **www.londoncandies.com**
- ❑   Tours: Monday-Friday 10:00am-3:00pm.
- ❑   Admission: $2.00-$3.00 (age 3+).
- ❑   Tour: 45 minutes. Reservations suggested (if group tour). Tours leave about every half hour. School tours follow Ohio Proficiency guidelines.
- ❑   Miscellaneous: Chocolate Hall of Fame, Largest Chocolate Store in the Midwest. Learn about cocoa beans and the history of chocolate (did you know the beans grow in pods on trunks of trees near the equator?). Live the fantasy of making, molding, wrapping, and boxing chocolate candy, fudge, and butterscotch. Be sure to try a London Mint (money wrapped candy) or a London Buckeye.

MAPS AIR MUSEUM

Canton, North - *5359 Massillon Road, Akron-Canton Airport (I-77 to Exit 113), 44720. Phone: (330) 896-6332.* **Web: www.mapsairmuseum.org**. *Hours: Monday-Saturday 9:00am-4:00pm and Wednesday evenings until 9:00pm. Admission: $3.00-$5.00 per person.* The staff here are pilots, mechanics, officers, and crew who desire to preserve the legacy of America's aviation heritage. Their slogan "Rebuilding History – One Rivet At a Time" really describes their dedication to acquire and renovate some of the world's greatest military aircraft. MAPS offers not just displays of mint condition aircraft, but also a truly unique "hands on" view of the restoration of some of the world's greatest aircraft by people who may have flown them years ago.

BLUEBIRD FARM TOY MUSEUM AND RESTAURANT

190 Alamo Road (at the bottom of the Square, take 332 south for
two blocks, turn left on 3rd Street S.E.), **Carrollton** 44615

- ❏ Phone: (330) 627-7980, **Web: www.bluebird-farm.com**
- ❏ Hours: Tuesday-Sunday 11:00am-4:00pm (April-December).
  Lunch or Tea served in restaurant.
- ❏ Admission: Museum $2.00 adult, FREE child.
- ❏ Miscellaneous: Great reasonable gift ideas in the gift shop barn.
  Christmastime is magical here.

A century old farmhouse restaurant featuring a fresh, daily menu
of family-priced, old-fashioned dishes like ham loaf, Swiss steak,
and chicken casserole cooked only as Grandma could. Walk off
your homemade dessert on the nature trail. The Toy Museum
features playthings available to American children from the 1800's
to the present (brightly, cleverly displayed). Look for some popular
dolls like Raggedy Ann and Andy, Shirley Temple, Mickey and
Minnie Mouse, and the beloved Teddy Bear...many made abroad.
Ask for the scavenger hunt pages to play a game in the museum.
This entire property is a wonderful haven for families...don't miss
it when in Amish / Swiss area of Ohio!

MCCOOK HOUSE

Carrollton - *Downtown Square (west side of square), 44615.*
*Web: www.ohiohistory.org/places/mccookhse. Phone: (330) 627-
3345 or (800) 600-7172. Hours: Friday-Saturday 9:30am - 5:00pm,
Sunday 1:00 - 5:00pm (Summers); Weekends only (Labor Day to
mid- October). Admission: $3.00 adults, $1.00 child (6-12).
Miscellaneous: History of Carroll County lifestyles and industry
portrayed upstairs - the clothing will appeal to girls.* The family
earned the name of "Fighting McCooks" due to their extensive
military service in the Civil War. Daniel McCook built this home
and his family lived here until 1853. During the Civil War, Daniel's
family contributed nine soldiers to the Union cause including 5
generals. Four of Daniel's family including Daniel himself died in
the conflict. You're greeted by the painting in the front room. Each
son and their father are portrayed. What's unique about the one son,

John James I? In the hallway, you'll find an 1838 large map of Ohio. Can you find your home town or was it even around then? Look for the real tree trunk with cannon balls stuck in it from the Civil War.

ROSCOE VILLAGE

311 Hill Street (State Route 16 and 83, near US 36 - I-77 exit 65)

Coshocton 43812

❑   Phone: (740) 622-9310 or (800) 877-1830
     Web: www.roscoevillage.com

❑   Hours: Daily, Most village shops open at 10:00am Special events May-December. History Tour Buildings Closed (January-March) for cleaning. Visitor Center daily 10:00am-5:00pm. Shops and Center closed major winter holidays.

❑   Admission: "Living History Tour" $5.00-$10.00 (ages 5+). Just Browsing is FREE! Additional charge $3-$6 for canal boat ride.

❑   Tours: Guided 11:00am and 2:00pm. Summer tours are called Leisure Tours and are more self-guided.

❑   Miscellaneous: Monticello III Canal Boat-A horse drawn replica of a 1800's canal boat, offers narrated trips on the 1 1/2 mile restored section of the original Ohio-Erie Canal. 1pm - 5pm daily from Memorial Day - Labor Day. Weekends only Labor Day to mid-October. Part of the Coshocton Park District (740) 622-7528.

Historic buildings offer a glimpse into the daily life of these craftsmen and their families. Maybe take a lesson in the one-room school or see the trappings of the 1800's daily life in the doctor's house. Watch craftsmen practice their trades of broom making, weaving, pottery, bucket making and more. Kids can try their hand at candle dipping, tin punching or rope making in the Hands-On facility. They can "discover" the sights and sounds of the canal era with games, puzzles, music and activities in the Discovery Room. Look over the realistic dioramas and working lock models in the Visitor Center complex. Spend gobs of time in the General Store where you can play with and buy old-fashioned toys like harmonicas, paper dolls and wooden toys. Plan to have the kids bring their allowance (and you can too) because you won't be able to resist! The Johnson-Humrickhouse Museum is full of prehistoric American Indian tools and pottery or Ohio Pioneer house or Oriental decorative arts (Samurai swords). During the summer, visit the Hillside where demonstrations of brick-making and woodworking take place. Grab baked goods or a light lunch at Captain Nye's Sweet Shop.

WILDS, (THE)

14000 International Road (I-70 exit 155, Zanesville or exit 169, SR 83 - follow signs), **Cumberland** 43732

- ❑   Phone: (740) 638-5030, **Web: www.thewilds.org**
- ❑   Hours: Hours vary, call first (November-April). Wednesday-Sunday 10:00am-4:00pm. (June-August). Weekends only (May, September, October).
- ❑   Admission: $14.00 adult, $13.00 senior(60+), $9.00 child (4-12). Parking fee $2.00.
- ❑   Tours: 1 hour tours in a shuttle bus - safari at 11:00am, 1:00pm and 3:00pm. School and Group Tours available almost any day (May-October).

Once a strip mine (donated by American Electric Power) it is now home to the International Center for the preservation of wild animals. Over 9000 acres of forest and grassland with 150 lakes is home to animals in a protected open range habitat (no pens, stables, and cages) designed to create an environment for reproduction. You'll see many animals you don't see in zoos like African gazelles, reticulated giraffes, mountain zebras, tundra swans and red wolves in herds. With lots of "tender loving care" and adaptation exercises, injured animals may now roam free. You might also see real wild horses that look like a rhinoceros and a horse. They are very strong and tough (yet beautiful to watch) animals. Other opportunities available to visitors include an education center where you can learn from interactive computer kiosks and various displays that focus on the relationship between humans and their environment.

DENNISON RAILROAD DEPOT MUSEUM & CANTEEN

Dennison - *400 Center Street (off SR 250 or SR 36, Dennison exit to Second St.-turn right along tracks), 44621. Phone: (740) 922-6776 or (877) 278-8020. **Web: www.dennisondepot.org**. Hours: Tuesday-Sunday 11:00am-5:00pm. Miscellaneous: Special train rides depart each season. Check website for events.* During WW II the Dennison Depot was located on the National Railway Defense Route. It was the main stopping point on the route because it was the exact mid-point between Columbus and Pittsburgh. One evening, a town's lady noticed the servicemen seemed sad, so she organized a few other friends to start a GI canteen. The community became so popular among the soldiers that it was called Dreamsville, USA. The canteen for WW II servicemen is now used as a museum of local history, a gift shop, an old fashioned candy counter and a theme restaurant. Lunch served at the Canteen Restaurant, a unique 1940s family restaurant offering Victory Garden Salads and Dreamsville Desserts (groups: ask about the "hobo lunch" served in a souvenir bandana). Small admission to the museum includes kids being able to ring a steam locomotive bell, swing a lantern, climb a caboose and watch trains run on the model train layout.

BROAD RUN CHEESEHOUSE

6011 County Road 139 NW (4 miles west of I-77, old SR 39)

Dover 44622

❑   Phone: (330) 343-4108 or (800) 332-3358
      Web: www.broadruncheese.com
❑   Admission: $1.50 per person (age 5+).
❑   Tours: Monday – Saturday (Mornings), by reservation usually.
      20 minutes long with samples.
❑   Miscellaneous: Gift Shop with novelties, cheese and sausage.

Not just a window view but an actual tour of Swiss, Baby Swiss, Brick, and Muenster productions. They make 640,000 pounds of cheese from 8,000,000 pounds (yes, pounds!) of milk each year. After your factory tour you can sample cheese and as a souvenir, get an official cheesemaker paper cap (the one you wore during the tour). What happens to the cream that is separated off from the cheese? (hint: its made into another tasty product). Ever seen thick, warm milk cut into cubes? (forms "curds" and "whey"). What makes the holes?

WARTHER CARVINGS TOUR

331 Karl Avenue (I-77 to exit 83 to State Route 211 east)

Dover 44622

- ❑ Phone: (330) 343-7513, **Web: www.warthers.com**
- ❑ Hours: Daily 9:00am-5:00pm (March-November). Monday-Saturday 10:00am – 4:00pm (December – February)
- ❑ Admission: $9.00 adult, $5.00 student (7-17).
- ❑ Tours: Last tour begins one hour before closing.
- ❑ Miscellaneous: Tree of Pliers – 500 interconnecting pairs of working pliers carved out of 1 piece of walnut wood! Mrs. Warther's Button Collection – Over 70,000 in museum! Gift Shop and garden trails. Short videos throughout the tour keep it interesting.

A must see tour of the visions of a master craftsman! Mr. Warther started carving at age 5 with a pocketknife while milking cows and during breaks working at a mill. Before your tour begins, take a peek into the original 1912 workshop or at the display of wood carved postcards. A favorite carving of ours was the steel mill (3 x 5 feet) with moving parts depicting the foreman raising a sandwich to eat, and another worker sleeping on the job. The Abraham Lincoln Funeral Train has thousands of mechanized movements powered by a sewing machine motor. See models of steam locomotives and trains using mostly walnut, ivory, and arguto (oily wood) for moving parts which still run without repairs for over 60 years! The late Mr. Warther loved entertaining children with his carvings (George actually met him in 1970) and he would carve a pair of working pliers with just a few cuts in a piece of wood in only a few seconds! Now, one of the family members still carves pliers for each child visiting. This is "Where enthusiasm is caught, not taught." Truly amazing!

BEAVER CREEK STATE PARK

East Liverpool - *12021 Echo Dell Road (8 miles North of East Liverpool off State Route 7), 43920. Phone: (330) 385-3091. **Web:** www.dnr.state.oh.us/parks/parks/beaverck.htm.* 3,038 acres of camping, hiking trails, fishing and winter sports. Approximately sixteen miles of hiking trails take the visitor to historic canal locks and through a steep walled gorge. Hikers will find several beautiful waterfalls by exploring the many tributary streams. A short trail from the campground to Oak Tree Point gives an excellent panorama of the scenic valley. Approximately sixteen miles of hiking trails take the visitor to historic canal locks and through a steep walled gorge. Hikers will find several beautiful waterfalls by exploring the many tributary streams. A short trail from the campground to Oak Tree Point gives an excellent panorama of the scenic valley. The park includes Little Beaver Creek, a state and national wild and scenic river, and acres of forest wilderness. The rich history of the area invites visitors to explore Gaston's Mill, pioneer village and abandoned canal locks.

MUSEUM OF CERAMICS

East Liverpool - *400 East 5th Street (corner of Broadway), 43920. **Web:** www.ohiohistory.org/places/ceramics. Phone: (330) 386-6001 or (800) 600-7880. Hours: Wednesday-Saturday 9:30am-5:00pm, Sunday and holidays Noon-5:00pm. Closed Thanksgiving Day, Christmas and New Year's Day. Admission: $7.00 adult, $6.00 senior, $3.00 student (all ages).* The exhibits in the museum depict the growth and development of East Liverpool and its ceramic industry from 1840 to 1930, the period when the city's potteries produced over 50% of the ceramics manufactured in the United States. Displays cover good and bad times of the ceramic industry and the effects on its people. Life- sized dioramas of kiln, jigger and decorating shops with a collection of old and new ceramics make the museum easy to follow. Slide presentation.

LONGABERGER MUSEUM & FACTORY TOUR

5563 Raiders Road (on State Route 16)

Frazeysburg 43822

- ❑ Phone: (740) 322-5588, **Web: www.longaberger.com**
- ❑ Hours: Monday-Saturday 9:00am-5:00pm. Sunday Noon - 5:00pm. Extended hours in the spring and summer and during special events. Closed holidays.
- ❑ Admission: FREE
- ❑ Tours: Arrive before 1:00pm. Monday – Friday to see actual production. No production on Saturday or Sunday. Weaving demonstrations daily in the Gallery with same setup as one of the factory stations.
- ❑ Miscellaneous: Their festivals at the Homestead are nicely done (check their website for events). Gift shops with tour baskets and eateries on campus.

CORPORATE HEADQUARTERS: (State Route 16) Newark. A giant 7-story Market Basket design with towering heated handles (to melt the winter ice) on top and painted / stenciled to look like wood. Incredible!

HOMESTEAD: Gift shops with tour baskets for sale, lots of home furnishings and eateries. Tour a replica of the Longaberger Family Home where Dave grew up with his 11 brothers and sisters. JW's workshop may be toured also. The Make a Basket Shop is where you can pay a fee to actually create your own hardwood maple Longaberger basket with the help of a Master artisan (takes one hour). All children (any age) can romp around at "The Lookout Treehouse" (located within the Homestead). Listen to the owl and the sights and sounds of nature. Outdoor Playground and special indoor Kid's shopping areas.

FACTORY TOURS: Fascinating tours and lots to see in this tiny little town. Longaberger - manufacturers high quality, handmade hard maple baskets. The one-quarter mile long factory is home to 1000 weavers who make over 100,000 baskets per week (each initialed and dated). It's best to watch a 13 minute video of the company's history and the manufacturing process that takes sugar maple logs (poached and debarked) that are cut into long thin strips. You'll be mesmerized when you go upstairs to the mezzanine to view 400 crafters, each with their own station, weaving damp wood strips around "forms", Each basket takes about 20-30 minutes to make. Can you guess what a weaving horse is?

GNADENHUTTEN MUSEUM AND PARK

352 South Cherry Street (I-77 to SR 36 east)

Gnadenhutten 44629

❑   Phone: (740) 254-4143

   Web: http://gnaden.tusco.net/history/History.htm

❑   Hours: Monday-Saturday 10:00am-5:00pm, Sunday 1:00-5:00pm
   (June-August). Weekends only (September-October).

❑   Admission: $1.00 donation.

❑   Miscellaneous: A "friendly" cemetery tour on the premises. Look
   at the graves tombstone hands- why are they turned in different
   directions-what does it mean?

Gnadenhutten (Huts of Grace) was settled five months after Schoenbrunn on October 9, 1772. Joshua, a Moravian Mohican Elder, brought a large group of Christian Mohican Indians from Pennsylvania to this location. This settlement grew rapidly and the group worked hard and prospered, their standard of living was high for that era on the frontier, their cabins had glass windows, basements, they used pewter household utensils, they were adept in crafts and artwork, and loved music. It was here that the Roth child (first white baby in this territory) was born, July 4, 1773. All went well until the Revolutionary War began and the English at Detroit wanted all Indians to fight against the Americans. The local Indians refused. When they would not leave, in September 1781, troops and Indian warriors rounded up all the Indians living in New Schoenbrunn, Gnadenhutten, and Salem and took them to Captives town. During the winter in the captive town many died of diseases. Permission to go home was granted to 150. They arrived back home in February 1782 and were gathering food and belongings, when Pennsylvania Militiamen under Colonel Williamson surrounded them. After a night of prayer and hymn singing, ninety men, women and children were massacred, then all cabins were set afire on March 8, 1782. Two boys escaped to warn others and to tell the story. See the sites of the two buildings where the Indians spent the night before their death. Those buildings, the Mission House and Cooper Shop (the actual basement foundation where one boy hid - it will take your breath away!), have been restored and are located on their original sites. The story of the massacre is told in the outdoor drama "Trumpet in the Land".

QUAIL HOLLOW STATE PARK

Hartville - *Congress Lake Road (2 miles North of Hartville), 44632.* ***Web:*** *www.dnr.state.oh.us/parks/parks/quailhlw.htm. Phone: (330) 877-6652.* Quail Hollow is a landscape of rolling meadows, marshes, pine and deciduous woodland trails surrounding a 40-room manor. Now called the Natural History Study Center, the former Stewart family home is primarily used for educational, nature-oriented and community activities. The home is open on weekends 1:00-5:00 pm. Quail Hollow has over 19 miles of trails ideal for hiking, jogging, nature study or cross-country skiing. Eight interpretive nature trails explore the unique natural habitats for which each is named. There is also a five-mile, day-use bridle trail and four-mile mountain bike trail. The Nature For All trail is a 2000 ft. paved interpretive trail for those visitors with a physical challenge. Interpretive audio tapes and brochures are available at the visitors center as well as along the trail.

GUILFORD LAKE STATE PARK

Lisbon - *6835 East Lake Road (6 miles Northwest of Lisbon off State Route 172), 44432. Phone: (330) 222-1712.* ***Web:*** *www.dnr.state.oh.us/parks/parks/guilford.htm.* Guilford Lake State Park is a quiet fishing lake located in northeastern Ohio on the west fork of the Little Beaver Creek. The gentle rolling terrain of the area offers a serene escape for park visitors year round. A half-mile hiking trail skirts the scenic lakeshore and provides opportunities for exercise and wildlife observation. 488 acres of camping, boating, fishing, swimming and winter sports.

ELSON FLOURING MILL

Magnolia - *261 North Main Street (SR 183, southwest edge of town), 44643. Web: www.elsonmill.freeservers.com. Phone: (330) 866-3353.* Visit this picturesque red mill in the center of a canal village. Founded in 1834 by the great-great grandfather of the present owners, it gives a glimpse of industry in the 1800's. Built of virgin timber cleared from the land on which the mill stands, it has been in continuous operation by the Elson Family. Corn meal has been made at the mill since 1834 and can be purchased still today. Tours Every Thursday at 10:00am and 2:00pm, April through November. Admission is $2.00 per person.

GUGGISBERG CHEESE FACTORY

Millersburg - *5060 State Route 557 (Off State Route 39, I-77 exit 83), 44654. Phone: (330) 893-2500. Web: www.guggisberg.com. Hours: Monday-Saturday 8:00am –6:00pm, Sunday 11:00 am – 4:00pm) (April – December) Monday-Saturday 8:00am – 5:00pm (December – March).* Home of the original Baby Swiss – you can watch through a window as cheese is being made (best time to view is 8:00 am – Noon weekdays). We learned milk is brought in the early mornings from neighboring Amish farms. Cultures and enzymes are added to form curd. Curd is pressed into molds and brine salted. Each cheese is aged at least a month for flavor. A short video is always playing that details this process if you can't view it personally.

ROLLING RIDGE RANCH

Millersburg - *3961 County Road 168 (Weaver Ridge Road) (I-77 exit Rte. 39 west to SR 62 north to CR 168), 44654. Phone: (330) 893-3777. Hours: Monday-Saturday 9:00am-One hour before sunset (April - mid-October). Admission: Drive thru in own car $5.00-$8.00 per person. $12.75 adult, $7.75 child (wagon ride tours). Only cash or check accepted.* The ranch features 400-500 animals & birds from around the world. Take a 2-mile safari ride in your own vehicle or a horse drawn wagon to see animals from 6 continents. Feed the animals from a guided horse-drawn tour or from the safety of your own car. You are welcome to bring along your camera, as you will be up close to the animals and birds. You may see zebras, water buffalo, African and Indian antelope, African Watusi cows, and Indian and Oriental deer. There is a petting zoo adjacent to the wildlife area and a gift shop. There are also picnic tables.

YODER'S AMISH HOME

Millersburg - *6050 State Route 515 (between Trail and Walnut Creek), 44654. Web: www.yodersamishhome.com. Phone: (330) 893-2541. Hours: Monday-Saturday 10:00am-5:00pm (mid-April thru October). Admission: Tours $3.50 Adult, $1.50 Children (under 12). Buggy Rides $2.00 Adult, $1.00 Children (under 12).* This home was built in 1866 and shows authentic furnishings from that period. Learn what a "hoodle stup" is. Then step into an 1885 barn with animals to pet. Most popular tends to be the turkeys – (Yes, you can try to pet turkeys!). Buggy rides are given by retired real Amish farmers who are personable and tell stories during the ride.

JOHN & ANNIE GLENN HISTORIC SITE & EXPLORATION CENTER

New Concord - *68 West Main Street (I-70 to New Concord exit, across from library), 43762. Phone: (740) 826-3305   Web: www.johnglennhome.org. Hours: Wednesday-Saturday 10:00am-3:00pm, Sunday 1:00-4:00pm. Closed major holidays. Admission: $5.00 adult, $4.00 senior, $2.00 student.* John Glenn, astronaut and politician, spent his boyhood in this home that has been moved and restored to its late 1930's appearance as a museum dedicated to telling 20th century American history through the lives of John and Annie Glenn. The backdrop are displays on the Cold War and the Space Race. Kids will like to view models of an F86 airplane, which John Glenn flew, and a Russian MIG, of which Glenn downed three in Korea. John Glenn's brand of heroism is steeped in small-town values. These values, along with patriotism, public service, and commitment to family are interpreted at the museum. "Grit is the theme of the museum," according to The New York Times.

MUSKINGUM WATERSHED CONSERVANCY DISTRICT LAKES

New Philadelphia, *44663. Phone: (330) 343-6647 or (877) 363-8500. Web: www.mwcdlakes.com.* All of the MWCD parks feature camping all year long, so a getaway for a day or weekend is easy. Stays in family vacation cabins also are available for a few weeks at Pleasant Hill and Seneca parks, several months at Tappan Lake Park and all year at Atwood Lake Park. Contact the park of your choice for details. Hiking trails, boating and rentals, fishing, swimming, visitor center, lodge or cabins and food service. Nature programs.

SHOENBRUNN VILLAGE STATE MEMORIAL

State Route 259, East High Avenue (4 miles East of I-77 exit 81)

New Philadelphia 44663

❑ Phone: (330) 339-3636 or (800) 752-2711
   Web: www.ohiohistory.org/places/shoenbr
❑ Hours: Wednesday-Saturday 9:30am-5:00pm; Sunday Noon-5:00pm (Summer).
❑ Admission: $7.00 adult, $3.00 student (all ages).
❑ Miscellaneous: Museum. Video orientation. Gift Shop. Picnic facilities. A special, interactive event is usually held one Saturday each month. Tape recorded tours available at no extra cost.

Take a self-guided tour of the reconstructed log building village founded by a Moravian missionary in 1772. The Moravian church founded Schoenbrunn ("beautiful spring") as a mission to the Delaware Indians. Being the first settlement in Ohio, Schoenbrunn claims the first civil code, the first church (learn about the love feast still occasionally held here, especially near Christmas), and the first school. Problems associated with the American Revolution prompted Schoenbrunn's closing in 1777. Today the reconstructed village includes seventeen log buildings and gardens...many occupied by costumed interpreters demonstrating period crafts and customs.

TRUMPET IN THE LAND

New Philadelphia - *Shoenbrunn Amphitheatre (-77 to Exit 81), 44663. Phone: (330) 339-1132. Web: www.trumpetintheland.com. Hours: Several performances per week (except Sunday) 8:30 pm (mid-June to late August). Admission: $15.00 adult, $13.00 senior, $7.00 child (under 12). Backstage tours a few dollars extra. Bargain days on Mondays and Tuesdays ($5.00-$10.00 per person). Miscellaneous: Read our write-up on Gnanenhutten to review more detailed history of this saga before you go.* In an Ohio Frontier setting (the first settlement at Schoenbrunn), meet historical characters like David Zeisgerber (missionary converting Indians), Simon Girtz (renegade), Captain Pipe (young warrior who hated white men) and John Heikewelder (explorer)...all vital historical figures in the founding of Ohio. The Revolutionary War breaks out and Moravian Indian Christians would not take sides. Feel their stress and desires to try to remain neutral in a hostile environment. Sadly, in the end, American militia brutally massacre 90 Christian Indians at Gnadenhutten.

TUSCORA PARK

New Philadelphia - *South Broadway Street (I-77 to US 250 east), 44663. Phone: (800) 527-3387. Web: www.tuscora.park.net.* The central feature is the antique big carousel or the summer showcase concert series or swimming pool. What draws little ones and families is also the Ferris wheel, 6-8 kiddie rides (including a train ride and mini roller coaster), batting cages and putt-putt - all at low prices. Most rides are 50 cents and activities are around $1.00. Great alternative to higher priced amusement "vacations" during Summer Break (only open summertime).

NATIONAL ROAD ZANE GREY MUSEUM

8850 East Pike (U.S. 40 / I-70 Norwich Exit)

Norwich 43767

❑   Phone: (740) 872-3143 or (800) 752-2602
      Web: www.ohiohistory.org/places/natlroad
❑   Hours: Wednesday-Saturday 9:30am-5:30pm, Sunday &
      Holidays Noon-5:00pm (Memorial Day weekend-Labor Day).
❑   Admission: $7.00 adult, $3.00 student (all ages).

"Head West Young Man" in a Conestoga wagon as you explore
the history of US-40 National Road. Built based on a concept of
George Washington, it stretches between western territories in
Illinois to the eastern state of Maryland. It was vital to the
development of the frontier heading west and later called
"America's Main Street". Play a game where children locate all the
different types of bridges on this route (examples: the "Y" and "S"
Bridge).   The facility also commemorates author Zane Grey and
his western novels and the area's ceramic heritage.

JEFFERSON LAKE STATE PARK

Steubenville - *501 Twsp Rd 261A (16 miles Northwest of
Steubenville of State Route 43), 43944. Phone: (740) 765-4459.
Web: www.dnr.state.oh.us/parks/parks/jefferso.htm*. In the sandstone
bedrock can be found layers of coal which were formed by
decaying swamp vegetation. 933 acres of camping, rough hiking
trails, boating, fishing, swimming and winter sports.

CREEGAN COMPANY ANIMATION FACTORY

510 Washington Street (I-70 to State Route 7 North)

Steubenville 43952

❑   Phone: (740) 283-3708 **Web: www.creegans.com**
❑   Tours: Reservations Preferred. (45 minute tour). Monday-Friday
      10:00am-2:00pm. Saturdays only 10:00am-2:00pm. (during
      Christmas season). Walking on three levels with stairs.

❏ Miscellaneous: Christmas Shop (year round). Retail store sells Creegan's most recent animated figures and scenery.

Start with the Craft Area where ribbon, yarn, and puppet props abound everywhere. Then, to the Art Department where workers paint faces on molded plastic heads and make costumes. (To make the plastic heads they use a machine press that uses molds to form faces out of sheets of plain white plastic.) In the sculpting area, shelves of hundreds of character head, feet, and hand molds line the walls and a woman sculpts new molds. Finally, peek inside some of the bodies of automated figures to view the electronics that produce body movements (some are a little scary for young ones). A costumed mascot (Beary Bear) greets and guides your pre-arranged tour of Animation "Behind the Scenes". Their theme is "We Make Things Move" and they're the nation's largest manufacturer of animated and costumed characters. (Some customers are Hershey Park and Disney World). An amazing place and tour…it's like Santa's workshop!

FERNWOOD STATE FOREST

Steubenville - *(north of SR-151, southwest of Steubenville), 43952. Phone: (330) 339-2205 (New Philadelphia office). Web: www.dnr.state.oh.us/forestry/Forests/stateforests/fernwood.htm.* 3,023 acres in Jefferson County. 3 mile hiking trail, several picnic areas, 22 family campsites (no fee).

STEUBENVILLE CITY OF MURALS

Steubenville - *120 South Third Street (Old Fort Steuben) (CVB offices - maps), 43952. Phone: (740) 282-0938 or (800) 510-4442. Web: www.steubenvilleoh.com.* During a self-guided tour (free) you can see 25 giant full color (almost 3D) murals with the theme "Preserving a Piece of America" on the sides of downtown buildings. Each has its own name with some of the most interesting being Stanton Park, Ohio River Oil Company and Steam Laundry – these all "jump" right off the wall and appear almost like a photograph.

ALPINE HILLS MUSEUM

Sugarcreek - *106 West Main Street, 44681. Phone: (888) 609-7592. Hours: Daily 9:00am-4:30pm, except Sundays (March-November). Extended summer hours.* Three floors of Swiss, German and Amish heritage. Many audio-visuals & push buttons "spotlight" parts of well-explained dioramas of an Amish kitchen, Swiss cheesehouse and a woodshop & printshop. Nearby, the best Swiss steak & mashed potatoes in town are at the Swiss Hat restaurant.

COBLENTZ CHOCOLATE COMPANY

Walnut Creek - *4917 State Route 515 and State Route 39, 44687. Phone: (330) 893-2995 or (800) 338-9341. Hours: Monday – Saturday 9:00am – 6:00pm (July – October). Close at 5:00pm (November-May). Best viewing is from 9:00am-3:00pm.* Watch through the kitchen windows as chocolate is stirred in large vats with automatic paddle stirs. They have a window going 65 feet along the side of the kitchen so you can see candy being made, from cooling to pouring onto tables to wrapping. Caramels, fruits, and nuts are hand dipped and layered on large trays to cool and dry. Also, see molds for chocolate forms used to create bars of barks and holiday shapes. Savor the sweet smell of fresh milk and dark chocolate as you decide which treats to buy. Our favorite was the chocolate covered Dutch pretzels with sprinkles or nuts on top.

GRANDMA'S ALPINE HOMESTEAD RESTAURANT & CLOCK SHOP

Wilmot - *1504 US 62, 44689. Phone: (330) 359-5454 or (800) 546-2572. Web: www.grandmashomestead.com Hours: Daily 9:00am-8:00pm (Spring-Thanksgiving). Serving lunch and dinner beginning at 11:00am.* This is home of the "World's Largest Cuckoo Clock". The Guinness Book of World Records has it listed as 23 ½ feet high, 24 feet long and 13 ½ feet wide. Trudy, a life-size mannequin with a German accent, opens shutters to greet you. The Swiss Village Market has viewing windows (to watch cheese-making), restaurants and shops.

AMISH DOOR DINNER THEATRE

Wilmot - *1210 Winesburg Street, US 62, 44689. Phone: (800) 891-6142. Web: www.amishdoor.com. Hours: Doors open at 6:15pm. Shows generally begin around 7:00pm.* Come celebrate the joy of dinner and a show at the Amish Door. Through original plays, classic stories and festive songs, you'll experience light-hearted, fun biblical "twists" of classic themes and musicals. Tickets are $28.00-$35.00 per person and include a bountiful, all inclusive meal featuring all the Amish Door favorites.

BUGGY HAUS

Winesburg - *County Road 160 (off Route 62), 44690. Phone: None (Amish). Hours: Monday – Saturday 8:00am – 5:00pm.* See the world's largest buggy or take a one hour guided tour of a working Amish buggy shop and three floors of warehouse and displays. You'll see over 500 units of buggies, carts, sleighs, and wooden riding horses for sale. Climb aboard them to test them out. Their tour includes the history and cultural differences of buggies around the country.

HARTZLER FAMILY DAIRY

Wooster - *5454 Cleveland Road, 44691. Phone: (330) 345-8190. Web: www.hartzlerfamilydairy.com. Tours: All tours are by appointment only. Mostly weekdays, some Saturdays. Group/Bus Tours (30 or more) $2.50 per person. Small Tours (15-29 people) $3.00 per person. [Both include single dip ice cream cone].* A true "family affair" with oodles of generations of kids working all about. Get the "scoops" from Mom Hartzler at the Ice Cream Shoppe. Tour the processing plant that is adjacent to the ice cream shoppe. Learn The History of Hartzler Farms, Their Family, and Their Dairy Business. Guided by a Hartzler Family Member.

OHIO AGRICULTURAL RESEARCH AND DEVELOPMENT CENTER

1680 Madison Avenue (off I-71 exit SR 83 or US 30)

Wooster 44691

❏   Phone: (330) 202-3503 or (330) 263-3700
    Web: www.oardc.ohio-state.edu
❏   Hours: Monday-Friday 7:30am-4:30pm (Summer). Monday-
    Friday 8:00am-5:00pm (September – June).
❏   Admission: FREE
❏   Tours: Guided tours for groups of 10+ by appointment.
    Weekdays 9:00am-4:00pm. Self guided maps at visitor center.

This center is the foremost, nationally known agricultural research Ohio State University facility with inventions to their credit such as crop dusting and adding vitamin D to milk. Many experiments on insects, greenhouses, honeybees and composting are going on. See how animals are raised, how the right wheat is important for successful bread making (maybe make some), how laser beams detect the size of water droplets in pesticide applications, and how a jellyfish gene can help soybean scientists. Most importantly, they teach you how agriculture impacts everyone-everyday. If self-guided tours are your option, you can see the Center which contains some activities for children such as a microscope and computer display as well as the bug zoo. You can also visit the 88 acre Secrest Arboretum which has many walking trails and a children's play area. This might spark the future scientist within your child.

WAYNE COUNTY HISTORICAL SOCIETY MUSEUM

Wooster - *546 East Bowman Street, 44691. Phone: (330) 264-8856. Web: www.waynehistorical.org. Hours: Wednesday-Sunday 2:00-4:30pm. Closed January and holidays.* Early 1800's Carriage Barn, Log Cabin (early settlers home life), Schoolhouse (McGuffy Readers, dunce cap and stool, and potbelly stove, it accurately recreates the atmosphere of a late 1800's learning center), Indians, Women's Vintage Dress Shop, and Outdoor Bake Oven (typical of the massive outdoor ovens which were once found on virtually all German farms in the area during the 19th century).

LORENA STERNWHEELER

Zanesville - *Moored at Zane's Landing Park (West End of Market Street – I-70 to Downtown Zanesville Exit – Follow signs), 43701.* ***Web: www.visitzanesville.com/lorena.htm****. Phone: (740) 455-8883 or (800) 246-6303. Hours: Wednesday and Saturdays (June – August). Weekends Only (September to mid-October). Admission: School Groups $3.00 student. $15.00-$30.00 lunch and dinner cruises.* There was a mythical sweetheart of the Civil War named Lorena who inspired a song written by the famous Zanesvillian, Rev. Henry Webster. The 104' long, 59-ton boat was christened "Lorena" after that popular song. A one-hour cruise on the Muskingum River at a very reasonable rate for students.

MAPLETREE BASKETS

Zanesville - *705 Keen Street, 43701. Phone: (740) 450-8824 or (888) 2BASKET. www.mapletreebaskets.com. Hours: Weekdays 8:00am-5:00pm. Saturday by appointment. Manufacturing tours given for groups of 12 or more by advanced reservation only.* Watch local artisans hand weave fine quality maple hard wood baskets.

BLUE ROCK STATE PARK

Zanesville (Blue Rock) - *7924 Cutler Lake Road (12 miles Southeast of Zanesville off State Route 60 and County Road 45), 43720. Web: www.dnr.state.oh.us/parks/parks/bluerock.htm. Phone: (740) 674-4794.* Rugged hills and rich green forests provide 350 acres of camping, hiking trails, boating, fishing, swimming and winter sports. A public beach is located on the north end of the lake. Swimming is permitted during daylight hours only. Change booths, lockers, restrooms and snacks are available.

MUSKINGUM RIVER PARKWAY STATE PARK

Zanesville (Blue Rock) - *(120 acres along 80 miles of the Muskingum River extending from Devola to Ellis Locks), 43720. Web: www.dnr.state.oh.us/parks/parks/muskngmr.htm. Phone: (740) 452-3820.* The Muskingum River is formed by the confluence of the Walhonding and Tuscarawas rivers in Coshocton flowing south through Zanesville where it joins the Licking River. The river travels 112 miles in all and its 10 locks are still hand-operated in the same manner as 150 years ago. Along with such majestic institutions as Hoover Dam, The Empire State Building and the Golden Gate Bridge, the Muskingum River's 10 hand-operated locks are now recognized as one of America's great engineering accomplishments. Visitors are offered camping, hiking trails, boating, and fishing.

DILLON STATE PARK

Zanesville (Nashport) - *5265 Dillon Hills Drive (8 miles west of Zanesville off State Route 146), 43830. Phone: (740) 453-4377.* **Web:** *www.dnr.state.oh.us/parks/parks/dillon.htm.* The wooded hills and valleys of the area offer outdoor adventure with 7690 acres of camping, hiking trails, boating and rentals, fishing, swimming (sandy beaches), and winter sports. The Ruffed Grouse Nature Trail is approximately 3/4-mile long and introduces the hiker to the varied habitats of the area. This trail is a branch of the 6-mile long Licking Bend Trail which skirts the lakeshore. Three other fascinating trails--Blackberry Ridge Trail (1 mile), King Ridge Loop (1.1 miles) and Hickory Grove Loop (1.5 miles) are located very near the camping and cottage area. Family deluxe cottages with A/C and cable. Nearby, in the Blackhand Gorge, carved by the Licking River, a sandstone cliff bore a soot blackened (Black Hand Sandstone) engraving of a human hand. This mysterious petroglyph is thought to have served as a guide marker for Indians searching for Flint Ridge.

ZOAR VILLAGE

Zoar - *198 Main Street (State Route 212 – I-77 to Exit 93), 44697.* **Web:** *www.ohiohistory.org/places/zoar.* *Phone: (800) 262-6195 or (330) 874-3011. Hours: Wednesday-Saturday 9:30am-5:00pm, Sunday, Holidays Noon-5:00 pm (Summer). Weekends Only (April, May, September, October). Restricted hours for FREE Museum. Admission: $7.00 adult, $3.00 student (all ages). Miscellaneous: Video presentation first explains Zoar history. Probably best to tour with an emphasis on early Ohio home and community life (w/German-American heritage) theme vs. a focus on their political and religious practices (cult-like aspects).* Zoar means "a sanctuary from evil". They, as a society of Separatists (separation between church and state), were known for their bountiful gardening designs based on the bible. The 12 block district of 1800's homes and shops include a dairy, bakery, museum, gardens, storehouse, tin shops, wagon shops, and blacksmith. They are actual original buildings in a real town of 75 families. Some buildings are staffed, others open by guided tour. Volunteers give craft demonstrations during the many yearly special events. Walk along streets dispersed with restored residences and shops for modern clients.

SUGGESTED LODGING AND DINING

ATWOOD LAKE RESORT – Dellroy. (330) 735-2211 or (800) 362-6406 or **www.atwoodlakeresort.com**. Camping, hiking trails, boating & rentals, fishing, swimming, visitor center and winter sports. Beach with paddle boat rentals & food service. Dining and accommodations with indoor/outdoor pool at lodge. Comfortable, spacious 4 bedroom cabins with trails! Bring along the extended family and plan a mini-reunion. Because the cabins are spacious and have separate bedrooms, everyone can have their "space", yet convene in the center gathering area for games, conversation or television. Summertime kids activities, too. (off SR 212 to SR 542 or off SR 39 entrance)

Chapter 3
Central West Area

Our Favorites...

* Boonshoft Museum of Discovery - Dayton
* Dayton History & Carillon Park - Dayton
* Sunwatch - Dayton
* National Museum of USAF - Dayton/Fairborn
* Piqua Historical Area - Piqua
* Freshwater Farms - Urbana
* Armstrong Air & Space Museum - Wapakoneta
* Blue Jacket / Tecumseh History - Xenia
* Young's Jersey Dairy - Yellow Springs

A Historical Chair from Tecumseh's past...

ZANE SHAWNEE CAVERNS

Bellefontaine - *7092 State Route 540 (5 miles east of town), 43311.* **Web: *www.zaneshawneecaverns.org.*** *Phone: (937) 592-9592. Hours: Daily 10:00am-5:00pm. Admission: Caverns $8.00 adult, $4.00 child (under age 12). Museum $7.00 adult, $4.00 child. Cavern & Museum package rate. Miscellaneous: There are a lot of extras like hayrides, gift shop, snack bar, and camping. Remember to dress appropriately because the temperature in the caverns is a constant 48-50 degrees F.* See crystals in objects formed like straws, draperies, and popcorn. They boast the only "cave pearls" found in Ohio. This property is now owned and operated by the Shawnee People. The Museum has artifacts from actual tribe members and some from prehistoric Indian digs (Hopewell, Ancient). Separate display cases give a special look to other Native American cultural areas including: Great Lakes Tribes, Northern Iroquois, Southwestern Tribes, Great plains, Southeastern Tribes and the Eskimo People. Also on display is the evolution of corn - Zea Maize to modern corn and Native American weapons along with several dioramas.

CLIFTON MILL

75 Water Street (I-70 West to SR 72 South)

Clifton 45316

❑ Phone: (937) 767-5501 **Web: www.cliftonmill.com**

❑ Hours: Monday-Friday 9:00am-4:00pm, Saturday-Sunday 8:00am-4:00pm, Restaurant closes one hour earlier. (November-March). Weekdays 9:00am-5:00pm, Weekends 8:00am-6:00pm (April-October). Closed Christmas, New Year's, Easter &Thanksgiving Day. Note: December hours they close the restaurant at 2:00pm and giftshop at 3:00pm.

❑ Admission: Restaurant serves kids meals around $3.00-$5.00. Adult meals are double.

❑ Miscellaneous: Restaurant and store. Walk off your meal by parking down the road at Clifton Gorge Nature Preserve and "hiking" the small sand/gravel walkway past bridges and on platforms that give you a "crows nest" view of the gorge - beautiful.

Clifton Mill (*cont.*)

A surprise treat tucked away in a small town where Woody Hayes grew up. Built in 1802 on the Little Miami River, it is the largest operating water powered gristmill in the nation. Before or after a yummy breakfast or lunch overlooking the river, take a self-guided tour for a small fee. There are 5 floors to view. The 3rd floor (main operations) is where you see how everything on the other floors above and below come together. The turbine takes the flowing water's energy to move a system of belts to the grindstones. As the stones rotate, raw grain is poured into the hopper, through a chute and into a space between the stones which grind it. The most interesting part of the tour is the belt to bucket elevators that are the "life of the mill" transporting grain and flour up and down 5 levels. Restaurant seating with a view of a waterwheel, river and covered bridge. Pancakes, mush, grits and bread are made from product produced at the mill. Best pork barbecue sandwich ever! Breakfast and lunch only. Be sure to buy some pancake mix to take home!

DAYTON SPORTS

Dayton

DAYTON BOMBERS HOCKEY - Erwin J. Nutter Center, Fairborn. (937) 775-4747 or **www.daytonbombers.com**. East Coast Hockey League.

DAYTON DRAGONS BASEBALL - Fifth Third Field. (937) 228-BATS or **www.daytondragons.com**. Class A team. Check out the new FunZone. Located behind the batters eye, the Dragons FunZone consists of : Pop-a-Shot (challenge a friend and winners can take home bragging rights); Speed pitch (unleash your fastball); Inflatable Bounce house (features a slide). Tickets are $1 each.

DUNBAR STATE MEMORIAL, PAUL LAWRENCE

219 North Paul Lawrence Dunbar Street (2 blocks north of 3rd Street, east of US35), **Dayton** 45401

❑ Phone: (937) 224-7061 or (800) 860-0148
   Web: www.ohiohistory.org/places/dunbar
❑ Hours: Wednesday-Saturday 9:00am-5:00pm, Sunday & Holidays Noon-5:00pm (Memorial Day-Labor Day). Weekends Only (April, May, September, October).
❑ Admission: $6.00 adult, $3.00 student (all ages).

The restored home of the first African American to achieve acclaim in American literature. From a young poet at age 6 to a nationally known figure (until his death at age 33 of tuberculosis), the guide helps you understand his inspiration especially from his mother and her stories of slavery. Personal belongings like his bicycle built by the Wright Brothers and a sword presented to him by President Roosevelt lead you to his bedroom where he wrote 100 novels, poems and short stories.

> *"We smile, but, O great Christ, our cries*
>
> *To thee from tortured souls arise.*
>
> *We sing, but oh the clay is vile*
>
> *Beneath our feet, and long the mile;*
>
> *But let the world dream otherwise,*
>
> *We wear the mask!"*

- Paul Laurence Dunbar, from the poem, We Wear the Mask

CITIZENS MOTORCAR PACKARD MUSEUM

Dayton - *420 South Ludlow Street - Downtown (I-75 to US 35 exit, head east a few blocks), 45402. Phone: (937) 226-1917. Web: www.americaspackardmuseum.org. Hours: Monday-Friday Noon-5:00pm, Saturday and Sunday 1:00-5:00pm. Admission: $5.00 adult, $4.00 student.* See the world's largest collection of Packard automobiles in an authentic showroom. The art deco Packard dealership interior exhibits are spread through 6 settings, including the service area and period decorated salesman's office.

DAYTON PHILHARMONIC ORCHESTRA

Dayton - *125 East First Street (many performances at the Schuster Center for the Performing Arts), 45402.* Phone: *(937) 224-9000.* **Web:** *www.daytonphilharmonic.com.* Plays classical, pops, and Summer outdoor concerts. The Family Concert Series often features Side-by-Side appearances with the Youth Orchestra with themes like Clowns or Mozart for the Mind.

METRODUCKS & RIVERSCAPE

Dayton - *111 E. Monument Avenue (MetroPark's RiverScape, Ride the River rentals), 45402. Phone: (937) 278-2607.* **Web:** *www.metroducks.com/dayton.htm or www.riverscape.org. Admission: $15.00 adult, $14.00 senior and active military, $10.00 child (4-12), $1.00 child (3 and under). Tours: Tuesday-Sunday 1:30pm, 3:00pm, 4:30pm and 7:00pm Thursday-Sunday only. Duck tours last approximately one hour and are held rain or shine.*

METRODUCKS: These vintage WWII re-supply crafts can travel up to 50 mph on land and up to 7 mph on water. They drive directly into, and out of, the Miami River, giving riders a thrill and spectators a gasp! On land, they'll take you through downtown and point out significant historical facts.

RIVERSCAPE: Before or after you duck tour, enjoy the RiverScape landscaped gardens, a free summer concert, major community festivals and family walks and bike rides along the river corridor recreation trails. A focal point of RiverScape is the Five Rivers Fountain of Lights, a series of five fountains that shoot water upwards of 200 feet and 400 feet across at the confluence of the Great Miami and Mad Rivers (May through October). And, don't forget your bathing suit. A popular spot for visitors looking to cool off on hot summer days is the Interactive Fountain where multiple fountain jets shoot water as high as 15 feet into the air choreographed to the sounds of family friendly music. And, the fun isn't over when it gets cold -MetroParks' invites you to come "Skate the Scape" as RiverScape becomes home to the regions only outdoor ice skating rink, festive light displays and other family winter activities. Concessions available.

DAYTON ART INSTITUTE

Dayton - *456 Belmonte Park North (I-75 exit 53B), 45405.* **Web:** *www.daytonartinstitute.org.* Phone: *(937) 223-5277 or (800) 296-4426.* Art collection spanning 5000 years. Experiencenter (features 20 hands-on activities) encourages interaction with art and experimentation with artistic elements of line, pattern, color, texture and shape. A gallery bag and an alphabet book are also available at the Entrance Rotunda desk allowing families to further explore featured special exhibits through the use of games and learning activities.

WRIGHT CYCLE COMPANY

22 South Williams Street (off West 3rd Street)

Dayton 45407

- ❏ Phone: (937) 225-7705, **Web: www.nps.gov/daav/**
- ❏ Hours: Daily 8:30am-5:00pm except major winter holidays.
- ❏ Admission: Donation

The bicycle craze in America began in 1887 with the introduction from England of the safety bicycle (two wheels of equal size) It made the freedom of cycling accessible to a much wider market. The Wright brothers' best known pre-aeronautical occupation was bicycle repair and manufacture. This building is the actual site where the Wright Brothers had a bicycle business from 1895-1897 and developed their own brand of bicycles. On this site, they also developed ideas that led to the invention of flight almost 7 years later. You'll walk on the same floorboards that the brothers did and see actual plans for a flying bicycle!

DAYTON HISTORY AT CARILLON PARK

1000 Carillon Blvd. (I-75 to Exit 51)

Dayton 45409

- ❏ Phone: (937) 293-2841 **Web: www.carillonpark.org**
- ❏ Hours: Monday-Saturday 9:30am-5:00pm. Sunday and Holidays Noon - 5:00pm, closed on Thanksgiving, Christmas Eve, Christmas Day, New Year's Eve, and New Year's Day.

Dayton History At Carillon Park (*cont.*)

- ❑ Admission: $8.00 adult, $7.00 senior, $5.00 child (3-17).
- ❑ Miscellaneous: Museum Store sells period toys, snacks and candy. Wooded park with Ohio's largest bell tower, the Carillon Bell Tower (57 bells), also has many shaded picnic areas. CULP'S CAFE, reminiscent of Culp's Cafeteria located in downtown Dayton in the 1930s and 1940s, serves soup, salads, and sandwiches, ice cream and sodas. (937) 299-2277.

A must see - very comfortable and educational - over 65 acres of historical buildings and outdoor exhibits of history, invention and transportation. Called the "Little Greenfield Village" in Miami Valley and we definitely agree! Inventions like the cash register, innovations like flood control, and industries like Huffy Corporation are represented throughout the Park. Many of the oldest buildings from the early 1800's are represented too (tavern, home, school). As you enter most buildings, a costumed guide will orient you to colorful stories of the famous people who once occupied them. The highlight of the collections is the 1905 Wright Flyer III, the world's first practical airplane. Our favorites are the Deed's Barn (learn about the Barn Gang and the big companies they started) and the rail cars that you can actually board-the Barney & Smith is ritzy!

AULLWOOD AUDUBON CENTER AND FARM

Dayton - *1000 Aullwood Road, 45414. Phone: (937) 890-7360.* ***Web: www.audubon.org/local/sanctuary/aullwood/aacfhome.html****. Hours: Monday-Saturday 9:00am-5:00pm, Sunday 1:00-5:00pm. Closed holidays. Admission: $4.00 adult, $2.00 child (2-18).* The Discovery Room has more than 50 hands-on exhibits. Visitors can begin walks on five miles of hiking trails here. Around the building are special plantings of prairie and woodland wildflowers and a butterfly - hummingbird garden. The nearby Farm (9101 Frederick Pike) is the site of many special events. Cows, pigs, horses, chickens, turkeys, sheep, goats and barn swallows can all be found here if you come at the right time. The sugar bush, organic garden, herb garden and access to the trails are here. The glacial erratics are the start of the Geology trail. On it, you can explore the recent erosion of the land and the water cycle, the leavings of the continental glacier, and the old bedrock with its load of Ordovician fossils.

BOONSHOFT MUSEUM OF DISCOVERY

2600 DeWeese Parkway (North of downtown I-75 to exit 57B, follow signs), **Dayton** 45414

❑   Phone: (937) 275-7431, **Web: www.boonshoftmuseum.org**

❑   Hours: Monday-Friday 9:00am-5:00pm, Saturday 11:00am-5:00pm, Sunday Noon-5:00pm. Closed major winter holidays.

❑   Admission: $8.50 adult, $7.00 senior, $7.00child (2-12). $1.00-$3.00 additional for Space Theater.

❑   Miscellaneous: With memberships here, you also can get free or discounted admissions to many museums in Ohio and surrounding states. Vending area. Discovery Shop.

A Children's Museum, a Science Center, Nature Center AND Planetarium all in one place! Here's highlights of each space:

ECOTREK - mastodon bones, desert animals (daytime vs. nighttime creatures using flashlights!), touch tide pool (ever seen a red sea cucumber? Touch one!), rainforest and treehouse within campsite and binoculars window views.

WILD OHIO – An indoor zoo with small animals in natural surroundings. Visit the den of bobcat Van Cleve or a coyote, river otter, groundhog, fox or turtle. A Falcon nest Web Cam is a popular area - something new is always happening with that family. Both parents will tend to the chicks so keep an eye out for both Mercury and Snowball at the nest.

ANCIENT WORLD – Egyptian artifacts with 3000 year old mummy.

SCIENCE CENTRAL – Inventions stations (water table w/ sticky water, airfort and force (tubes & funny windbag blower machines), chemistry lab, and a climbing discovery tower (nets, tubes & slide) provides hands on adventures.

KIDS' PLAYCE - baby garden, pioneer cabin, dig, slide & little creatures. Dress up spot.

LEARNING TREE FARM

Dayton - *3376 South Union Road, 45418. Phone: (937) 866-8650.*
Web: *www.learningtreefarm.org. Hours: Dawn to Dusk. Best weekdays when most facilities are open or during special programs. Admission: Hands on the Farm: $5.00 general self-guided. Special Programs: guided $7.00 general. $1.00 discount per person for groups (12+).* The history of the family which originally owned the farm, from their initial voyage to Ohio to the present day, has been researched and displayed. Visitors may tour the house, visit the farm animals, hike on the farm's land, and participate in hands-on activities like caring for animals, crafts, and sheep shearing. Special programs like "Finding Freedom on the Farm" highlights storytelling, quilts used by escaping slaves, clue game thru nearby land and daily activities of the safe house station.

SUNWATCH

2301 West River Road (I-75 to Exit 51, west on Edwin C. Moses Blvd., cross South Broadway, turn left), **Dayton** 45418

- ❑   Phone: (937) 268-8199, **Web: www.sunwatch.org**
- ❑   Hours: Tuesday-Saturday 9:00am-5:00pm. Sunday and Holidays Noon – 5:00pm.
- ❑   Admission: $5.00 adult, $3.00 child (6-17) & senior (60+).
- ❑   Tours: Guided tours daily at 1: 30 p.m. (Summer)
- ❑   Miscellaneous: Occasional Family Days are best. Orientation video suggested first.

Archaeological excavations at a site near the Great Miami River uncovered evidence of an 800-year-old village built by the Fort Ancient Indians. The reconstructed 12th Century Indian Village has self-guided tours of the thatched huts, gardens and artifacts of the lifestyle of a unique culture. In the museum exhibits study the trash pits - you can learn a lot from people's trash. Study their ancient calendars - can you tell the season? Some activities include story telling, archery, toys and games, harvesting, a multi-media presentation, and best of all, learn to tell time by charting the sun. See how the Indians used flint and bone to create jewelry and tools - then buy some as souvenirs.

COX ARBORETUM

Dayton - *6733 Springboro Pike, 45449. Phone: (937) 434-9005.*
Web: *www.metroparks.org.* *Hours: Daily 8:00am to dusk. Visitor*
Center weekdays 8:30am-4:30pm and weekends 1:00-4:00pm.
170 acres including the nationally recognized Edible Landscape
Garden.   Every season has something special to offer, from
spring's splashes of bright color to winter's textures. The
Arboretum hosts nine specialty gardens. In addition to exploring
gardens, hike trails through mature forests and colorful meadows.

NATIONAL MUSEUM OF THE US AIR FORCE

Wright Patterson Air Force Base (I-75 to State Route 4 East to
Harshman Road Exit)

Dayton (Fairborn) 45433

☐   Phone: (937) 255-3286, **Web: www.wpafb.af.mil/museum**
☐   Hours: Daily 9:00am-5:00pm. Closed Thanksgiving, Christmas
     and New Years.
☐   Admission: FREE
☐   Tours: The free USAF Heritage Tour begins at 1:30 p.m. Monday
     through Friday. Saturdays 10:30 a.m. & 1:30 p.m. No reservation
     required.
☐   Miscellaneous: Largest Gift Shop imaginable. Concessions.
     IMAX THEATER - 6 story with hourly 40 minute space/aviation
     films - feel like you're flying with the pilots. Fee. (937-253-IMAX.
     Morphis MovieRide Theater - actually move, tilt & shout.
     HUFFMAN PRAIRIE FIELD - Rte. 44 (937-257-5535). See
     where The Wright Brothers first attempted flight.

For the best in family entertainment / educational value, this
museum is definitely a must see! You'll have a real adventure
exploring the world's oldest and largest military aviation museum
that features over 50 vintage WWII aircraft (even the huge 6-
engine B-36) and 300 other aircraft and rockets. See everything
from presidential planes, to Persian Gulf advanced missiles and
bombs, the original Wright Brothers wind tunnel, to the original
Apollo 15 command module. Look for the observation balloon

(easy to find—just look up ever so slightly), Rosie the Rivetor and "Little Vittles" parachuted goodies. Discovery Hangar Five follows a common museum trend and focuses on the interactive learning of why things fly and different parts of airplanes. Continuous films played at stations throughout the complex (with chairs-take a break from all the walking). National Aviation Hall of Fame is next door.

CARRIAGE HILL FARM AND MUSEUM

Dayton (Huber Heights) - *7860 East Shull Road (I-70 to Exit 38 - State Route 201 north), 45424. Phone: (937) 278-2609. Web: www.metroparks.org. Hours: Monday-Friday 10:00am-5:00pm, Saturday-Sunday 1:00-5:00pm. Admission: Donation. Miscellaneous: Picnic area, fishing, horseback riding, cross country skiing, hayrides and bobsled rides. No bikes on trails, though.* Stop at the Visitor Center for exhibits highlighting lifestyles of a century ago, a children's interactive center and the Country Store gift shop. The self-guided tour of an 1880's working farm is a great benefit to the community. The farm includes a summer kitchen, workshop, black smith and barns. Household chores and farming are performed as they were 100 years ago and a variety of farm animals fill the barn. They are best to visit when workers are planting or harvesting gardens.

MIAMISBURG MOUND

Dayton (Miamisburg) - *(I-75 to State Route 725 exit 42, follow signs), 45342. Web: www.ohiohistory.org/places/miamisbur. Phone: (937) 866-5632. Hours: Daily Dawn to Dusk. Admission: FREE. Miscellaneous: Park, Picnic tables and playground.* Take the 116 stairs up a 68-foot high and 1.5 acre wide mound built by American Indians. This is the largest conical burial mound in Ohio. Archaeological investigations of the surrounding area suggest that it was constructed by the prehistoric Adena Indians (800BC - AD100). The mound measures 877 feet in circumference.

WRIGHT B. FLYER

Dayton (Miamisburg) - *10550 Springboro Pike (State Route 741 – Dayton Wright Airport), 45342. Phone: (937) 885-2327. Web: www.destinationdayton.com/wrightb/hanger.html. Hours: Tuesday, Thursday, and Saturday 9:00am-2:00pm. Admission: Aircraft ride certificates may be purchased for $150.00. This entitles the certificate bearer to an orientation ride replicating the Wright Brothers' original flight patterns over Huffman Prairie! Otherwise, only donations.* A group decided to build a flying replica of the first production aircraft ever built - the Wright Brothers B Model Airplane. The result is a fully operational flying aircraft that closely resembles the original Wright B Model that flew over Huffman Prairie in 1911. This hangar houses a flyable replica of the 1911 plane built by Wilbur and Orville Wright. They also have a half scale model of the plane and other aviation exhibits and souvenirs.

FORT RECOVERY STATE MEMORIAL

Fort Recovery - *One Fort Site Street (State Route 49 and State Route 119), 45846. Phone: (419) 375-4649. Web: www.ohiohistory.org/places/ftrecovr. Hours: Daily Noon-5:00pm (Summer). Weekends Only (May and September). Admission: $1.00-$3.00 (student and adult).* The remaining blockhouses with connecting stockade wall are where General Arthur St. Clair was defeated by Indians in 1791. Later, in 1794, General "Mad" Anthony Wayne defended the fort successfully. A museum with Indian War artifacts and dressed mannequins is also displayed on the property.

BEAR'S MILL

Greenville - *Bear's Mill Road (5 miles East on US 36 then South), 45331. Phone: (937) 548-5112. Web: www.bearsmill.com. Tours (self-guided): Tuesday-Sunday 11:00am – 5:00pm (March-December), extended morning hours on Saturdays. Weekends only (January-February). Guided tours by appointment. Miscellaneous: Store-sells flours ground at the mill, gift baskets, handmade pottery.* Bear's Mill, built in 1849, is an authentic example of a stone grinding flour mill of its time. It is still in use today to grinding cornmeal, whole-wheat flour, and rye flour. Tour the mill built in 1849 by Gabriel Bear where grinding stones (powered by water flowing beneath the building) grind flour and meal. The process is slow and kept cool to retard deteriorating wholesome nutrients. Everyone who comes to Bear's Mill during business hours is welcome to take a self guided tour of the 4 story structure and take a walk in the scenic woods surrounding the mill.

GARST MUSEUM, DARKE COUNTY HISTORICAL SOCIETY

Greenville - *205 North Broadway, 45331. Phone: (937) 548-5250. Web: www.garstmuseum.org. Hours: Tuesday-Saturday 11:00am -5:00pm, Sunday 1:00-5:00pm. (March-November). Admission: $1.00-$3.00 (age 6+).* The main feature of the museum are Darke County's most-famous daughter sharp-shooter and entertainer Annie Oakley (artifacts from her professional AND private life - newly renovated Center). View displays about: world-traveler, broadcaster, author and adventurer Lowell Thomas; pioneering aviator Zachary Lansdowne; The Treaty of Greeneville and much other history of the county including 30 individual room settings. Even something on Lewis and Clark. Anthony Wayne, Native American artifacts and Village of shops, too.

KITCHENAID EXPERIENCE & FACTORY TOURS

Greenville - *423 South Broadway/ 1701 KitchenAid Way (I-70 exit US 127 north to town), 45331. Phone: (888) 886-8318. Web: www.KitchenAid.com/experience. Hours: Experience store Monday - Saturday 10:00am-6:00pm, Sunday Noon-5:00pm. Admission: Tours are $5.00 per person. Tours: Weekdays at 10:00am and 1:00pm (subject to manufacturing schedules) or groups over 8 with appointment. Enclosed footwear required. Safety glasses provided, must be at least 12 years old.* The site that houses the KitchenAid Experience was the Turpin House Hotel and later a five and dime store. The Greenville connection started way back in 1908 with a mixer produced for commercial bakers. Visit the heritage exhibits, take a kids cooking class, or tour. The work force produces hundreds of mixers every day. Walk through the whole process, peeking over workers shoulders.

INDIAN LAKE STATE PARK

Lakeview - *12774 State Route 235 N (US 33, 20 miles east of I-75), 43331. Web: www.dnr.state.oh.us/parks/parks/indianlk.htm. Phone: (937) 843-2717.* The present and much larger lake lies along one of the country's major avian migration routes. Indian Lake is an important resting stop for birds such as Canada geese, ducks, grebes, swans, egrets and herons. Many stay over the summer to nest. The Cherokee Trail, a 3-mile easy walk through brushy habitat, is located west of the camp. The Pew Island Trail, a 1-mile path, encircles Pew Island. Access is available to Pew Island from a causeway. This trail affords a spectacular view of Indian Lake. A paved bikeway is located on the West Bank between Old Field Beach and Lakeview Harbor. The bikeway is 3 miles long. Walkers and joggers are welcome to use the bikeway. Two public beaches, Old Field Beach and Fox Island Beach, invite swimmers to relax in the cool waters of Indian Lake. 6448 acres of camping, hiking trails, boating, fishing, swimming and winter sports.

LOCKINGTON LOCKS STATE MEMORIAL

Lockington - *5 miles North of Piqua-Lockington Road (I-75 to exit 83 West on State Route 25A), 45356. Phone: (800) 686-1535. Web: www.ohiohistory.org/places/lockingt/index.html. Hours: Daily Dawn to Dusk. Admission: FREE.* These stair step locks, among the best preserved in Ohio, were part of the Miami and Erie Canal System, which opened for navigation in 1845 and connected Cincinnati and the Ohio River to Toledo and Lake Erie. For several decades, the canal provided Ohio with valuable transportation and waterpower. View portions of five original locks (elevation adjusters for canal boats) and the aqueduct that lowered boats 67 feet into the Miami-Erie Canal.

LAKE LORAMIE STATE PARK

Minster - *4401 Ft. Loramie Swanders Road (3 miles Southeast of Minster off State Route 66), 45865. Phone: (937) 295-2011. Web: www.dnr.state.oh.us/parks/parks/lkloramie.htm.* One of the original canal feeder lakes, Lake Loramie State Park offers visitors a quiet retreat in rural Ohio. Swim from the sandy beach, hike along the old canal towpath, stay a night in a shaded campsite or boat the lazy waters of Lake Loramie. The hiking opportunities at Lake Loramie include more than eight miles of trail. A portion of the trail system follows the Miami-Erie Canal from the park to Delphos. This route is also a part of the Buckeye Trail and the North Country National Scenic Trail.

BICYCLE MUSEUM OF AMERICA

New Bremen - *7 West Monroe Street (SR 274), 45869. Phone: (419) 629-9249. Web: www.bicyclemuseum.com. Hours: Monday – Friday 11:00am - 5:00pm (til 7:00pm in the summer). Saturday 11:00am – 2:00pm. Admission: $3.00 adult, $2.00 senior, $1.00 student.* A department store has been converted into a showcase of the world's oldest bike (w/out pedals) to the Schwinn family collection (including the 1,000,000th bicycle made). High-wheelers to side-by-side doubles and quads. Celebrity bikes and bikes from balloon tire to banana seat bikes will amuse you.

PIQUA HISTORICAL AREA TOUR

North Hardin Road (I-75 to exit 83 County Road 25A West to State Route 66 North), **Piqua** 45356

- ❑ Phone: (937) 773-2522 or (800) 752-2619
  Web: www.ohiohistory.org/places/piqua
- ❑ Hours: Wednesday-Saturday 9:30am-5:00pm, Sunday and Holidays Noon-5:00pm (Summer). Weekends Only (September and October).
- ❑ Admission: $7.00 adult, $3.00 student (all ages). Includes canal boat ride.
- ❑ Miscellaneous: Canal rides a few times during the afternoon in the summer.

Tour the Johnston Farm which includes an 1808 massive log barn which is probably the oldest such barn in Ohio. In the farmhouse, the kids will probably be most interested in the beds made of rope and hay filled sacks. Eight girls slept in one room (ages 2-20) and three boys in another. Many youth games of that time period are displayed. The Winter Kitchen is also very interesting – especially the size of the walk-in fireplace. The Farm buildings have costumed guides describing and interacting with youth as they demonstrate chores on the farm. Before you visit the canal, stop in the museum where excellent exhibits, inside and out, explain the treacherous job of building a canal and why. The General Harrison canal boat is powered by two mules which pull the boat down and back on a section of the Old Miami-Erie Canal (Cincinnati to Toledo). The cargo boat was once used to transport produce and meat at a speed limit of 4 MPH. The boats were fined $10.00 for speeding although many paid the fine and continued going 10 MPH. Once the railroads came, canals became obsolete.

CLARK STATE PERFORMING ARTS CENTER

Springfield - *300 South Fountain Avenue, 45501. Phone: (937) 328-3874. Web: www.clarkstate.edu/pac/.* Hosts national and regional performers, recording artists, Broadway shows, circuses, and Family Stages (Dinosaurs!) or Sunday Funday programs. (September- June)

BUCK CREEK STATE PARK

Springfield - *1901 Buck Creek Lane (4 miles East of Springfield on State Route 4), 45502. Phone: (937) 322-5284. Web: www.dnr.state.oh.us/parks/parks/buckck.htm.* Buck Creek State Park lies in a fertile agricultural area, rich in Ohio's history. The park's recreational facilities center around the 2,120-acre lake, offering endless water-related opportunities. The spotted turtle, a state endangered animal, is found in the area. The northernmost region of the park is an excellent area to observe waterfowl. The shallow waters provide a stopover for thousands of migrating ducks. More than 7.5 miles of hiking trails offer opportunities for nature study, bird watching and other wildlife observation. A scenic 7.5-mile bridle trail is also open to snowmobiling, weather permitting. The U.S. Army Corps of Engineers manages a visitor center and recreational site near the dam. The center provides displays, programs and dam operation tours. 4030 acres of camping, hiking trails, boating and rentals, fishing, swimming and winter sports. 26 family cabins with A/C.

GRAND LAKE ST. MARY'S STATE PARK

834 Edgewater Drive (2 miles West of St. Mary's on State Route 703), **St. Mary's** 45885

❑   Phone: (419) 394-3611

Web: www.dnr.state.oh.us/parks/parks/grndlake

Originally constructed as a feeder reservoir for the Miami-Erie Canal, Grand Lake St. Mary's was for many years recognized as the largest man-made reservoir in the world. Nature programs. 14,000 acres of camping, boating and rentals, fishing, swimming, sport courts, putt-putt and winter sports. Ohio's largest inland lake.

ST. MARY'S FISH FARM: After boating or swimming on Grand Lake (man-made), wander through 52 acres of ponds where pike, catfish, etc. are raised. The farm is one of the only three in Ohio and is the only farm with a large mouth bass and yellow perch hatchery. (East Side of Grand Lake, Phone: (419) 394-5170, Hours: Daily 7:00am-3:30pm)

KISER LAKE STATE PARK

St. Paris - *4889 N. St. Rt. 235 (17 miles Northwest of Urbana on State Route 235), 43072. Phone: (937) 362-3822. Web: www.dnr.state.oh.us/parks/parks/kisrlake.htm*. The rolling wooded hills and diverse wetlands add to the beauty of this scenic lake known for its clean, clear waters. Five hiking trails are located within the park and provide 5.1 scenic miles of walking pleasure. Red Oak and the Nature Preserve Boardwalk trails are located near the family camp area at the east end of the lake. The North Bay Trail follows the lake shoreline for 1.5 miles. Seven miles of horse trails are located near State Route 235. 870 acres of camping, hiking trails, boating and rentals, fishing, swimming and winter sports.

SYCAMORE STATE PARK

Trotwood - *4675 N. Diamond Mill Road (1 mile North of Trotwood on State Route 49), 45426. Phone: (937) 854-4452 Web: www.dnr.state.oh.us/parks/parks/sycamore.htm*. The meadows, woodlots and still waters of Sycamore State Park provide the perfect setting for picnicking, hiking, fishing, camping, snowmobiling and horseback riding. The 3-mile Ghost Hedge Nature Trail offers the hiker an opportunity to explore the Wolf Creek Valley. Giant sycamore trees form a picturesque canopy over the trail. The 1.5-mile Beech Ridge Trail explores the surrounding woodlots and meadows. Horsemen can enjoy 15 miles of bridle trail, including the snowmobile routes when not snow covered. The trails pass through scenic meadows and woodlots.

BRUKNER NATURE CENTER

Troy - *5995 Horseshoe Bend Rd. (Exit # 73 off of I-75, west on SR 55 3 miles), 45373. Phone: (937) 698-6493.* **Web: www.tdn-net.com/brukner.** *Hours: Monday-Saturday 9:00am-5:00pm, Sunday 12:30 - 5:00pm. Admission: Small admission charged on Sundays.* This 164 acre nature preserve's attractions include 6 miles of hiking trails, a wildlife rehabilitation center and the interpretive center. The 1804 Iddings log house was built by the first settlers in Miami County. The Center's animal rehabilitation has over 65 permanent residents on display. The top floor contains a glass-enclosed vista room for watching and listening to birds as they feed. A ground-level viewing station for mammals also is available.

CEDAR BOG AND NATURE PRESERVE

Urbana - *980 Woodburn Road (off Route 68 North / I-70 to Springfield / off State Route 36), 43078. Phone: (937) 484-3744.* **Web: www.ohiohistory.org/places/cedarbog.** *Hours: Friday-Sunday 9:00am-4:30pm (April-September). Volunteer staffing so call ahead to be sure open. Admission: $3.00-$4.00 per student or adult.* A bog is a remnant of the Ice Age (glaciers and mastodons) and public tours take you to the boardwalk over this bog. Below, you'll see the black, wet, slimy muck and chilly dampness created by a constant water table and cool springs. In contrast, see excellent orchid, prairie and woodland wildflowers.

FRESHWATER FARMS OF OHIO

2624 US 68 (north of downtown circle)

Urbana 43078

- ❑   Phone: (937) 652-3701 or (800) 634-7434
  Web: www.fwfarms.com
- ❑   Hours: (Store) Monday-Saturday 10:00am-6:00pm. Closed major holidays.
- ❑   Tours: FREE. Self-guided tour
- ❑   Miscellaneous: Bring a cooler if you plan to purchase any fish. Supplies for ponds at home - compatible fish, frogs. Produces several hundred thousand trout sold to premium restaurants. The Douglas Inn (111 Miami St., 937-653-5585) downtown Urbana serves this wonderful fresh trout in a historic early 1800s bldg.

Start your tour by petting a sturgeon fish. Why can you touch them, but not catfish? They raise rainbow trout that are bred in large water tanks. Farmer Smith, a marine biologist with a doctorate in nutrition, and his father (an engineer), developed a system of tracks and tanks using re-circulated pure cleaned water. The fish are really spoiled with a special diet and solar-heated hatchery. View the spring water "ponds" with gravel bottoms (outside) and put a quarter in the machine to get fish food to feed the fish. Other newer exhibits of live fish are the jumbo freshwater shrimp and their "loopy" eyes! These fish are really spoiled, aren't they?

ARMSTRONG AIR AND SPACE MUSEUM

500 South Apollo Drive (I-75 to Exit 111)

Wapakoneta 45895

- ❑   Phone: (419) 738-8811 or (800) 860-0142
  Web: www.ohiohistory.org/places/armstron
- ❑   Hours: Tuesday-Saturday 9:30am-5:00pm. Sunday Noon – 5:00pm. Closed Winter Holidays.
- ❑   Admission: $7.00 adult, $3.00 student (all ages).

The museum honors Neil Armstrong (a Wapakoneta native) and other area aeronauts (like the Wright Brothers) and their flying machines. After greeted by a NASA Skylaneer flown by

Armstrong in the early 1960's, trace the history of flights from balloons to space travel. Look at the Apollo crew spacesuits, a real moon rock, or watch a video of lunar space walks. In the Astro Theater, pretend you're on a trip to the moon. Try a lunar or shuttle landing interactive. Look at Space Food, even dessert! Another favorite is the Infinity Cube – 18 square feet covered with mirrors that make you feel like you've been projected into space. Interactives and videos are abundant. Blast OFF!

MAC-O-CHEE AND MAC-A-CHEEK CASTLES (PIATT CASTLES)

State Route 245 (Route 33 West to State Route 245 East)

West Liberty 43357

❏ Phone: (937) 465-2821, **Web: www.piattcastles.org**
❏ Hours: Daily Noon–4:00pm (April-October), 11:00am-5:00pm (Summer). Weekends only in March.
❏ Admission: $7.00 adult, $6.00 senior (60+),$5.00 student (13-21), $4.00 child (5-12). Prices listed are for each castle. Discount combo prices for both castles.
❏ Miscellaneous: Hands-on activities for families (summer).

Castles in Ohio? Catch the eerie, yet magnificent old castles furnished with collections ranging from 150-800 years old. Both castles were built in the mid-1800's and give a good sense of what the lifestyle of the upper-class Piatt brothers family was like. This self-guided tour is very manageable for school-aged (pre-schoolers not suggested) children and includes lots of land to explore outside. Telling friends they were in a castle is fun too. Because the furniture is original, the homes have an old smell and the rooms look frozen in time. Ceiling paintings and the kitchen/dining area were most interesting.

MAD RIVER THEATER WORKS

West Liberty - *319 North Detroit, 43357. Phone: (937) 465-6751. Web: www.madrivertheater.org*. Their purpose is to create and produce plays that explore the concerns of rural people and to perform these works for multi-generational, primarily rural audiences. They interview local residents and research historical issues with contemporary relevance (i.e. John Henry, slavery, Casey Jones). This material is used to craft plays with music that are drawn from and produced for the people of the rural Midwest.

OHIO CAVERNS

West Liberty - *2210 East State Route 245 (I-70 to US 68 north to SR 507 east), 43357.* **Web:** *www.cavern.com/ohiocaverns. Phone: (937) 465-4017. Hours: Daily 9:00am-5:00pm (April-October). 9:00am – 4:00pm (November – March). Admission: $10.50 Adult, $5.50 Children (5-12). Historic tour costs more. Miscellaneous: On the premises is a park and gift shop.* This tour is a 45 minute guided regular or historic tour of the largest cave in Ohio. The temperature here is 54 degrees F. constantly so dress appropriately. Look for the Palace of the Gods and stalagmites that look like cacti or a pump.

NATIONAL AFRO-AMERICAN MUSEUM AND CULTURAL CENTER

Wilberforce - *1350 Brush Row Road (off US 42 - Next to Central State College), 45384.* **Web:** *www.ohiohistory.org/places/afroam. Phone: (800) BLK-HIST. Hours: Tuesday-Saturday 9:00am-5:00pm. Closed holidays except MLK holiday. Admission: $4.00 Adult, $1.50 Children.* Wilberforce was a famous stop on the Underground Railroad and became the center (Wilberforce University) for black education and achievements. The University was the first owned and operated by Afro-Americans. Best feature is the "From Victory to Freedom - the Afro-American Experience of 1950 - 1960's". This exhibition chronicles the trends, struggles and social changes that occurred within this crucial period in American history through a variety of photographs and artifacts, but also through life-sized scenes of a typical fifties lifestyles. These include a barber shop, a beauty salon, and a church interior complete with pews, pulpit and choir stand. These exhibits are made real to the visitor through the accompaniment of recorded speaking voices and gospel music.

BLUE JACKET

Caesar's Ford Park Amphitheater (SR 35 to Jasper Road, south to Stringtown Road), **Xenia** 45385

❑   Phone: (937) 376-4318 or (877) 465-BLUE

   Web: www.bluejacketdrama.com

❑   Hours: Tuesday-Sunday at 8:00pm (mid–June – Labor Day). Dinner at the Pavillon 5:30-7:30pm. Backstage guided tours at 4:00 and 5:00pm

❑   Admission: $9.00-$15.00 adult, $8.00-$13.00 senior, 6.00-$8.00 child (1-12). $3.50 Adult, $2.00 child additional for backstage tour. Picnic Basket Dinners are ~$5-$9.00 per person and yummy and filling.

❑   Tours: Backstage guided tours at 4:00 and 5:00pm. Members of the cast whimsically teach you the theatrical effects (like revolving stages and underground tunnels) and tricks to make it look real! Suggested for children to ward against fright during drama.

❑   Miscellaneous: During dinner, they present Blue Jacket 101 (learn basic, interesting history) and a Frontier Musical Review. These are something not normally presented at these dramas and they're FREE. This keeps the kids from getting bored before the show and everyone is in the mood to watch and learn! The Holiday Inn Xenia is close by for lodging (Main St., 937-372-9921)

Over two hour outdoor drama recounts the true story of a pure white man adopted by Indians. Named for the unique clothes he wore at the time of his capture, Duke was named Blue Jacket. Blue Jacket became a Shawnee Indian Chief and fought to keep the land and heritage from frontiersmen like Daniel Boone, Simon Kenton and whites. To add life to the drama, they use live horses, real muskets, cannons, lots of flaming arrows and torches. Horses thunder across the stage in the largest horse charge in outdoor drama during the siege of Ft. Boonesborough. Lots of Ohio Territory history here (and good explanations of why each character acted as they did). This family drama is not only for everyone in the family, but has multiple threads of Blue Jacket's family life. The acting is filled with enough humor to keep from getting too serious.

GREENE COUNTY HISTORICAL SOCIETY MUSEUM

Xenia - *74 Church Street (near center of town), 45385. Phone: (937) 372-4606. Hours: Tuesday-Friday 9:00am-Noon, Saturday and Sunday, 1:00-3:00 pm (Summer). Weekends Only (Rest of Year). Admission: Donations suggested.* Restored Victorian home and 1799 James Galloway log house where Tecumseh tried to "woo" Rebecca Galloway (actually view the chair Tecumseh sat in near the fireplace!). First, pick herbs from a 1700's garden, smell them and then try to enter the front door of the log house. No door knob or latch? How did they open the door and why? The Carriage House has a wonderful display of farm equipment, general store (candy), china, books, furniture, toys, railroad exhibit, and school. In the Big House, easily explore the many rooms looking for old-fashioned toys, the kiddie potty, or, the old hair crimpers and curling irons - try one - how does it work?

JOHN BRYAN STATE PARK

Yellow Springs - *3790 State Route 370 (2 miles Southeast of Yellow Springs on State Route 370), 45387. Phone: (937) 767-1274. Web: www.johnbryan.org.* 750 acres of camping, hiking trails, fishing and winter sports. The park contains a remarkable limestone gorge cut by the Little Miami River which is designated as a state and national scenic river. Clifton Gorge State Nature Preserve is located adjacent to the park. The Clifton Gorge is a limestone gorge cut by the river (a national natural landmark). Nature lovers can enjoy any of the nine different trails found in the park. Trails follow the scenic river gorge and meander through majestic woodlands.

YOUNG'S JERSEY DAIRY FARM

6880 Springfield-Xenia Road (On Route 68, off I-70)

Yellow Springs 45387

❏   Phone: (937) 325-0629, **Web:** www.youngsdairy.com
❏   Hours: Daily 8:00am / 10:00am–10:00pm (April-October). Open later in the summer and closes earlier in the winter.
❏   Admission: Grounds are FREE. Each activity is between $2.00-$5.00 per person.

❑   Tours: Scheduled groups Monday – Friday (April – October). $3.50 Children – FREE for Teachers and Chaperones. The one hour tour starts with a short video in the barn full of small animals such as ducks, rabbits and chicks. The video shows the farming process: from feeding the cows (amazing how much food they need - 25 gallons of water, over 100 lbs of hay/grain), milking the cows, bottling the milk (quick chilled) and making the ice cream (what's their secret?), watching the operations through the processing window, to selling the milk and ice cream in the store and restaurant. The children then visit the animals in the big barn. They see what a cow eats, feed the goats (why can't they bite?), and visit with the other farm animals. The next step is a wagon ride. Finish the tour with some homemade ice cream. Add lunch or another activity for a small additional fee.

The Dairy store began in 1960 and is still operated by members of the Young family. Udders and Putters Miniature Golf, Driving Range, Batting Cage, Corny Maze (a 3 acre corn field maze open weekends, August thru October), Wagon Rides & Moo-ver & Shaker Barrel Cart rides on weekends, Petting Area – Baby Jersey (pretty-faced calves) cows, pigs and sheep; Water Balloon Toss (summertime). Go to the petting area and then the wagon ride with a treat at the end in one of the restaurants. Our family has fallen in love with this farm place amusement park!

MARMON VALLEY FARM

7754 SR 292 (off US 33 northwest, exit Mad River Mtn. Area)

Zanesfield 43360

❑   Phone: (937) 593-8051 **Web: www.marmonvalley.com**
❑   Hours: Call for details

Winter and summer activities are available at Marmon Valley Farm. They have live farm animals and a fun barn with rope bridges, rope swings and barn games. Hiking and horseback riding (year-round trail rides, on ponies, or in the indoor arena) are available. If it's very cold, try ice-skating. When there's snow, you may want to take your sled along for some great sled riding hills. Overnights combine activities with just enough time left to wander and make new friends. Activities like archery, fishing, a challenge course, indoor arena sports, and the new indoor barn rock climbing wall fill a sport gal or guy's day. An evening hayride followed by silly barn line dancing and s'mores by the fire pit are a great way to end the day. Overnighters ride the wagon each morning over to the cowboy chuck wagon camp for yummy, open-air cooked, big breakfasts followed by a nature hike with Wrangler Matt. Look to attend their seasonal events if you can't arrange a group visit. (See Seasonal & Special Events)

Chapter 4
North Central Area

Our Favorites...

* Mohican Area - Loudonville

* Edison's Birthplace - Milan

* Biblewalk - Mansfield

* Carousel Magic! - Mansfield

* Crystal Cave - Put-In-Bay

* Kelly's Island

* Great Wolf Lodge & Waterpark - Sandusky

Inside the World's Largest Geode - Crystal Cave

LYME VILLAGE

Bellevue - *5001 State Route 4 (south of SR 113), 44811. Phone: (419) 483-4949.* **Web:** *www.lymevillage.com. Hours: Tuesday-Sunday 1:00-5:00pm (Summer). Sunday only (May and September). Admission: $8.00 adult, $7.00 senior (65+), $4.00 child (6-12). Miscellaneous: Gift Shop and concessions. Best to visit during special events.* This 19th Century Ohio Village includes the Wright Mansion, Annie Brown's log home that she owned for 82 years (early Ohio settler exhibits inside), a blacksmith shop, schoolhouse, barns, a church, and the Cooper-Fries general store. All original buildings were moved to this location. Of special interest is the National Museum of Postmark Collector's Club (with the world's largest single collection of postmarks) in a restored post office.

MAD RIVER & NKP RAILROAD SOCIETY MUSEUM

Bellevue - *233 York Street (Just South of US 20), 44811. Phone: (419) 483-2222.* **Web:** *www.onebellevue.com/madriver. Hours: Daily Noon-4:00pm (Memorial Day-Labor Day). Weekends Only (May, September, October). Admission: $7.00 adult, $6.00 senior (60+),$4.00 child (3-12).* Look for steam engines, diesel engines, or the huge snow plow. Once you find them, browse through their collections of full-scale locomotives, cabooses, and mail cars – many that you can climb aboard. Tour guide volunteers are usually retired railway personnel who are knowledgeable and excited to tell you stories about the old railway days.

SENECA CAVERNS

Bellevue (Flat Rock) - *5248 Twp. Road 178 (SR 4 off turnpike, south of SR 269), 44811. Phone: (419) 483-6711* **Web:** *www.senecacavernsohio.com. Hours: Daily 9:00am-7:00pm (Summer). Weekends 10:00am - 5:00pm (May, September, October). Admission: $11.00 adult, $9.00 senior(62+), $5.50 child (5-12). Miscellaneous: Light jacket is suggested as the cave is a constant 54 degrees F.* Take a one hour tour of the 110 foot deep limestone cave with many small rooms, seven levels and the "Ole Mist'ry River". The cave is actually an earth crack discovered by two boys out hunting in 1872. To make the tour really fun, stop by Sandy Creek Gem Mining and let your little explorers pan for gems.

COOPER'S MILL APPLE BUTTER & JELLY FACTORY

Bucyrus - *1414 North Sandusky Avenue (U.S. Route 30 bypass and State Route 4), 44820. Phone: (419) 562-4215. Web: www.coopersmill.net. Hours: Open Monday - Saturday 8:30am-6:00pm. Admission: FREE. Tours: Monday-Friday 9:00am-11:30am and 1:00-3:30pm. Miscellaneous: Farm Market - taste test jellies and homemade fudge.* Jelly Factory tour lets you watch fruit spreads being made the old fashioned way. With "Grandma" recipes, watch the cooking of fine jams and apple butter. Take time to go into the screened-in porch to watch the apple butter bubbling in open 50 gallon copper kettles over a wood fire. Or, observe the delicious ripe fruits cooking into jelly. They cook in small batches and use home-canning jars.

MILLER BOAT LINE

Catawba - *Catawba Point (SR 2 to Route 53 north), 43456. Phone: (800) 500-2421 or (419) 285-2421. Web: www.millerferry.com.* Trips run spring, summer & fall, "family friendly" fares, free mainland parking, Put-in-Bay summer trips every half hour as late as 9:00pm service to Put-in-Bay and Middle Bass Island (late March-October). Low rates $5.50 adult, $1.00 child, one way), most frequent trips and the only ferry that takes vehicles. It is the only scheduled service to Middle Bass Island.

HAYES PRESIDENTIAL CENTER

1337 Hayes Avenue (Rt. 6), Spiegel Grove

Fremont 43420

- ❏ Phone: (419) 332-2081 or (800) 998-7737
  Web: www.rbhayes.org
- ❏ Hours: Monday-Saturday 9:00am-5:00pm. Sunday and Holidays Noon - 5:00pm. Closed Easter, Thanksgiving, Christmas & New Year's Day.

❑   Admission: $6.00 adult, $5.00 senior, $2.00 child (6-12) Home or
        Museum. Combo prices offered to tour both.

❑   Miscellaneous: Museum Store

Disputed Election? Contested Florida votes? Popular vote vs.
Electoral College vote? It all happened in 1876 with the campaign
of Rutherford B. Hayes. The iron gates that greet you at the
entrance were the same gates that once stood at the White House
during the Hayes administration. The 33-room mansion estate was
the home of President and Mrs. Rutherford B. Hayes and is full of
family mementos, private papers and books. They give you the
sense he dedicated himself to his country. The museum displays
the President's daughter's ornate dollhouses and the White House
carriage that the family used. As 19th President, Hayes contended
with the aftermath of Reconstruction in the South, the problems of
our black citizens, and the plight of the American Indian.

CAROUSEL MAGIC! FACTORY & RICHLAND CAROUSEL PARK

44 West 4th Street(behind the Gift Horse) (I-71 Exit State Route 13
North to downtown), **Mansfield** 44901

❑   Phone: (419) 526-4009 factory or (419) 522-4223 carousel
        Web: www.carouselmagic.com

❑   Admission: Factory Tour $5.00 adult, $1.50 child (5-12).
        Carousel $1.00 – (2) ride tokens.

❑   Tours: Factory tours start at the back of the Gift Shop Tuesday-
        Saturday 10:00am–4:00pm. 30-45 minutes long. (Early April–
        December 23, except Thanksgiving). Reservations necessary for
        parties of 10 or more.

❑   Miscellaneous: For lunch, stop at the Coney Island Diner on
        Main Street with its genuine old-time tables, stools and "Blue
        Plate" specials.

Watch the wood carousel horses being made starting from a
"coffin box" with a hollow center, then the carving with special
tools, and finally the painting. The artisans casually show off their
skill. Your tour guide will explain carousel history and
construction as they guide you through displays showing the
history of American carousels, and the process of creating magical

animals from a pile of boards. Why do some carousels run backwards? Why were they built in medieval times? Now that you know how they're made, walk over to the wonderful carousel in the center of town (Main & Fourth Street-indoor/outdoor style - open daily).

MANSFIELD SYMPHONY ORCHESTRA

Mansfield - *138 Park Avenue West, Renaissance Theatre, 44902. Phone: (419) 522-2726.* **Web:** *www.rparts.org.* Performs classical works, opera, pops, ballet (holiday Nutcracker) and special events in restored Renaissance Theatre. Summer musical and outdoor concerts. The Mansfield Symphony Youth Orchestra is comprised of over 100 student musicians, primarily from grades 9 through 12, representing Richland, Ashland, Wayne, Marion, Knox, Crawford and Holmes counties. In addition to two formal concerts each year, the group also performs four free "Lollipop" concerts in area schools.

RICHLAND ACADEMY

Mansfield - *75 North Walnut Street Richland Academy, west of carousel, downtown), 44902. Phone: (419) 522-8224.* **Web:** *www.richlandacademy.com. Hours: Monday-Thursday 10:00am-7:00pm, Friday-Saturday 10:00am-4:00pm. Admission: $2.00 to Discovery Center.* Showcases techno-art - hands-on. Play a gas-powered Fire Organ or follow the perpetual motion Wave Machine. Call before your visit for the daily activity and performance schedule. The Academy also has performances in black box theatre, recitals, musicals, choral concerts, and children's plays.

OHIO BIRD SANCTUARY

Mansfield - *3773 Orweiler Road (west of Lexington off SR 97, turn north on Bowers Rd, then east), 44903. Phone: (419) 884-HAWK.* **Web:** *www.ohiobirdsanctuary.com. Hours: Visitors Center open Tuesday- Saturday 10:00am-4:00pm, Sunday 1:00-5:00pm. Trails open daily during daylight hours, restricted winter hours, and group tours by reservation (small fee).* The Ohio Bird Sanctuary is located on the headwater of the Clearfork River. The marsh and old growth forest offers great birding and hiking. Enjoy seeing birds up close at the Birds Of Prey. The Sanctuary is also a wildlife rehabilitation for native bird species. Nine species of birds of prey including our national emblem, the Bald Eagle reside in large display areas. If you are a fan of songbirds you will enjoy the walk through Songbird Aviary where birds will alight on your hand in search of food. Groups can schedule "Falcon & Friends", a live bird presentation. Picnic tables, gift shop. FREE.

BIBLEWALK

500 Tingley Avenue (I-71 to US 30 West to State Route 545 North)

Mansfield 44905

❑ Phone: (419) 524-0139 or (800) 222-0139
   Web: www.livingbiblemuseum.org
❑ Hours: Monday-Saturday 9:00am-6:00pm, Sunday 3:00-7:00pm.
❑ Admission: $3.75-$4.50 adult, $3.50-4.25 senior (50+), $2.75-$3.50 youth (6-18), $10.00-$20.00 family. This is the price per adjoining museum. There are 4 museums: Life of Christ, Miracles of The Old Testament and Christian Martyrs, or Heart of Reformation (church history). Discount for families and for combo of all 4 museums.
❑ Miscellaneous: Gift Shop. Collection of rare bibles and religious woodcarvings.

The only life-size wax museum in Ohio – it features figures from the Old and New Testaments (non-denominational). Featured stories include the Life of Christ, Daniel in the Lions Den, Jonah and the whale, and Adam and Eve. You can choose to study more recent martyrs and figures in Christian history, too. The tour guide takes you through dimly lit hallways that add a theatrical, dramatic effect. Your personal tour guide will assist you through dioramas from the Bible, each with its own audio text, music, and some with special effects. At the end of the tour you will be left emotional (a small chapel is available to reflect). What an excellent way to dramatically, unforgettably, walk through the bible and church history.

KINGWOOD CENTER

Mansfield - *900 Park Avenue West (I-71 exit State Route 30), 44906. Phone: (419) 522-0211. Web: www.kingwoodcenter.org. Hours: 8:00am - 30 minutes before dusk.* Forty-seven acres of gardens, woods and ponds surrounding the King French Provincial mansion. Greenhouses with a specialty of tulips and perennials and short hiking trails are family friendly.

OHIO STATE REFORMATORY

100 Reformatory Road (I-71 to SR 30 west & SR 545 North)

Mansfield 44906

- ❏ Phone: (419) 522-2644, **Web: www.mrps.org**
- ❏ Hours: Sunday 1:00-4:00pm (Mid-May to September).
- ❏ Admission: $5.00 per person per tour.
- ❏ Tours: Phone Reservations Preferred. Children under 9 and pregnant women should use caution because of stairs and lead-based paint. 45 minutes. Daily group tours (10+) by appointment. Groups by reservation only

A castle prison? This 1886 structure was built as a boy's reformatory. The original cellblocks and offices remain intact and were used to film 4 major motion pictures including "The Shawshank Redemption" and "Air Force One" . The East Cell Block houses the world's largest free-standing steel cell block - 6 tiers. Tours to choose from:

TOWER TOUR - Travel the length of the East Cell Block. Strenuous. Includes guard tower and Catholic Chapel.

DUNGEON TOUR - Venture into the dark and dingy "Hole" in the detention wing. Hear the story of the seven-foot Jesus.

HOLLYWOOD TOUR - See the Shawshank Warden's Office and Andy Dufresne's escape tunnels. Hazard a trip into the sinister "Hole". View the 1886 West Cell Block used as a Russian prison in Air Force One.

"EASY TIME" TOUR - See the Visiting Room and hear the stories. View a video and hear prison stories from a second floor room in the Warden's residence. This is the least strenuous tour.

JOHNNY APPLESEED HERITAGE CENTER

Mansfield (Ashland) - *2179 State Route 603 (off US 30. The site is two miles south of Mifflin, just north of Charles Mill Dam), 44805. Phone: (800) 642-0388. Web: www.jahci.org.* An Outdoor Historical Drama focusing on Johnny Appleseed as a unique national hero as a humanitarian, philanthropist and conservationist. It focuses on his wanderings all across Ohio, Pennsylvania, Indiana, Illinois and Kentucky in the early 1800's, planting apple seeds and sharing his love and faith. However, because these were unsettled times, some scenes depict pioneer, savage violence. We would not recommend the current drama for children who are sensitive to rough, historical violence. That final decision can only ultimately be made by the parent or guardian. The staff here are hoping to add a less violent matinee in future years. They also hope to collect funds for educational exhibits in a museum on the premises. *Check their website periodically for details and warnings about the drama.* Performances are scheduled at 8:00pm nightly except Monday, from late June through Labor Day.

BOOKMASTERS

Mansfield (Ashland) - *2541 Ashland Road, 44905. Phone: (419) 281-8549 ask for plant manager. Web: www.bookmasters.com. Tours: Monday – Friday 10:00am – 2:00pm. Appointment necessary. Group size (6 – 40).* While visiting, kids will learn step-by-step how books (*like this "Kids Love" book*) are produced. Start by seeing what materials are needed, then see the pre-press division, the printing area (with huge, monster-like printers), and the final book binding area. See all phases of books being made through production and view finished books at the end of the tour.

MID OHIO SPORTS CAR COURSE

Mansfield (Lexington) - *Steam Corners Road (I-71 exit SR 97 or SR 95, follow signs). 44904. Phone: (419) 884-4000 or (800) MID-OHIO. Web: www.midohio.com.* Indy Car, Sport Car, AMA Motorcycles, Vintage Car Races. General, Weekend, Paddock (walk through garages & see drivers) passes available. Weekends (June – mid September)

MOHICAN STATE PARK RESORT

Mansfield (Loudonville) - *3116 State Route 3, 44842. Phone: (419) 994-4290 or (419) 938-5411 Resort.* **Web: www.mohicancamp.com** *or* **Web: www.mohicanresort.com.** The striking Clearfork Gorge, hemlock forest and scenic Mohican River offer a wilderness experience while the resort lodge and cottages provide comfortable accommodations. Most people come to stay at riverfront family cabins (with A/C, fireplaces and cable) or the Lodge rooms (with indoor/outdoor pools, sauna, tennis, basketball and shuffleboard facilities). Family playground activity center. Over 13 miles of trails take the visitor to the more interesting areas of the park and forest. Lyons Falls trail follows Clear Fork Gorge and features two waterfalls. The Hemlock trail leads to the scenic wooden bridge, and Pleasant Hill trail follows the lake shoreline and offers beautiful views of the lake (a favorite trail as it leaves from the lodge and is super scenic). Among the resort's most popular attractions are birds of prey presentations conducted by experts from the Ohio Bird Sanctuary. Nearby activities include visiting four canoe liveries, Mohican Water Slide, five golf courses, two horse stables, and downhill ski resorts. 1,294 acres of camping, bridle trails, boating and rentals, marina, bike rentals, fishing and winter sports.

MALABAR FARM STATE PARK

4050 Bromfield Road (I-71 to Exit 169, follow signs)

Mansfield (Lucas) 44843

- ❑ Phone: (419) 892-2784, **Web: www.malabarfarm.org**
- ❑ Hours: Tuesday-Saturday 10:00am-5:00pm, Sunday Noon-5:00pm. (May-December)
- ❑ Admission: Big House Tour, $4.00 adult,$2.00 child (6-18). Tractor Drawn Wagon Tour, $2.00 (6+). Tours begin at 10:00am, last tour at 4:00pm. Wagon tours are generally only on weekends (May-October).
- ❑ Miscellaneous: Malabar Inn. 1820's stagecoach stop restaurant. (Special note to grandparents… Humphrey Bogart & Lauren Bacall were married on these beautiful grounds).

A writer and lover of nature, Louis Bromfield, dreamed of this scenic land and home. Today, visitors can see the house and farm existing just as they did in Bromfield's time. The outbuildings and pastures still house chickens, goats and beef cattle. It is still a working farm and the place where Bromfield discovered new farming techniques. The guides at the Big House tell captivating stories. During seasonal events, kids can watch harvesting or planting, ride an authentic wagon, or help with daily chores @ 3:30pm. Easy to understand farm exhibits (even milk a mechanical cow!). There are twelve miles of trail for the hiker or horseperson to enjoy. Trails traverse scenic fields and forests. Bridle trails, fishing, hiking trails, camping and winter sports are also available park-wide.

MOHICAN-MEMORIAL STATE FOREST

Mansfield (Perrysville) - *3060 County Road 939, 44864. Web: www.dnr.state.oh.us/forestry/Forests/stateforests/mohican.htm. Phone: (419) 938-6222.* 4,498 acres in Ashland County. Hiking trails (24 miles), bridle trails (22 miles), "Park & Pack" camping sites (10), snowmobile trails (7 miles - weather permitting), state nature preserve. Also War Memorial Shrine and Mohican State Park is adjacent.

EAST HARBOR STATE PARK

Marblehead - *(8 miles East of Port Clinton on State Route 269), 43440. Web: www.dnr.state.oh.us/parks/parks/eharbor.htm. Phone: (419) 734-4424.* Located on the shores of Lake Erie, East Harbor State Park has unlimited opportunities for outdoor recreation. Boating, fishing, swimming (sandy beaches), picnicking and camping (large campground) are popular while nature enthusiasts will enjoy the abundance of waterfowl, shorebirds and other species of wildlife found in the park's scenic wetlands. Nature programs. 1,152 acres of hiking trails and winter sports.

KELLEYS ISLAND FERRY BOAT LINES

Marblehead - *510 W. Main St. (Take 163 E into Marblehead. We are located at 510 West Main St. (across from the Police Department, and Fire Station.), 43440. Phone: (419) 798-9763 or (888) 225-4325. Web: www.kelleysislandferry.com.* Daily passenger and automobile transportation to Kelley's Island from Marblehead, departing every half-hour during peak times. Available year-round, weather permitting. Admission fees.

MARBLEHEAD LIGHTHOUSE STATE PARK

110 Lighthouse Drive, **Marblehead** 43440

❑   Phone: (419) 798-4530 or (800) 441-1271
   Web: www.dnr.state.oh.us/parks/parks/marblehead.htm
❑   Hours: Monday-Friday 1:00-5:00pm, and on the second Saturday of the month (June-Labor Day). Some Saturdays there are pioneer demos at the lightkeeper's house.

The oldest working lighthouse on the Great Lakes. Marblehead Point has been known for having the roughest weather along Lake Erie. To warn ships of the danger of being dashed against the rocks by winds from the north, the federal government constructed the Marblehead Lighthouse in 1821. Built of native limestone, it is the oldest light in continuous operation on the Great Lakes. The reflector lamp originally burned whale oil, lard oil, coal oil, and now it's electric. Their stories of old lighthouse keepers lugging 40# buckets of whale oil up those 77 stairs are so interesting. From the top, you can see Cedar Point rides, Kelley's Island and Put-in-Bay. The cute little museum and gift shop (in the lightkeepers house) have many inexpensive coloring books and puzzles to buy and artifacts to explore.

PREHISTORIC FOREST & MYSTERY HILL

8232 East Harbor Road - State Route 163 (8 miles East of Port Clinton off State Route 2), **Marblehead** 43440

❑   Phone: (419) 798-5230, **Web: www.mysteryhill.com**
❑   Hours: Daily 10:00am-Dark (Memorial Day-Labor Day). Weekends Only (May and September).

❑   Admission: $5.95-$7.95 (4 and over) - Mystery Hill and
     Prehistoric Forest. Coupons on website.

❑   Miscellaneous: "Sleep with the Dinos" sleeping cabins (w/AC)
     sleep up to 5 available to rent. Mini golf course.

PREHISTORIC FOREST: Learn the eating habits and lifestyles
of dinosaurs in a forest full of them. Start your walk in the forest
by going through the volcano with a 35 foot waterfall. The volcano
rumbles and smokes and look out for the creatures that live in this
place. There are Dino bones, serpent, Pterodactyl, dino egg nest
and a little guy that likes to hide, he will show himself at just the
right time, can you find him? Dig for dinosaur footprints and bones
or get your picture taken with dinos. The T-Rex now "follows"
you, the Stenonychosaurus is the brainiest, and the dinosaurs are
pretty much life-size!

MYSTERY HILL: The "Illusion of Nature" House where water
runs uphill and chairs stick to the walls. Is it Magnetic or Magic?
In one place you feel OK and only a few inches away you feel
strange. They will answer any question that have an answer. Be
sure to volunteer for the fun demonstrations at Mystery Hill.

TRAIN – O – RAMA

Marblehead - *6732 East Harbor Road (Route 161 East), 43440.
Phone: (419) 734-5856. **Web: www.trainorama.net**. Hours: Monday -
Saturday 11:00am-5:00pm, Sunday 1:00 – 5:00pm. Admission:
$5.00 adult, $4.00 senior, $3.00 child (4-11). Miscellaneous: Train
Gift Shop.* Ohio's largest operating model train display open to the
public.

LAKESIDE

Marblehead (Lakeside) - *236 Walnut Avenue, 43440. Phone:
(419) 798-4461 or (866) 9-LAKESIDE. www.lakesideohio.com.*
Chautauqua – like resort with programs in a historic enclave on
Lake Erie. (June – September). The entire area is a Christian
family retreat of shops, eateries, entertainment, lectures, worship
services and family-rated movies. Daily, weekly and season pass
admission prices are charged (avg. $10.00 per person per day-ages
10+). This gated community is safe for families and offers a huge

dock, lake swimming, a sailing area (learn to sail), mini-golf, a town movie theatre, and seasonal festivals. It is like stepping back in time!

EDISON BIRTHPLACE MUSEUM

North Edison Street (off State Route 250, Downtown, near exit 7 off Turnpike), **Milan** 44846

- ❑ Phone: (419) 499-2135, **Web: www.tomedison.org**
- ❑ Hours: Tuesday-Saturday 10:00am-5:00pm, Sunday 1:00-5:00pm (Summer). Tuesday-Sunday 1:00-5:00pm (April-May and September-October). Wednesday-Sunday 1:00-4:00pm (February-March & November-December). Closed Easter & January.
- ❑ Admission: $5.00 adult, $4.00 senior (59+), $2.00 child (6-12).
- ❑ Miscellaneous: The Milan Historical Museum Complex is across the street.

Edison was born here in 1847 and raised in this home until age 7. Your tour guides are two of Edison's great-great-great-grandnieces. The original family mementos give you a feeling of being taken back in time. The room full of his inventions (he had 1,093 American patents) gives you a sense of his brilliance! Most famous for his invention of the light bulb and phonograph (1st words recorded were "Mary had a little lamb"), you may not know he was kicked out of school for being a non-attentive/slow learner! So, his mother home-schooled him. Part of the Edison family belongings include slippers, Derby hat, cane, Mother Edison's disciplinary switch (still hanging in the original spot in the kitchen), butter molds and "Pop Goes the Weasel" yarner. Two practical inventions of the time you'll want to see are the pole ladder (a long pole that pulls out to a full size ladder) and the slipper seat (a cushioned little seat, low to the ground, so it is easier to put your slippers or shoes on). Ask about one of our favorite Edison inventions...the Power Nap!

MILAN HISTORICAL MUSEUM

Milan - *10 Edison Drive (off SR 113, Turnpike exit 118), 44846. Phone: (419) 499-2968.* **Web: www.milanhist.org**. *Hours: Tuesday-Saturday 10:00am-5:00pm, Sunday 1:00-5:00pm (Summer).*

Tuesday-Sunday 1:00-5:00pm (May, September) Admission: $5.00 adult, $4.00 senior, $2.00 child (6-12). Miscellaneous: Gift Shop with video and slide presentations. Provide excellent school tour packets of study. Tour includes several buildings in a complex featuring different themes like the Galpin Home of local history, dolls, toys and a collection of mechanical banks. There are several other homes along with a blacksmith and carriage shop and everything you might want to buy from the 1800's is sold in the general store. Be sure to add this to your visit to Edison's Home, one block away.

VEGGIE U EDUCATION CENTER

Milan - *12304 Mudbrook Road, 44846. Phone: (419) 499-7500. Web: www.vegieu.org.* With the rise in childhood and adolescent obesity, along with wide variety of unhealthy food choices, it is more important than ever for parents to provide guidance on making healthy food choices for their children. The Veggie U curriculum is provided free to all 4th grade classrooms. While focusing on Life Sciences and Health and Nutrition issues, teachers using the curriculum have also integrated the unit in areas of Language Arts and Mathematics.

OBERLIN HERITAGE TOUR

Oberlin - *73 South Professor Street, James Monroe House (State Route 38 and State Route 511), 44074. Phone: (440) 774-1700. Web: www.oberlinheritage.org/visit.html. Hours: Tuesday, Thursday, Saturday 10:30am and 1:30pm. The tour is of most interest to adults and children above the age of 7 years.* Learn about abolition and the Underground Railroad, student life around campus through the years, and a little red school house with a collection of lunch pails and McGuffey Readers. Start the tour in James Monroe's home. He was an important abolitionist, advocate of voting rights for African Americans, and friend of Frederick Douglass. Monroe taught at Oberlin College. On display in the Jewett House is an exhibit on "Aluminum: The Oberlin Connection" that includes a recreation of Charles Martin Hall's 1886 wood shed experiment station.

AFRICAN SAFARI WILDLIFE PARK

267 Lightner Road (Off State Route 2 exit SR 53, follow signs)

Port Clinton 43452

- ❑ Phone: (419) 732-3606 or (800) 521-2660
  Web: www.africansafariwildlifepark.com
- ❑ Hours: Daily 10:00am-5:00pm (April, May, September, October). Daily 9:00am-7:00pm (Memorial Day-Labor Day).
- ❑ Admission: $10.00-$16.00 per person (summer). $3.00 discount (spring & fall). Admission ages 3+.
- ❑ Miscellaneous: Safari Grill and gift shop. Jungle Junction Playland and petting zoo.

See more than 400 animals (including llamas, alpacas, and zebras) as they wander freely around your vehicle as you drive through a 100-acre park. This is the only drive through safari park in the Midwest. The giraffe lean their long necks over to check you out through your car windows. The friendliest animals are the camels and ponies and you can ride them, too (at no additional charge). The ugliest are probably the warthogs. Another favorite is the "Porkchop Downs" pig races. Boy, do they snort loud when they're trying to win!

CRANE CREEK STATE PARK & MAGEE MARSH WILDLIFE AREA

Port Clinton - *(Rte. 2, west of Port Clinton), 43452. Phone: (419) 898-0960. Web: www.dnr.state.oh.us/odnr/parks/cranecrk.htm. Hours: Open dawn to dusk, year-round.* We loved the boardwalk viewing, the beach and especially, the Eagle's Nests and spring migration. It's amazing how many birds come thru this area!

GREAT LAKES POPCORN COMPANY

Port Clinton - *115 Madison Street (downtown), 43452. Web: www.GreatLakesPopcorn.com. Phone: (419) 732-3080 (866) 732-3080. Hours: Daily 10:00am-5:30pm (Sunday 10:00am-4:00pm). Extended Seasonal hours. Tours: Tours are available for school-age children.* Look for the bright red & white awning and listen for the "island music" as you and your children find this fun adventure! All of their equipment is located within view of customers standing at the counter. They turn the coaters at an angle so you can see inside of them and see the popcorn churning in the machines. Sample many varieties of popcorn including "Bubble Gum", "Root Beer", "Jelly Bean" and "Wild Walleye". The "Popcorn Tasting Station" is where kids and families alike can sample any, or all, of the 30 plus flavors.

JET EXPRESS

Port Clinton - *5 North Jefferson Street (docks at foot of Perry Street Bridge, SR 163), 43452. Phone: (800) 245-1JET. Web: www.jet-express.com. Admission: Children 12 and under ride FREE! Each way is $11.00 for adults, $3.00 more for bikes. (April-October).* Indoor and outdoor seating on the fastest catamaran to Islands. 22 minute trip with some boat facts weaved in. Nice ride and the docks are located right in the hub of activity. Free parking nearby or parking fee at terminal.

LAKE ERIE ISLANDS REGIONAL WELCOME CENTER

Port Clinton - *770 S.E. Catawba Road (just off Rte. 2 & Rte. 53 N), 43452. Phone: (800) 441-1271. Web: www.lake-erie.com.* The clever silhouette building design and replica dioramas inside really orient you to all the area has to offer. The staff are very friendly. The kids can gaze at the 600 gallon aquarium or do nature rubbings while the parents work out a visitors plan. Their movie theater highlights the Lake Erie region. A Kids play area resides within a replica of Oliver Hazard Perry's flagship, THE LAWRENCE, from the Battle of Lake Erie during the War of 1812. Gander at replicas of the Tin Goose, the first airplane to service the Lake Erie Islands. The Birdwatching display has an interactive telescope. Look for the replica of the Marblehead Lighthouse or listen for a Talking walleye, plus more surprises. They can also tell you about eateries in the area that specialize in perch and walleye...any way you like it. The Crow's Nest has their famous, warm Hot Apple Walnut Pie and Nate's has the tangy Sunburst Salad...both great add-ons to your fresh fish meal.

LAKE ERIE ISLANDS STATE PARK

4049 E. Moores Dock Road

Port Clinton 43452

❑   Phone: (866) 644-6727 for camping

     Web: www.dnr.state.oh.us/parks/parks/lakeerie.htm

❑   Hours: Daylight hours.

Limestone cliffs, historic wineries, crystal caverns and a shimmering Great Lake greet visitors to the Lake Erie Islands state parks. These five state parks offer unique island retreats with an atmosphere both festive and casual. Fishing, boating and swimming can be enjoyed at each park.

<u>CATAWBA ISLAND STATE PARK</u>: (419) 797-4530, off SR 53.

<u>SOUTH BASS ISLAND</u>: (419) 285-2112 seasonally. Some overnight camping is available.

<u>KELLEY'S ISLAND STATE PARK</u>: (reached only by ferry or boat) Six miles of hiking trails lead to scenic vistas, historic sites and two nature preserves. The islands were formed during the glacial period when massive ice sheets entered Ohio. GLACIAL GROOVES STATE MEMORIAL is a must see and a great way to study Ohio geology. Located on the north side of the island, the largest easily accessible grooves were formed when ice once covered solid limestone bedrock. Looking safely over fence, you see a giant groove passage that seems unbelievable. Placards along the trail detail the history of glaciers moving through the area. Prior to the War of 1812, the Lake Erie Island region had been occupied by Ottawa and Huron (Wyandot) Indian tribes. A testimony to their existence on the islands is carved in INSCRIPTION ROCK STATE MEMORIAL. The flat-topped limestone slab displays carvings of animals and human figures. Discovered partly buried in the shoreline in 1833, the 32 feet by 21 feet rock is now entirely exposed (protected by a roof and viewing platform). Archaeologists believe the inscriptions date from sometime between AD 1200 and 1600. (419) 746-2546 or (419) 797-4530 (Rock) or (419) 797-4025 (Grooves).

MONSOON LAGOON

Port Clinton - *1530 S. Danbury Rd. N (Danbury N Road exit off Rte. 2), 43452. Web: www.monsoonlagoonwaterpark.com. Phone: (419) 732-6671. Hours: Generally 11:00am-dusk (Memorial Day weekend-Labor Day). Admission: Rates range $10.00-$15.00 per day. Golf, boats and go-carts $5.00 extra. Miscellaneous: Picnics and coolers are not allowed as well as any outside food. Monsoon Lagoon offers a concession stand with very reasonable prices.* If your kids like water and the outdoors, head over to the Monsoon Lagoon. They have Adventure Island with 150 water toys, a lazy river, two giant water slides plus eatery, mini-golf, bumper boats, go-karts and a game room. Take a ride on the six great waterslides, including the three stories tall Typhoon Rush Slide Tower or.... Splash around on the Adventure Island Tree House with one-hundred and five water play stations on seventeen different levels. Little ones can splash and play in the Little Squirts Play Pool. And Mom and Dad can relax in the adult pool.

AQUATIC VISITORS CENTER

Put-in-Bay - *Peach Point, 43456. Phone: (419) 285-3701 or (419) 625-0062. Hours: Tuesday-Saturday 11:00am - 6:00pm. (May - August). Admission: FREE.* The Ohio Division of Wildlife invites kids to learn about fish and fishing. Displays highlight the story of this historic fish hatchery, live fish exhibits, Ohio's fishery resources, the wealth of recreational fishing activity offered on Lake Erie, and hands-on children's activities. Kids can fish off the docks with rod and bait provided.

BUTTERFLY HOUSE

Put-in-Bay – *43456. Phone: (419) 285-CAVE. Hours: Daily 9:00am-7:00pm (summer). Admission: $7.00 adult, $3.50 child (6-12).* Walk among hundreds of exotic butterflies in their fully-enclosed garden. Enjoy the tranquil environment with soothing fountain, Koi fish pond & lush flowers. 15-minute Educational Butterfly Video. Unique educational gift shop including framed butterfly specimens, nature gifts, candles & ceramics, butterfly & Put-in-Bay souvenirs.

CHOCOLATE CAFÉ & MUSEUM

Put-in-Bay - *820 Catawba Avenue, 43456. Phone: (419) 734-7114.* **Web:** *www.chocolateohio.com. Hours: Daily 7:00am-10:30pm (May-September). Miscellaneous: Golf Cart Rentals available. Receive one free pound of chocolate with a daily cart rental.* Visit a fun Chocolate Museum and learn the history and making of chocolate! Featuring South Bend Chocolate Company handmade chocolates (our favorite Indiana chocolate factory tour!) Learn the history and making of chocolate while viewing a fine collection of antique chocolate collectibles. Learn even more about chocolate - watch a film, or have your picture taken with Lucy at the Chocolate Factory. The unique bistro celebrates fine chocolate & coffee. Decadent cheesecakes and ice cream treats guarantee something for everyone.

CRYSTAL CAVE & HEINEMAN'S GRAPE JUICE WINERY

Catawba Avenue, **Put-in-Bay** 43456

- ❑   Phone: (419) 285-3412
- ❑   Hours: Daily (early May-Late September). Call for schedule (basically 10:00am-5:00pm except Noon on Sundays)
- ❑   Admission: $6.00 adult, $3.00 child (6-11).

The Crystal Cave (located below the factory) is well worth the visit! Discovered by workers in 1897 while digging a well for the winery 40 feet above them. The walls of this cave are covered in strontium sulfate, a bluish mineral called celestite. These crystals range from 8 to 18 inches long. The original cave was much smaller than what appears today, as crystals were harvested and sold for the manufacturing of fireworks. You'll walk right into the world's largest geode! Every crystal (mostly bluish green) has 14 sides. We promise a WOW on this one! Another tour option is the juice/wine factory. Although you may be hesitant to have children tour a winery, they really put emphasis on the grapes (varieties, flavor, color, etc.) and the chemistry of making juice. Did you know they use air bags to press the juice out of grapes?

LAKE ERIE ISLANDS MUSEUM

441 Catawba Avenue (adjacent to the Put-in-Bay Town Hall parking lot), **Put-in-Bay** 43456

- ❏ Phone: (419) 285-2804, **Web: www.leihs.org**
- ❏ Hours: Daily 11:00am-5:00pm (May, June and September). Daily 10:00am-6:00pm (July and August). Weekends only in October.
- ❏ Admission is $1.00 (age 12+).
- ❏ Miscellaneous: Island Bike Rental, 419-285-2016. Bicycles can be rented near both boat docks. Rates are $3 per hour and $9 per day. Children's seats and helmets are available. Golf carts are also available. Rates range from $10 to $16 per hour, depending on the number of seats.

Boating, sailors, and shipping industry artifacts. Video shown is an excellent trip to the past. Why did so many Grand Hotels burn? What are the major industries on the island...a hint...one is a fruit! Usually live displays of Box Turtles, Painted Turtles, and island snakes can be seen at the wildlife building. Look for ship models scattered throughout.

PERRY'S CAVE & FAMILY FUN CENTER

Put-in-Bay - *979 Catawba Avenue (South Bass Island, 1/2 mile from town), 43456. Web: www.perryscave.com. Phone: (419) 285-2405. Admission:$7.00 adult, $3.50 child (6-12). Lantern Tours $20.00 per person (includes t-shirt) - must have at least 4 in group. Tours: Daily 10:30am - 6:00pm. Tours leave every 20 minutes in the summer. Fewer times rest of year.* Inside the cave you'll see walls covered with calcium carbonate (the same ingredient in antacids) that has settled from years of dripping water. Rumor says Perry kept prisoners and stored supplies in the cave during the Battle of Lake Erie. At the Gem Mining Company, mine for real gems and minerals. After-hours lantern tours available by reservation. Chart your course around the War of 18 Holes, the brand new 18-hole miniature golf course with a War of 1812 theme. In the Antique Car Museum, stroll through the past as you view Ford Model A's & T's as well as the island's oldest automobile.

PERRY'S VICTORY AND INTERNATIONAL PEACE MEMORIAL

93 Delaware Avenue (Ohio Turnpike to SR 53 and SR 2. There are several ferry lines that service the island, the Jet Express, The Miller Boat Line, and the Rocket), **Put-In-Bay** 43456

- ❑ Phone: (419) 285-2184, **Web: www.nps.gov/pevi**
- ❑ Hours: Daily 10:00am-7:00pm (Mid-June - Labor Day). Daily 10:00am-5:00pm (Late April - Mid-June & September and mid-October). Daily 10:00am-6:00pm (mid-May to mid-June).
- ❑ Admission: Observation Deck by elevator, $3.00 per person (age 17 and up). Must climb two flights of stairs first.

Built of pink granite, 352 feet high and 45 feet in diameter, this memorial commemorates the Battle of Lake Erie and then the years of peace. Commodore Perry commanded the American fleet in the War of 1812. In September of 1813 he defeated the British and Perry then sent his famous message to General William Henry Harrison "We have met the enemy and they are ours". Interpretive actors outside chat with you on busy days and weekends. The new Visitors Center facility has extensive exhibits, an auditorium featuring a film with surround sound, and an expanded bookstore. The exhibits will tell the story of the Battle of Lake Erie, the War of 1812, construction of the monument and the international peace that it represents. A live feed camera system will provide views from the top of the monument enabling those who are unable or decide not to make the trip to the observation deck to witness the view. The DVD presentation of the War of 1812 and the Battle of Lake Erie are so worth seeing.

PUT-IN-BAY TOUR TRAIN

(South Bass Island), **Put-In-Bay** 43456

- ❑ Phone: (419) 285-4855 **Web: www.put-in-bay-trans.com**
- ❑ Hours: Daily 10:00am-5:00pm (Memorial Day-Labor Day). Weekends Only (May and September).
- ❑ Admission: $8.00 adult , $1.50 child (6-11)

❑   Miscellaneous: South Bass Island State Park, (419) 797-4530, (419) 285-2112, Reservations: (866) OHIOPARKS. Stone beach, ice skating, flush restrooms with showers (summer only), ice fishing, campsites, cabents (a combination of cabins & tents, picnic shelter, launch ramp, and fishing pier.

A tram departs frequently from the village depot for an one hour tour of the island. Stops include Perry's Cave, Heineman's Winery, Crystal Cave, War of 18 Holes Miniature Golf Course, Alaskan Wildlife Museum, and Perry's Victory and International Peace Memorial. Departing every 30 minutes, the train trolley allows passengers to depart and re-board (without additional cost) at any time. The tour is especially interesting and gives a clear understanding of all that occupied the island thru the years.

STONE LABORATORY

Put-in-Bay - *Field Station, Box 119, 43456. Phone: (614) 247-6500 or (419) 285-2341.* **Web:** *www.stonelab.ohio-state.edu. Hours: Workshops (open mid-April thru October). Wednesdays in the summer, they co-host Put-in-Bay Eco-History (a.k.a.Passport) tours open to everyone. Admission: Workshops: $20.00-$40.00 per student (4th grade and up). Meals and lodging extra. Field Station Tours: $10.00 per person. All workshops and tours are prearranged and require transport to the Island from Put-in-Bay or privately. Tours: Four-Site Passport Package (includes only South Bass Island Lighthouse, ODNR. Aquatic Visitors Center, Lake Erie Islands Historical Society, and Perry's Victory & International Peace Monument) Five-Site Passport Package (includes admission to the all of the sites above, including Stone Laboratory on Gibraltar Island).* Stone Lab's science workshop program offers a variety of activities ranging from water sampling on a research vessel in the lake, to identifying microscopic aquatic organisms you've collected or dissecting fish in a lab. You can specialize island activities by adding an invertebrate walk, bird walk, edible plant walk, exotic species slide show, or seining. Groups may arrange a one-hour historical/scientific tour of the Gibraltar Island facilities. Cooke Castle, Perry's Lookout, glacial grooves, and brief classroom activities will provide participants with a well-rounded program overview.

CASTAWAY BAY

Sandusky - *(at the entrance to Cedar Point Causeway), 44870.*
Phone: (419) 627-2106. **Web:** *www.cedarpoint.com*. The newly
opened waterpark is the state's largest. In the elaborate enclosed
natural setting of palm trees, huts, inland lagoons and plenty of
water lies numerous water attractions. Highlights include a tall
water roller coaster that propels riders uphill, then downhill; a
dozen water slides; a large wave pool w/ 3 foot waves; an action
pool with water basketball and floating logs; concessions and the
center attraction: a gigantic multi-story interactive play are including
a 1,000 gallon tipping bucket that downpours every few minutes.
The waterpark is only open to overnight guests at the resort featuring
rooms starting at $200 per night. Each overnight stay includes park
admission for three to six, depending on the size of room. All rooms
feature extras such as microwave and mini-frig. The resort has two
mid-priced restaurants, an indoor pool, whirlpool, exercise room,
arcade and adjacent marina within the property.

CEDAR POINT & SOAK CITY

SR 4 (I-80 to Exit 118 or 110. Follow Signs), **Sandusky** 44870

- ❑   Phone: (419) 627-2350. **Web: www.cedarpoint.com**
- ❑   Hours: Vary by season. (May-October). Generally open at 10:00
   or 11:00am until dark.
- ❑   Admission: $25.00-45.00, Small children (under 48") – General
   (ages 4-59). Separate admission for Soak City ($16.00-$28.00).
   Combo, 2 day & Starlight rates. Parking $8.00.
- ❑   Miscellaneous: Stroller rental. Picnic area. Food Service.
   Miniature golf. Challenge Park.

More rides than most other parks in the world! The amusement
extravaganza on the shores of Lake Erie includes 15 Roller
Coasters and a total of 68 rides. Most new rides are super thrillers,
not for kids, but maybe the parents. Here are some of the themed
areas or rides: SOAK CITY – wave pool, water slides, Adventure
Cove, Eerie Falls (get wet in the dark). CHALLENGE PARK –
Rip cord Sky coaster (fall 150 feet and then swing in a 300-foot
arc.   Grand Prix Raceway. LIVE SHOWS – 50's, Motown,
Country, Ice Shows. CHAOS – turn sideways & upside down at

the same time. MILLENNIUM & MAGNUM XL - tallest and best coasters. CAMP SNOOPY - with piped-in kids music and child sized play like Red Baron airplanes, Woodstock's express family coaster, Peanuts 500 Speedway. Also Sing-along Show with Peanuts characters. Cedar Point continues to hold the title of "Best Amusement Park in the World."

GOODTIME I

Sandusky - *(docked at Jackson Street Pier), 44870. Phone: (419) 625-9692 or (800) 446-3140.* **Web: *www.goodtimeboat.com.*** *Admission: $13.00 - $23.00 (ages 4 and up). Tours: Depart 9:30am, Arrive back 6:30pm (Memorial Day-Labor Day).* Island hopping 40-meter sight seeing cruise to Kelley's Island and Put-In-Bay. Stop for awhile at each island.

GREAT WOLF LODGE INDOOR WATERPARK

4600 Milan Road (SR250) (Ohio Turnpike, exit 7, north on SR250)

Sandusky 44870

❑ Phone: (419) 609-6000 or (888) 779-BEAR
  Web: www.greatwolflodge.com
❑ Hours: Waterpark daily 9:00am-10:00pm. Wristbands are good day of arrival until closing the next day. Checkout is 10:30am.
❑ Admission: Lodge room suites include 4-6 waterpark passes. Rooms vary from $169-$300+ per night. Additional waterpark passes $15.00 each. Check out the Kroger or Tops discounts online at www.greatwolflodge.com for $75.00 plus off room rates.
❑ Miscellaneous: All suites: Family, KidCabin (log cabin in room with bunk beds), microwave, refrigerator. Arcade and outdoor pools, gift shops. Bring Coast Guard approved swim vests for non-swimmers (limited number of vests available at park, too).

Well, we've gone to explore this family-friendly resort several times....and the verdict...we are always VERY impressed! Even though it's a resort...it still was comfy for the both kids and parents. Bring you own food to prepare or eat in one of two on site restaurants - GITCHIE GOOMIE GRILL and LUMBER JACK'S

COOK SHANTY (pass it around family style). All the kid's menu prices for both restaurants are around $5.00 and includes beverage & dessert. BEAR TRACK LANDING Indoor Waterpark is the highlight! The minute you step into the Outdoor/Northwoods ambiance (and gently heated, no musty or chlorine smell-they ozonate the water) you have hours of fun. Your favorite treehouse, Fort Mackenzie, is now home to two new Otter Run body slides. Play as you may in the 4-story interactive fun center featuring 12 levels of water based antics or get "dunked" by the giant bucket. If you don't scream from excitement in the Fort, you're sure to on the giant inner tube slides (best for elementary ages and up). In 5 pools (all age levels), 7 waterslides, and the water fort you'll find watchful and helpful lifeguards - there for safety and are excellent for crowd control. Smaller guests will delight in the redesigned Soak'n Oak Springs, a water play fort, just for toddlers, complete with slides and water spouting bear cubs. Teens and Tweeners can take on the challenge of climbing an Aqua Rock Wall (additional fee required). Take breaks. Two areas for the 10 and under crowd are the nightly Story time by the lobby fireplace (come in your pajamas) or the craft room, Cubs Cabin. Each month they change the seasonal theme of the crafts offered and most are free. The staff and quality of craft received high ratings from our crew! With a little planning of resources, you will get your money's worth in memories and fun for sure!

KALAHARI RESORT & INDOOR WATERPARK

7000 Kalahari Drive (located on State Route 250, just 10 minutes south of Cedar Point), **Sandusky** 44870

- ❑   Phone: (419) 433-7200 or (877) KALAHARI
  Web: www.kalahariresort.com
- ❑   Admission: Overnight packages (lodging, waterpark, dry play area included) run $129.00-$349.00 per night. Waterpark only: $29.00-$34.00 for all day pass.
- ❑   Miscellaneous: Check-in is 4:00pm, Checkout is 11:00am. You may stay to play after checkout until 3:00pm that day.

Ohio's largest Indoor Waterpark, Kalahari is a brand new authentic African-themed Resort featuring the 80,000 sq. ft Great Kalahari

Waterpark, Crocodile Cove (for younger set and sport game area), Madagascar Indoor Mini-Golf and 4-story Tree Top Dry Play area, Huge Game Room, four retail shopping outlets and scheduled activities and events for the whole family (try cookie decorating, crafts or just hanging out in the Game Room). Zoom along on the "Zip Coaster" – the only water coaster in the entire world! Or Surf Indoors – the only indoor surfing spot in Ohio! They have Family Tube rides and long, swirling tube rides. Indoor and outdoor hot tubs. Including nearly 600 Guest Rooms and Suites (at least a micro/frig in every room, some suites have mini-kitchens), Kalahari also offers eight unique dining and lounge options including a family buffet.

LAGOON DEER PARK

Sandusky - *1502 Martins Point Road,State Route 269 (between State Route 2 and US 6), 44870. Phone: (419) 684-5701.* **Web: www.sanduskyfunspots.com/deerpark.** *Hours: Daily 10:00am-6:00pm (May - mid-October). Admission: $8.00 adult, $4.00 child (3-12). Pay Fishing available in stocked lake.* Hand feed and pet hundreds of deer, llamas, miniature donkeys and other tame species. Altogether, They have 250 exotic animals from Europe, Japan, Asia, South and North America. Approximately 75 baby animals are born here each year.

MERRY-GO-ROUND MUSEUM

West Washington and Jackson Streets (State Route 6, downtown)

Sandusky 44870

- ❏ Phone: (419) 626-6111
  Web: www.merrygoroundmuseum.org
- ❏ Hours: Monday-Saturday 11:00am-5:00pm. Sunday Noon - 5:00pm (Summer). Weekends Only (January & February). Wednesday - Sunday (Rest of the Year).
- ❏ Admission: $5.00 adult, $4.00 senior (60+), $3.00 child (4-14). Includes carousel ride.
- ❏ Miscellaneous: Gift Shop

This colorful, bright, big museum was the former Post Office. Once inside, you'll see all sorts of carousel memorabilia and history.   Each year, a new exhibit space is highlighted with colorful displays of carousel designers or companies. Next, tour the workshop to watch craftsman make carousel horses with authentic "old world" tools.   Finally, ride the Herschel 1930's indoor merry-go-round.

INDIAN MILL

Upper Sandusky - *State Route 23 and State Route 67 to Route 47 (along the banks of the Sandusky River), 43351.   Phone: (419) 294-3349 or (800) 600-7147.   www.ohiohistory.org/places/indian. Hours: Friday – Sunday 1:00 – 6:00pm (Memorial Day – Labor Day), weekends only in September and October. Admission: $1.00 Adult, $.50 Youth (6-12).* In a scenic location along the Sandusky River, Indian Mill, built in 1861, is the nation's first educational museum of milling in its original structure. The restored three-story structure replaces the original one-story building that the U.S. government built in 1820 to reward the loyalty of local Wyandot Indians during the War of 1812. Many exhibits are placed around the original mill machinery. The restored miller's office displays the history of milling from prehistoric times to the present.

INLAND SEAS MARITIME MUSEUM & LIGHTHOUSE

Vermillion - *480 Main Street (2 miles North of State Route 60 / OH 2 intersection), 44089. Phone: (440) 967-3467 or (800) 893-1485.   Web: www.inlandseas.org. Hours: Daily 10:00am-5:00pm. Admission: $5.00 adult, $4.00 senior, $3.00 child (6-15).* The museum celebrates adventures of the Great Lakes including models, photographs, instruments, a steam tug engine, and a 1905 pilothouse.   Special artifacts are the timbers from the Niagara (Admiral Perry's 1812 ship) and an 1847 lighthouse built with a 400 foot catwalk to the mainland. Take the family on a unique underwater adventure as an interactive exhibit lets you dive the Great Lakes shipwreck of your choice.

FINDLEY STATE PARK

Wellington - *25381 State Route 58 (3 miles South of Wellington on State Route 58), 44090. Phone: (440) 647-4490.   Web: www.dnr.state.oh.us/parks/parks/findley.htm.* Once a state forest,

Findley State Park is heavily wooded with stately pines and various hardwoods. The scenic hiking trails allow nature lovers to view spectacular wildflowers and observe wildlife. One area of the park is set aside as a sanctuary for the Duke's skipper butterfly, an extremely rare insect. 931 acres of camping, hiking trails, bike rentals, nature programs, boating and rentals, fishing, swimming and winter sports.

CELERYVILLE, BUURMA VEGETABLE FARMS

Willard - *4200 Broadway (Route 224 West to Route 103 South to Celeryville), 44890. Phone: (419) 935-3633. Web: www.buurmafarms.com. Hours: Weekdays (June-September) just watching. Tours: 20+ people required.* Judged one of the best industrial tours in the state, this is a 3000-acre organic "muck" vegetable garden.   On tour you'll see greenhouses, celery and radish harvesting machines in action, and vegetable processing (cleaning, pruning) and packaging.   You'll love the facts and figures it takes to produce veggies. Although started with celery growing, the area now never grows celery (soil conditions prevent it).

SUGGESTED LODGING AND DINING

SPRUCE HILL INN & COTTAGES. **Mansfield**. 3230 O'Possum Run Road (I-71 exit 169, Rte. 13 turn up the hill beside Cracker Barrel). (419) 756-2200 or **www.sprucehillinn.com**. Right next to Snow Trails Ski Resort are sets of cottages (rent for $125 peak) and a lodge or house (for groups or extended families) to rent overnight while in the area. Nestled on the hill overlooking the ski trails, you'll have easy access to the slopes. The cottages include a jacuzzi tub in the bathroom, a queen bed and some have a tower room w/ futon bed or an outside deck. Walking around the sloped property and pond is an activity. They serve a light continental breakfast at the carriage house/office each morning. Just minutes from attractions or nearby Mohican Country - canoeing, hiking and other outdoor sports.

LANDOLL'S MOHICAN CASTLE - **Mansfield (Loudonville)** -. 561 Twp. Rd 3352. **Web: www.landollsmohicancastle.com**. Phone: (800) 291-5001. If you really want an upscale, enchanted getaway in the Mohican Area... Landoll's Mohican Castle complex is the place! Stay overnight in a castle with royal family suites or cottages! Castle suites have fireplaces, jacuzzis, mini-kitchens, heated tile floors, and complimentary euro-style continental breakfast. Euro-gardens and cobblestone paths lead into the 30 miles of hiking/golf cart trails (golf cart rentals available). The royal suites are great for small families, but the newly remodeled royal cottages are the best for large families extended family and friends. The patio, two-floor, two-bedroom cottages connect in the middle and each unit sleeps 6+. We loved visiting with friends in the connecting great rooms and were up until late playing "Yahtzee" and "Life" and watching DVD's (one player in most every room, by the way). Both floors have a large deck to sit and watch the leaves change or the flowers bloom. In colder weather (mid-November thru March), the Landoll's have nearly one million lights outside the castle and all the "kingdom structures". Every season has its own natural enchantment set around the intriguing castle. Along with the indoor pool/fitness/gameroom complex, there is also a wonderful restaurant/gift shop serving lunch and dinner. You must try the blueberry piefin (made with fresh organic blueberries grown on the property) for dessert and our table especially loved the pork loin, walleye and the pecan chicken (lunch $8.00-$10.00, dinner $15.00-$25.00, kids menu $4.95) entrees. Overnight stays begin around $200 up to around $400 per night. A unique treat!

Chapter 5
North East Area

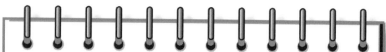

Our Favorites...

* Inventor's Hall of Fame - Akron

* Hale Farm & Village - Bath

* Cuyahoga Valley Nat'l Park/Train - Brecksville to Peninsula

* Cleveland Museum of Natural History-Cleveland

* Malley's Chocolates - Cleveland

* Fairport Marine Lighthouse - Fairport Harbor

* Lake Farm Park - Kirtland

* Mill Creek Park - Youngstown

Canal Lock in Cuyahoga Valley

STAN HYWET HALL

Akron - *714 North Portage Path (I-77 or I-71 to State Route 18, follow signs into town), 44303. Phone: (330) 836-5533.* **Web:** *www.stanhywet.org. Hours: Daily 10:00am-4:30pm (April-New Years). Closed January-March for maintainance. Admission: $12.00 adult, $6.00 child (6-12). Miscellaneous: Museum Store, Carriage House Café. Special event Nooks and Crannies tour is more of an adventure into secret passages and doors.* Want to pretend you're visiting old rich relatives for tea? – this is the place. The long driveway up to the home is beautifully landscaped. You can park right next to the home and carriage house (vs. a block away) and are greeted as an invited guest. The actual family photographs of the Seiberling Family (Frank was the co-founder of the Goodyear Tire and Rubber Company) scattered throughout the home make you feel as if you know them. Stan Hywet means "stone quarry" referring to the stone quarry the house was built on and the stone that was supplied for building. Being an English Tudor, it is rather dark inside with an almost "castle-like" feeling (the detailed wood panels and crown molding are magnificent). Try to count the fireplaces (23) and discover concealed telephones behind the paneled walls. The Corbin Conservatory, a 7,600 square-foot Gothic replication of the original 1915 building, is a complimentary addition to the grounds. Track Butterflies in Flight (seasonally) or explore other garden exhibits.

AKRON ZOO

Akron - *500 Edgewood Avenue (Perkins Woods Park), 44307. Phone: (330) 375-2525.* **Web: www.akronzoo.com**. *Hours: Daily 10:00am-5:00pm (April-October). Daily 11:00am-4:00pm (November-March). Closed New Year's Day, end of October, Thanksgiving, Christmas Eve and Christmas Day. Admission: $8.00 adult, $6.50 senior, $5.00 child (2-14). Small parking fee. Reduced winter admission.* When you visit the zoo, you'll come nose-to-nose with more than 700 animals, including endangered Humboldt penguins, snow leopards, Sumatran tigers, jaguars and Komodo dragons. The zoo features Monkey Island, The River Otter Exhibit, and an Ohio Farmyard petting area. Visit the Asian Trail with Tiger Valley, the red pandas, and the barking deer. The exhibit "Wild Prairie" includes prairie dogs and black-footed ferrets.

AKRON AEROS

Akron - *Canal Park, downtown, 44308. Phone: (330) 253-5151 or (800) 97-AEROS. Web: www.akronaeros.com.* Minor league baseball with ticket prices ranging $5.00-10.00. AA affiliate of the Cleveland Indians. Special events like Little League Nights and fireworks. Orbit, the Akron Aeros loveable mascot, invites you to become a member of the Akron Aeros Kids Club that includes souvenirs, free game tickets and special parties.

AKRON ART MUSEUM

Akron - *70 East Market Street & High Street, 44308. Phone: (330) 376-9185. Web: www.akronartmuseum.org. Hours: Daily 11:00am-5:00pm.* A new open, crystal glass setting for discovering beautiful, new art dating from 1850 to the present. Kids "Drop-in" programs allow for hands-on exploring contemporary art. The Sculpture Courtyard serves as an outdoor gallery with large-scale sculptures. Summer Family Fun nights.

AKRON CIVIC THEATRE

Akron - *182 S. Main St, 44308. Phone: (330) 535-3179. Web: www.akron-civic.com.* The ornate interior features a mighty Wurlitzer organ and resembles a Moorish garden complete with blinking stars and moving clouds. The theater features first-rate productions, films and concerts like Fantastic Fridays. Group tours of the theater are available and are interesting for all ages.

AKRON SYMPHONY ORCHESTRA

Akron - *17 North Broadway (performances at E.J. Thomas Performing Arts Hall on Univ. of Akron campus), 44308. Phone: (330) 535-8131. Web: www.akronsymphony.org.* Professional orchestra offers pops, classical and educational concerts. Family Series of concerts, Picnic Pops in the Park and Youth Symphony. (September – July)

NATIONAL INVENTORS HALL OF FAME

221 South Broadway Street (I- 77 south to Akron. Take Exit 22A.
Go straight through the first light and turn left at the second light
onto Broadway), **Akron** 44308

- ❏   Phone: (330) 762-4463, **Web: www.invent.org**
- ❏   Hours: Wednesday-Saturday 10:00am-4:30pm. Closed major
  winter holidays.
- ❏   Admission: $8.75 adult, $7.75 senior (65+), $6.75 youth (3-17),
  $29.00 family.
- ❏   Miscellaneous: Hall of Fame (4 floors of exhibits) with open
  architecture with 5 tiers of steel and windows. Next door is
  Quaker Square shops and the Depot Diner, a former Railway
  Express Train and model train display sit-down lunch and dinner
  (330-253-5970).

Start with the Inventor's Workshop. A sign says it all - *"This is a place to mess around. No rights. No wrongs. Only experiments and surprises!"* This is honestly the most hands-on, exploring creativity area we've visited in Ohio. Kids' (and adults') minds open before your eyes. Therefore, plan to spend at least 2 hours exploring. In the wood shop you can actually work with a hammer, nails, and saws (all real) to build a mini-boat, house, or new instrument. A favorite exhibit was the "untitled" (metal grasses) which was sculpted of iron powder and danced to music in a magnetic field. Also see the animation area where we each made our own "Toy Story" type movies.

WEATHERVANE PLAYHOUSE

Akron - *1301 Weathervane Lane, 44313. Phone: (330) 836-2626. Web: www.weathervaneplayhouse.com.* Offers mainstage and children's productions, Youth Theatre shows, Spring Puppet show (ex. Snow White, Sound of Music).

GOODYEAR WORLD OF RUBBER

Akron - *1144 East Market Street (Downtown, Goodyear Hall, 4th floor of headquarters), 44316. Phone: (330) 796-7117. Web: www.goodyear.com. Hours: Monday-Friday 8:00am-4:30pm. Tour: Introductory film (by request) of tire production. 1 hour. Groups of 10 or more should call ahead for a reservation.* Discover how Charles Goodyear vulcanized rubber in his kitchen in a replica of his workshop. Other attractions include a simulated rubber plantation (hands on), Indy race cars, an artificial heart, a moon buggy, history of blimps, history of the trucking industry, and of course an array of Goodyear products. Everyone leaves knowing about at least one unusual new product made from rubber to tell his or her friends about.

PORTAGE LAKES STATE PARK

Akron - *5031 Manchester Road (SR 93), 44319. Phone: (330) 644-2220. Web: www.dnr.state.oh.us/parks/parks/portage.htm.* The wetlands of the park attract thousands of geese and waterfowl during spring and fall migration periods. Mallards, wood ducks and Canada geese nest in the wetlands each year. 4,963 acres of camping, hiking trails, boating, fishing, swimming and winter sports.

SUMMIT COUNTY HISTORICAL SOCIETY/JOHN BROWN HOME/PERKINS STONE MANSION

Akron - *550 Copley Road, 44320. Phone: (330) 535-1120. Web: www.summithistory.org. Hours: Wednesday-Sunday 1:00-4:00pm. Closed January and February.* The fight to free slaves governed abolitionist John Brown's life from his hometown days in an 1830's house to the 1859 raid on Harpers Ferry (WV). The house features photos from the time, a reconstruction of a canal boat captain's quarters and changing exhibits about the area. Just across the street is the Perkins Mansion with a décor illustrating Akron and Summit County's history.

ASHTABULA MARINE MUSEUM

Ashtabula - *1071 Walnut Blvd. (Point Park in Ashtabula Harbor),
44004. Web: www.ashtcohs.com/ashmus.html. Phone: (440)
964-6847. Hours: Friday-Sunday Noon-5:00pm (June-August).
Weekends only (September). Admission: $3.00-$4.00 (age 6+).*
Holds treasures of the Great Lakes. Housed in the former residence
of the Lighthouse Keepers and the Coast Guard Chief, built in
1898. Contains models, paintings, marine artifacts, photos of early
Ashtabula Harbor and ore boats and tugs, miniature hand-made
brass tools that actually work, and the world's only working scale
model of a Hulett ore unloading machine. Expansive view of the
harbor from the hill. Feel like you're captain of the high seas in the
actual pilothouse from the steamship.

HUBBARD HOUSE AND UNDERGROUND
RAILROAD MUSEUM

Ashtabula - *Walnut Boulevard and Lake Avenue (near the
Ashtabula Harbor), 44004. Phone: (440) 964-8168. Web:
www.hubbardhouseugrrmuseum.org. Hours: Friday-Sunday
1:00-5:00pm (Memorial Day weekend-September). Closed on
holidays. Admission: $3.00-$5.00 (age 6+).*   There are three
distinct features of the Hubbard House: the circa 1841 home of
William and Catharine Hubbard on the first floor, the Underground
Railroad exhibit area on the second floor; and the Civil War and
Americana exhibit area in the basement. This is recognized as a
northern terminal that was part of the pathway from slavery to
freedom in the pre Civil War era. The Hubbard House, known as
Mother Hubbard's Cupboard and The Great Emporium, is the only
Ohio Underground Railroad terminus, or endpoint, open to the
public. Ashtabula County was instrumental in John Brown's
famous attack on the Federal arsenal at Harper's Ferry, Virginia.
Of the nineteen men who charged the arsenal with John Brown,
Sr., thirteen were from Ashtabula County.

PYMATUNING STATE PARK

Ashtabula (Andover) - *Lake Road (6 miles Southeast of
Andover off SR 85), 44003. Phone: (440) 293-6329. Web:
www.dnr.state.oh.us/odnr/parks/parks/pymatuning.* In a setting

that highlights the mystery of an old swamp forest and the excitement of a water recreation area, Pymatuning State Park invites outdoor lovers of all ages to enjoy one of the finest walleye and muskellunge lakes in the country, camping, swimming and boating opportunities as well. Hiking trails and an assortment of casual, furnished family cabins.

GEAUGA LAKE & WILDWATER KINGDOM

1060 Aurora Road, St. Rte. 43 (9 miles north of Turnpike Exit 13)

Aurora 44202

- ❑ Phone: (330) 562-8303 or (877) 989-3389
  Web: www.geaugalake.com
- ❑ Hours: Open 10:00am. Closes after dark. Weekends Only (May, September, October).
- ❑ Admission: ~$25.00 general. ~$15.00 for kids (under 48" and Seniors (61+). Kids age 2 and under FREE. $8.00 for Parking.
- ❑ Miscellaneous: Lockers and changing rooms. Stroller and wagon rental. Picnic area. Food service. Towel rental. Proper swimwear required. Swimwear available in gift shops. Restaurants.

Here you will find more than 60 rides and attractions, including ten roller coasters and a water park! For the daredevils in all of us, Geauga Lake features Texas Twister, X-Flight, and The Raging Wolf Bobs. Take a ride on a backward loop or 13-story plunge roller coaster. Water play at Wildwater Kingdom: 2½ acre pool with surfs, water chutes, wet slides, toboggan run, or white water rapids. Little ones can splash in mini-waterfalls and slides (even a feeding area for babies) at Happy Harbor. Newer or refurbished rides are: Escape from Dino Island, Robots from Mars 3D, Thunderhawk and Starfish or Thriller Bees. Snoopy and the Peanuts Characters area is here with entertainment.

HALE FARM AND VILLAGE

2686 Oak Hill Road (I-77 exit 226 or I-271 exit 12 (Rte. 303),follow signs), **Bath** 44210

- ☐ Phone: (800) 589-9703 or (330) 666-3711
  Web: www.wrhs.org
- ☐ Hours: Wednesday-Saturday 11:00am-5:00pm (9:30am-2:00pm in September/October); Sunday and Holidays Noon-5:00 pm. Memorial Day - October (Regular Season). Special Weekends November-March.
- ☐ Admission: $12.00 adult, $10.00 senior (60+), $7.00 child (3-12).
- ☐ Miscellaneous: Museum Shop (you can purchase crafts made on site) and Cafe. Map and sample questions to ask towns people provided. Summer Family Fun days are old-fashioned fun geared towards kids. Remember, authentic dirt roads throughout the village.

Jonathan Hale moved to the Western Reserve from Connecticut and prospered during the canal era building an elaborate brick home and farm typical of New England. The gate house prepares guests with an orientation movie, then begin your adventure around the homestead area. Wheatfield Village is a small Ohio town struggling with the impact of the War Between the States. Period tools and machines provide wood- working demonstrations. Other barns serve as shops for a blacksmith, glass-blower, candle or broom-maker and basket maker. The Hale House (bricks made on site by Hale family and still made today) has pioneer cooking (and sampling!) demonstrations. Across the street, visit with mothers, daughters, sons and fathers (they are first person 1860s) as they share with you thoughts of the day. You will feel like you're part of mid-1800's life as crops are planted and harvested, meetings attended, letters written, textiles spun, barters made, and church and school attended. Kids are asked to help with chores and schoolwork. Maybe you'll even get to "knead" the dough for bricks (with your feet!) or card wool or roll clay marbles. Samples of crafts worked on are given to the kids as souvenirs. We liked the mix of some buildings set in the present, some set in the Civil War era - it's amusing and interesting.

CUYAHOGA VALLEY NATIONAL PARK

15610 Vaughn Road (I-271 exit 12, Rte. 303)

Brecksville 44141

- ❑ Phone: (216) 524-1497 or (800) 257-9477 or (800) 445-9667
  Web: www.nps.gov/cuva/index.htm or **www.dayinthevalley.com**
- ❑ Hours: Visitor Center open at 9:00am-5:00pm. Park hours vary by season.
- ❑ Miscellaneous: Hale Farm & Village & Cuyahoga Valley Scenic Railroad all within park. See separate listings in this chapter for details. No overnight camping within the park, however some is available near the perimeter.

Visitors enjoy picnicking, hiking, bike trails, bridle trails, winter sports, golf, fishing, and ranger-guided programs. Some of the park attractions are:

CANAL VISITOR CENTER: Permanent exhibits illustrate 12,000 years of history in the valley, including the history of the Ohio & Erie Canal. The canal-era building once served canal boat passengers waiting to pass through Lock 38. A 20-minute slide program about the park is shown by request. Hours: 10:00am-4:00pm daily except winter holidays. (Canal Road 1.5 miles south of Rockside Road. Access off Hillside Road). Just down the street is the Frazee family home, typical of the era (only open summer weekends).

LOCK 38 DEMONSTRATIONS: Learn about the canal days in the museum and watch the canal lock demonstrations held afternoons every weekend during the summer and periodically in early fall. "Hoooooo!" is the command that mule drivers shouted as they approached Twelve-mile Lock. Step back in time and relive the canal era along the Ohio & Erie Canal. Imagine riding in a boat being raised or lowered in the old stone lock. Join volunteers and park rangers in 19th-century dress as they operate Lock 38.

OHIO & ERIE CANAL TOWPATH TRAIL: Once a mode of transportation of goods and people, the canal (dry and overgrown in places) makes for a nice path for over 19 miles of biking, hiking, running or walking. As you enjoy the Towpath Trail each summer, you may chance upon musicians playing banjo, harmonica, and other instruments.

BRANDYWINE FALLS: A boardwalk trail allows a close view of the roaring water (best after lots of rain).

THE LEDGES OVERLOOK: Hikers can climb to the top of the valley walls to view lots of greenspace.

BOSTON STORE: 1836 gas station store functions as a museum with exhibits on canal boat construction.

MAPLESIDE FARMS

294 Pearl Road, US 42 (on US 42, between Rte. 82 and Rte 303 off I-71 exits), **Brunswick** 44212

- ❑   Phone: (330) 225-5577 store **Web: www.mapleside.com**
- ❑   Tours: Scheduled. Minimum 12 people. $4.00-$7.00 per person. Teachers are FREE. Monday-Friday (Labor Day-October)
- ❑   Miscellaneous: Gift shop, bakery and ice cream parlor. See Suggested Lodging and Dining for Restaurant.

They harvest over 20,000 bushels of apples each year from 5,000 apple trees. Many of the 20 different varieties are kept fresh in controlled atmosphere storage so they can be enjoyed year around (what's the secret?). Fall group tours of the orchards include sample apples (some picked, some from packing room); a tour of apple orchards and production areas with explanation of growing and processing apples; a cup of cider and bakery; a visit to Harvest Hideout playland; and a small pumpkin for each child. Everything you ever wanted to know or never knew about apples!

CENTURY VILLAGE MUSEUM & COUNTRY STORE

Burton - *14653 E. Park Street (State Route 87 and State Route 700), 44021. **Web: www.geaugahistorical.org**. Phone: (440) 834-1492. Hours: Daily daytime hours spring and fall (mid-April, May, September/October). Weekends only in summer. Admission: $6.00 adult, $4.00 child (6-12). Tours: Friday - Sunday 1:00 and 3:00pm (mid-April to mid-November).* Tour the magnificent century homes on the Village grounds, hear stories of early settlers, and view a collection of 9,000 toy soldiers. A restored community with 12 buildings (log cabin, church, barns, schoolhouse, marshal's office and train station) containing 19th Century historical antiques and a working farm. Best to attend during Apple Syrup Festivals, Civil War Festival, or Pioneer School Camp when the village comes alive with visiting "villagers."

YELLOW DUCK PARK

Canfield - *10590 Columbiana Canfield Road (3 miles north of SR1, on SR 46), 44406. Web: www.yellowduckpark.com. Phone: (330) 533-3773. Hours: Daily 11:00am-7:00pm (Summer). Admission: $7.00-$10.00 (Ages 5+). Season passes or member guest only.* Yellow Duck Park is a "family" swim club and picnic fun land that offers a wide range of family fun attractions. The park consists of 42 acres of wooded and well trimmed lawn areas. Shaded picnic areas encircle a wide variety of both wet and dry attractions and activities in a family atmosphere. Enjoy a family swim club, Little Tikes Beach, Yellow Duck and Jackrabbit Waterslides, or the new Family Pool and Lazy River.

NOAH'S LOST ARK ANIMAL SANCTUARY

Canfield (Berlin Center) - *8424 Bedell Road (off SR 224), 44401. Phone: (330) 584-7835. Web: www.noahslostark.org. Hours: Tuesday-Friday 10:00am-5:00pm, Saturday-Sunday 10:00am-5:00pm (May-August). Weekends only until 4:00pm (September-October). Admission: $6.50 adult, $5.00 child (2-17).* Tour the no-frills Exotic Animal Park. The facility is dedicated to providing a permanent safe haven for unwanted and abused Exotic animals. Hands-on interaction with unusual, uncommon international animals (camels, pot-bellied pigs, antelope). Wagon rides thru farm. The newly constructed large cat compound featuring Tigers, Lions, Ligers, Servals, Leopards, Caracals and Bobcats or the Primate Area are favorites.

PIONEER WATERLAND AND DRY PARK

Chardon - *10661 Kile Road (off US 6 or SR 608/US 322), 44024. Web: www.pioneerwaterland.com. Phone: (440) 285-0910. Hours: Daily 10:00am-8:00pm (Memorial Day-Labor Day).*

Admission: $15.95 and up. Discount tickets available online. Dry activities are a few additional dollars each. Less than 40" tall FREE. Miscellaneous: Picnic Area, Food Service, and Video Arcade. Little ones frequent the toddler play area and waterland. Others can explore the water slides, paddleboats, inner tube rides, volleyball nets, Indy raceway, batting cages, miniature golf or driving range. All adjoining a chlorinated crystal clear lake with beaches.

CLEVELAND SPORTS

CLEVELAND BROWNS - Browns Stadium, lakefront. (440) 224-3361 tours. **www.clevelandbrowns.com**. NFL Football, New Dawg Pound. Largest scoreboard in NFL Football. Kids Club. Tours by appointment give you facts and figures plus a peek at locker rooms and press boxes. Tickets begin at $30.00. (September-December)

CLEVELAND CAVALIERS - Quicken Arena *(The Q)*. (216) 420-2200 or **www.nba.com/cavs**. Professional Basketball. (September – April).

CLEVELAND INDIANS - Jacobs Field. (866) 48-TRIBE or **www.indians.com**. Professional Baseball. Kids Club. $7.00-$27.00 tickets. (April – October). Tours (fee of $4.50-$6.50) include Kidsland, a press box, a suite, a dugout, a fun video...lasts one hour (Monday-Saturday 10am-2pm, some summer Sundays).

CHILDREN'S MUSEUM OF CLEVELAND

Cleveland - *10730 Euclid Avenue (University Circle, I-90 to MLK exit 177), 44106.* **Web:** *www.clevelandchildrensmuseum.org.* *Phone: (216) 791-KIDS. Hours: Tuesday-Saturday 10:00am-5:00pm, Sunday Noon-5:00pm, except Christmas and New Years. Admission: General admission (age 1yr +) is $6.00.* The Children's Museum of Cleveland offers innovative and educational exhibits for children. Splish! Splash! features a two-story climbing structure that is designed to teach basic principles of the water cycle (fun to climb into). Also in this area is the Kids' Forecast Center (predict weather, then present it before camera). Put on an apron & splash play in Water Works. Bridges to Our Community features areas that are joined together by bridges. Kids pretend to shop, bank, pump gas or drive a bus. Build with blocks or create art here, too. The Big Red Barn area is a child's book brought to life- infants & preschoolers play with lots of chutes and ladders. Temporary exhibits might be covering tools or trains or sand. Summer camps. Best for kids under 8.

CLEVELAND BOTANICAL GARDEN

Cleveland - *11030 East Blvd. (University Circle, I-90 to MLK exit), 44106. Phone: (216) 721-1600. Web: www.cbgarden.org. Hours: Monday-Saturday 10:00am-5:00pm and Sunday Noon-5:00pm. Closed Mondays in winter. (Hershey Children's Garden closes all winter). Admission: $7.50 adult, $3.00 child (3-12).* Display gardens changing each season (best April-October for color). Most like the Knot Garden and the newer areas: the spiny desert of Madagascar and the cloud forest of Costa Rica. With its wheelchair-accessible tree house, dwarf forests, scrounger garden, worm bins and watery bog, Hershey Children's Garden is an exciting destination for families. Lots of adventure paths to explore and splash in water spouts. Flowers in a bathtub - oh my!

CLEVELAND CENTER FOR CONTEMPORARY ART

Cleveland - *8501 Carnegie Avenue (2nd floor of Playhouse Complex), 44106. Web: www.contemporaryart.org. Phone: (216) 421-8671. Hours: Tuesday-Saturday 11:00am-6:00pm. Admission: FREE for children. $3.00-$4.00 student and adult (age 12+).* Displays of avant-garde paintings, sculpture, drawings, prints, and photographs by regional and national artists. From Warhol to Lichtenstein, Christo to Grooms - and every season they continue to tap into new trends.

CLEVELAND MUSEUM OF ART

Cleveland - *11150 East Boulevard (University Circle, near the Botanical Gardens), 44106. Phone: (216) 421-7340 or (888) 262-0033. Web: www.clevelandart.org. Hours: Tuesday, Thursday, Saturday & Sunday 10:00am-5:00pm. Wednesday & Friday 10:00am-9:00pm. Check website for updates on hours. Admission: Watch their website for admission updates as complete phases of the new museum open. Miscellaneous: Café open daytime.* New, renovated museum is open after almost a year of changes and improvements. See the large collection of objects from all cultures and periods including European and American paintings, medieval, Asian, Islamic, pre-Columbian, African masks, Egyptian mummies and Oceanic art. The kids really like the Armor Court (knights in shining armor).

CLEVELAND MUSEUM OF NATURAL HISTORY

1 Wade Oval Drive (University Circle, I-90 and Martin Luther King Dr. exit), **Cleveland** 44106

❑   Phone: (216) 231-4600 or (800) 317-9155
      Web: www.cmnh.org

❑   Hours: Monday-Saturday 10:00am-5:00pm, Sunday Noon-
      5:00pm. Also, Wednesdays open until 10:00pm (September-May
      only). Closed holidays.

❑   Admission: $7.50 adult, $5.50 youth (7-18) and senior (60+),
      $4.50 child (3-6).

❑   Miscellaneous: Gift shop. Modern Planetarium and interactive
      pre-show activities (extra fee) plus Observatory open Wednesday
      evenings. Live animal shows daily. Café lunch. Parking fee.

Meet "Happy" the 70 foot long dinosaur or "Lucy" the oldest human fossil. Look for real dino eggs and touch real dino bones! Highlights of Ohio Natural History are: Johnstown Mastodon -- A long-ago Ohio resident and Dunkle - this fearsome 16-foot-long armored fish with huge self-sharpening jaws is a native Clevelander found in the shale of the Rocky River Valley (look low, then look high - oh my!). The Ringler dugout is the oldest well-dated watercraft ever found in North America (found in 1976 in Ashland, OH). Also look for the Glacier that Covered Cleveland; the Diorama of Moundbuilders - shown in layers depicting what might be found (excellent examples-the most spectacular mounds were found in Ohio); or the Wildlife Center & Woods (outside, partially enclosed) where natural habitats are home to raptors (owls, hawks), songbirds, turkey, river otters, fox and many other species found in the state. The lower level of the museum has Ohio Botany, Ohio Birds & Insects and Ohio

Ecology. In the Discovery Center, kids can use microscopes or view live insects and reptiles. Lots of touch and feel toys and games. "Planet e" is an interactive area featuring actual footage from NASA space missions projected onto a large viewing monitor. Your "spacecraft" can take you to planets and moons in the solar system and launch a probe. Or, experience an earthquake in Ohio - are we ready? Kids visiting here are first amazed at the large scale of the prehistoric skeletons and also love that many prehistoric artifacts came from Ohio. As you might have guessed, you need several hours or many visits to explore every corner of this place!

CLEVELAND ORCHESTRA

Cleveland - *11001 Euclid Avenue, 44106. Phone: (216) 231-1111 or (800) 686-1141. Web: www.clevelandorchestra.com.* Concerts in beautiful Severance Hall (September-May), outdoors at Blossom Music Center (Summer). The COYO (Cleveland Orchestra Youth Orchestra) performs concerts also. Family Concerts are specially designed for children 6 and older. These narrated concerts are structured around a theme and include collaborative artist such as young musicians, singers, dancers and actors.

CLEVELAND PLAYHOUSE

Cleveland - *8500 Euclid Avenue, 44106. Phone: (216) 795-7000. Web: www.clevelandplayhouse.com.* America's longest running regional theatre presents contemporary and classical children's series plays during the school year.

WESTERN RESERVE HISTORY MUSEUM

Cleveland - *10825 East Boulevard, University Circle (I-90 to MLK exit 177), 44106. Web: www.wrhs.org. Phone: (216) 721-5722. Hours: Monday-Saturday 10:00am-5:00pm. Sunday Noon – 5:00pm. Admission: $8.50 adult, $7.50 senior, $5.00 student (age 6+). Includes Mansion, History, Costume Wing and Crawford Museum. Miscellaneous: We strongly suggest hands-on programs and guided tours for families.* Cleveland's oldest cultural institution boasts a tour of a grand mansion recreating the Western Reserve from pre-Revolution War to the 20th Century. The look (but mostly don't touch) displays include: farming tools, clothing and costumes (displayed with cute artifacts of the time) and over 150 classic automobiles (Cleveland built cars, oldest car, and heaviest car) and airplanes. Look for an original Morgan Traffic Signal (native Clevelander) or the Tinkerbelle - the smallest sailboat to cross the Atlantic.

CLEVELAND LAKEFRONT STATE PARK

Cleveland - *8701 Lakeshore Blvd., NE (off I-90, downtown), 44108. www.dnr.state.oh.us/parks/parks/clevelkf.htm.* Phone: *(216) 881-8141.* Cleveland Lakefront State Park provides natural relief to the metropolitan skyline. Sand beaches, tree-lined picnic areas and panoramic views of the lake are found within the park along the Lake Erie shoreline. The annual Erie fish catch nearly equals the combined catches of all the other great lakes. Dominant species are perch, smallmouth and white bass, channel catfish, walleye and freshwater drum. Facilities include: Edgewater Park - This park is divided into upper and lower areas connected by a paved bicycle path and fitness course; East 55th Marina; Gordon Park; Euclid Beach - 650-foot swimming beach with shaded picnic areas and a scenic observation pier; Villa Angela; and Wildwood. 450 acres of boating and rentals, fishing, swimming, and winter sports.

CLEVELAND METROPARKS ZOO & RAINFOREST

3900 Wildlife Way (I-71 exit Fulton Road or East 25th Street)

Cleveland 44109

- ❑ Phone: (216) 661-6500, **Web: www.clemetzoo.com**
- ❑ Hours: Daily 10:00am-5:00pm. Until 7:00pm Weekends (Summer). Closed only Christmas and New Year's Day.
- ❑ Admission: $9.00 adult (12+), $4.00 child (2-11). Free Parking. Free zoo only admission for Cuyahoga county residents on Mondays.
- ❑ Miscellaneous: Outback railroad train ride, camel rides and adventure rides are $1.50-$3.00 extra. Concessions and cafes. Zoo trams run daily for FREE.

A rainforest with animal and plant settings like the jungles of Africa, Asia, and South America is the most popular exhibit to explore. The rainforest boasts a storm every 12 minutes, a 25-foot waterfall, and a walk-through aviary. Altogether, the whole zoo holds thousands of animals from all continents including Africa and Australia. Wolf Wilderness is a popular educational study exhibit where you can view thru a giant window the wolves acting "naturally" in the day and night. The Australian Adventure has a kookaburra station, wallaby walkabout and koala junction (55 ft. treehouse and play area with petting yard). New animals are born here often so check their website for who's new!

LOLLY THE TROLLEY TOURS

1831 Columbus Road (Station: Powerhouse @ Nautica, west bank of Flats), **Cleveland** 44113

- ❏　Phone: (216) 771-4484 or (800) 848-0173
  Web: www.lollytrolley.com
- ❏　Hours: Early morning or afternoon departures. More available on weekends (even early evening). Weekends only in winter.
- ❏　Admission: $7.00-$10.00 (1 hr.) or $10.00-$15.00 (2 hr.).
- ❏　Tours: 1 or 2 hours, Reservations Required. 1 hour tour is suggested for preschoolers.
- ❏　Miscellaneous: Specialty tours with Cleveland authors traveling along to sites or Holiday Tours (see Seasonal & Special Events).

"Lolly the Trolley", an old fashioned bright red trolley, clangs its bell as you take in over 100 sights around the downtown area. The tour includes Cleveland's North Coast Harbor featuring the world's only Rock & Roll Hall of Fame and Museum and the Great Lakes Science Center; Downtown Cleveland; The Warehouse District, The Flats, a river port by day and a bustling entertainment center by night; Ohio City, with both Victorian homes renovated by "urban homesteaders"; and the West Side Market, one of the world's largest indoor/outdoor food and produce markets; Playhouse Square; University Circle, a focal point for cultural educational and medical institutions. Your tour concludes with a brief stop at the Rockefeller Greenhouse and a drive along the Lake Erie shoreline back to the station. A great way to show off the city to visitors or get an overview of sites to decide which you want to visit.

TOWER CITY CENTER OBSERVATION DECK

Cleveland - *50 Public Square, 42nd Floor, Terminal Tower, 44113. Phone: (216) 621-7981. Hours: Weekends 11:00am-4:30pm (Summer), 11:00am-3:30pm (Rest of Year). Admission: $2.00 adult, $1.00 child (6-16).* The 42nd floor deck offers a full view of the city (best if you choose a clear day) with a few displays of the history of the Terminal Tower and downtown.

GOOD TIME III

825 East 9th Street Pier (Behind Rock & Roll Hall of Fame)

Cleveland 44114

❏   Phone: (216) 861-5110, **Web: www.goodtimeiii.com**

❏   Admission: $15.00 adult, $14.00 senior, $9.00 child (age 2-11). Add $10.00 extra for lunch.

❏   Tours: Daily Noon, 3:00pm, Sundays at 6:00pm (mid-June to Labor Day). Weekends (Friday-Sunday) only in May and September.

❏   Miscellaneous: Food Service Available. Lower deck is air-conditioned and heated. Parking on the pier.

The quadruple-deck, 1000 passenger boat takes a two hour excursion of city sights along the Cuyahoga River and Lake Erie. The word Cuyahoga is Indian for "crooked". You'll see tugboats and the largest yellow crane boats in the country. See all the industry in the Flats including concrete, pipe, transportation, limestone, and coke businesses. Collision Bend used to be so narrow that many boats got tangled up. Since then, they have dredged the curve and it's now very wide.

GREAT LAKES SCIENCE CENTER

601 Erieside Avenue (E 9th Street and I-90, North Coast Harbor, Downtown), **Cleveland** 44114

❏   Phone: (216) 694-2000 **Web: www.glsc.org**

❏   Hours: Daily 9:30am-5:30pm. Only closed Thanksgiving and Christmas.

❏   Admission: $7.00-$9.00. Memberships Available. Omnimax additional $7.00-$9.00. Discount combo tickets.

Great Lakes Science Center (*cont.*)

❑   Miscellaneous: Gift Shop OmniMax Theater – 6 story domed screen image and sound. Bytes sandwich restaurant on location.

Over 400 interactive exhibits – especially fun on the second floor. Pilot a blimp, test your batting skills, or bounce off the walls in the Polymer Funhouse. The science playground museum focuses on the Great Lakes region and its environment (Sick Earth, Cloud Maker, Nitrogen Fixation). Young lab scientists (guests) can create a tornado or create light. Virtual Sports, Electric Shows & one of the largest video walls east of the Rockies.

NAUTICA QUEEN

Cleveland - *1153 Main Avenue (West Bank Flats), 44114. Phone: (216) 696-8888 or (800) 837-0604.* **Web: www.nauticaqueen.com**. *Hours: Monday – Thursday Noon, 7:00pm; Friday Noon, 7:30 pm; Saturday 11:00am, 7:30pm; Sunday 11:00am, 4:00 pm (April-December). Reservation Required. Admission: $14.00-19.00 child (Adult prices are about double).* 3 Hour Dinner Cruise or 2 hour Lunch/Brunch Cruise. Many cruises include entertainment with special themes like pirates or shipwrecks.

ROCK AND ROLL HALL OF FAME MUSEUM

Cleveland - *One Key Plaza (9th Street exit north, downtown waterfront), 44114. Phone: (216) 781-ROCK or (800) 493-ROLL.* **Web: www.rockhall.com**. *Hours: Daily 10:00am - 5:30pm (open until 9 p.m. on Wednesdays). Closed Thanksgiving and Christmas. Admission: $20.00 adult, $14.00 senior (60+), $11.00 youth (9-12). Free Museum admission for children 8 and under with the purchase of an adult admission.* As parents reminisce, kids will probably giggle, at most of the many exhibits including: Rock & Roll in the 50s,The Music of Ohio, Cinema (documentary films), Induction Videos, Radio Station and the Hall of Fame. Please check in with Visitor's Services before you explore here - they'll let you know which areas have PG and above ratings - you'll know which areas to overlook.

U.S.S. COD

1809 East 9th Street (North Marginal Road next to Burke Lakefront)

Cleveland 44114

- ❑ Phone: (216) 566-8770, **Web: www.usscod.org**
- ❑ Hours: Daily 10:00am-5:00pm (May-September).
- ❑ Admission: $6.00 adult, $5.00 senior (62+), $3.00 student (under 6 Free). FREE for military in uniform.
- ❑ Miscellaneous: Recommend airport parking lot.

We started our visit at the Aristotle periscope on shore that gives you a view of Lake Erie and puts you in the mood to explore the WW II submarine that sank enemy shipping boats. The ninety-man crew lived in cramped quarters - an amazing reminder of the price of freedom. The eight separate compartments, tight quarters, ladders to climb and plenty of knobs to play with give an authentic feeling of submarine life. The best part of this tour is the fact that the sub was actually used in wartime and still remains pretty much the same as during wartime...very authentic presentation.

WILLIAM G. MATHER MUSEUM

Docked at 305 Old Erieside Avenue (Dock 32 at Northcoast Harbor Park, just north of Science Center), **Cleveland** 44114

- ❑ Phone: (216) 574-6262
  Web: http://little.nhlink.net/wgm/wgmhome.html
- ❑ Hours: Daily 10:00am-5:30pm, except Sunday Noon-5:30pm (summer). Weekends (Friday-Sunday) Only (May, September, October).
- ❑ Admission: $6.00 adult, $5.00 senior (60+), $4.00 youth (5-18 and college w/ID).
- ❑ Miscellaneous: Best for preschoolers and older because of dangerous spots while walking. Films play continuously. After your visit, have lunch or dinner at Hornblowers Restaurant (216-363-1151). An actual barge restaurant on the water.

The floating Mather is an iron boat once used to carry ore, coal and grain along the Great Lakes. Little eyes will open wide in the 4 story engine room and they will have fun pretending to be the crew (or maybe guests) in the cozy sleeping quarters or the elegant dining room. Group tours are treated to programmed learning fun in the Interactive Cargo Hold area. Make a sailor hat or a boat made from silly putty (why does a boat float?). Learn to tie sailors' knots with real rope or pretend you're at sea as you move the ship's wheel. In the pilothouse area, kids use navigation charts, working radar, and a marine radio to plan a trip.

MALLEY'S CHOCOLATES

13400 Brookpark Road (I-480 and West 130th street)

Cleveland 44135

- ❑ Phone: (216) 362-8700 or (800) 835-5684
  Web: www.malleys.com
- ❑ Admission: $3.00 (age 3+).
- ❑ Tours: Monday-Friday 10:00am –3:00pm (By Appointment) excluding holidays. Summer hours vary. Strollers allowed, No cameras. 60 minute tour, 15-50 person limit.

See and hear about the story of chocolate from a professional at Malley's family business (since 1935). We learned it takes 400 cocoa beans to make one pound of chocolate. You'll watch them roast nuts, dip chocolates, and wrap goodies along with samples at the beginning and end of the tour (plus a candy bar to take home). They sell one half million pounds per year with the most sales at Easter, then Christmas, then Valentine's Day. Allow time to shop in their factory store.

NASA GLENN RESEARCH VISITOR CENTER

21000 Brookpark Road (I-480 to Exit 9, next to Cleveland Hopkins Airport, Lewis Field), **Cleveland** 44135

- ❑ Phone: (216) 433-2000 **Web: www.grc.nasa.gov**
- ❑ Hours: Weekdays 9:00am-4:00pm. Saturday & Holidays 10:00am-3:00pm, Sunday 1:00-5:00pm. Closed major winter holidays.
- ❑ Admission: FREE
- ❑ Tours: Available, call for details. Family programs and tours are offered most Saturdays.

The interactive exhibit space called the Aero Adventures houses displays on a space shuttle, satellites, zero gravity chamber, wind tunnels, and space environmental tanks. The Apollo Command Module (used on Skylab 3) is the most popular area. Look for the moon rock and space suit used by astronauts (audio explanation) and tribute to John Glenn. The Launch Control Center allows you to conduct a countdown sequence towards a simulated launch of a rocket. You can perform some of the steps that the astronauts performed when working with the Combustion Module. After following the steps, actual footage is played from one of the experiments conducted in space. The ACTS satellite control room and the space shuttle live broadcasts are a great reason for frequent visits.

MEMPHIS KIDDIE PARK

Cleveland - *10340 Memphis Avenue (I-71 to West 117th /Memphis Avenue Exit), 44144. Web: www.memphiskiddiepark.com. Phone: (216) 941-5995. Hours and Admission: 10:00am-8:00pm, seasonal. Pay per ride (~$1.00 each). Discounts for books of tickets. Riders must be under 50 inches tall for most rides.* With many of the original rides still in place, Memphis Kiddie Park is truly a landmark of the Cleveland area which has thrilled generations of children. Memphis Kiddie Park consists of eleven miniature amusement rides, a concession stand, an arcade, and an eighteen hole miniature golf course. The park is mainly for youngsters anywhere from about a year old on up to around eight. Little tots rides like a ferris wheel, roller coaster (our little girl's first!) and carousel.

MOSQUITO LAKE STATE PARK

Cortland - *1439 SR 305 (10 miles North of Warren off State Route 305), 44410. Web: www.dnr.state.oh.us/odnr/parks/parks/mosquito. Phone: (330) 637-2856.* Several hiking trails allow visitors to explore the woodlands and scenic shoreline of the park. Ten miles of bridle trails give horsemen access to the park's interior. Snowmobilers have access to 14 miles of shoreline and 15 miles of wooded trails. Mountain biking is permitted on 5 miles of multiple-use trails. 11,811 acres of camping, boating and rentals, fishing, swimming at sandy beach and winter sports. Near the lake, look for the 12 bald eagles that reside in the area.

FAIRPORT HARBOR MARINE MUSEUM
129 Second Street (I-90 to SR 44 north to SR 2)
Fairport Harbor 44077

❑ Phone: (440) 354-4825 **Web: www.ncweb.com/org/fhlh**

❑ Hours: Wednesday, Saturday, Sunday and Holidays. 1:00 – 6:00pm (Memorial Weekend – 2nd weekend in September)

❑ Admission: $3.00 adult, $2.00 senior and $1.00 child (6-12).

Pretend you're on a sea voyage as you explore an old pilothouse with navigation instruments, maps and charts and a large ship's wheel. Find out what number of whistles you use to indicate the ship's direction. This room is large enough to really romp around. The highlight of this museum has to be the real lighthouse (although it's a steep climb up and out to the deck). After you proudly climb the 69 steps, catch your breath with a beautiful view of Lake Erie. Our favorite lighthouse & museum combo!

ERIEVIEW PARK

Geneva-on-the-Lake - *5483 Lake Road (I-90 to Geneva Exit 218 to State Route 531), 44041. Phone: (440) 466-8650. **Web:** www.ncweb.com/biz/erieview. Hours: Daily 2:00-9:00pm (mid-June to late August). Admission: "Day Pass" $7.00-$15.00, Individual rides are ~$2.00. No admission into park to walk around.* Located on the "strip" with 20 old-fashioned classic rides, kiddie rides, bumper cars and water slides. Food service and picnic areas.

GENEVA STATE PARK

Geneva-on-the-Lake - *Padanarum Road (Shore of Lake Erie), 44041. Phone: (440) 466-8400 or (800) 801-9982 lodge. **Web:** www.dnr.state.oh.us/odnr/parks/jparks/geneva.htm.* Located on Ohio's northeastern shoreline, Geneva State Park reflects the charisma of Lake Erie. Vacationers enjoy fishing and boating, swimmers love the beautiful sand beach, while nature enthusiasts retreat to the park's freshwater marshes and estuaries. Three miles of multi-use trails traverse the park. They are used by hikers and cross-country skiers. 698 acres of camping, boating and jet ski rentals, and large cottages. The **LODGE & CONFERENCE CENTER** at

Geneva State Park (**www.thelodgeatgeneva.com**) is a newer upscale resort with a spectacular view of Lake Erie. The resort includes 109 guest rooms, a restaurant, indoor pool, fitness center, game room and gift shop. In addition, direct access to Lake Erie is available at the beach and marina located in the State Park.

AC & J SCENIC RAILROAD

Jefferson - *State Route 46 to East Jefferson Street (Rte. 11 north, exit @ Rte. 307 west), 44047. Phone: (440) 576-6346.* **Web:** *www.acjrscenic.net. Hours: Weekends departing 1:00 or 3:00 pm (mid-June - October). Only Sundays in September. One is a former long-distance car with air-conditioning. Two others are commuter cars having openable windows and ceiling fans. Several can be heated for cooler weather. There is one on-board lavatory. Admission: $9.00 adult, $8.00 senior (60+), $6.00 child (3-12).* Ride on a 1951 Nickel Plate train with a bright red caboose on a one hour ride through woodlands and farmland. Stop halfway at a staging yard for coal and iron ore in Ashtabula Harbor. Gift shop / concessions.

JEFFERSON DEPOT

Jefferson - *147 E. Jefferson Street (SR 46 and downtown), 44047. Phone: (440) 293-5532. www.members.tripod.com/jeffersonhome. Admission: $2.00 donation accepted. Tours: GUIDED TOURS every Sunday, 1:00-4:00pm during June, July, August and September.* Travel back in time to the 1800's Costumed kinfolk will let you peek back into the past! See the ornate 1872 LS&Ms Railroad Station on the National Register, the quaint 1848 "Church in the Wildwood," 1849 Church barn, 1918 Caboose, 1838 Spafford One-Room School House, Hohn's General Store, Early Pharmacy and 1888 House. The Blacksmith shop and Post Office are newer buildings on the property.

VICTORIAN PERAMBULATOR MUSEUM

Jefferson - *26 East Cedar Street (off State Route 46), 44047. Web: www.webspawner.com/users/carriage/ Phone: (440) 576-9588. Hours: Wednesday & Saturday 11:00am-5:00pm (Summer Only). Saturdays only (September-May).* First of all, do you know what a perambulator is? If you were like us, we just had to know! Answer…a baby carriage. Two sisters have collected and displayed almost 140 carriages dating from the mid- 1800's to the early 1900's. Some are shaped like swans, gondolas, seahorses, and antique cars (made from wicker, which was the Victorian style). This is the nation's only baby carriage museum. $3.50-$4.50 admission.

KENT STATE UNIVERSITY MUSEUM

Kent - *East Main & South Lincoln Streets (Rockwell Hall), 44242. Phone: (330) 672-3450. Web: www.kent.edu/museum. Hours: Wednesday-Saturday 10:00am-4:45pm. Sunday Noon-4:45pm. Closed most school holidays and breaks. Admission: $3.00-$5.00 (age 7+). Miscellaneous: Pufferbelly Train Depot Restaurant (330-673-1771) nearby.* Features work of the world's greatest artists and designers. Fashion, ethnic costumes, and textiles are highlighted along with whimsical artifacts from that time.

HOLDEN ARBORETUM

Kirtland - *9500 Sperry Road, 44094. Phone: (440) 946-4400. Web: www.holdenarb.org. Hours: Tuesday-Sunday 10:00am-5:00pm.* Tour the many trails, which offer a variety of lengths and difficulty, from easy to rugged; something for everyone. Walk through gardens, fields and woods, past ponds and down into the valley. Guided hikes are available year-round. 3000 acres of gardens and walking trails (focus on woody plants). Holden Butterfly Garden is directly behind the Visitor Center. This fabulous garden is over two acres and home to two ponds, a waterfall and a profusion of plantings geared to attract caterpillars, butterflies and hummingbirds. Guided or self-guided hikes begin at Visitors Center. $2.00 Tram Tour, by reservation.

LAKE FARMPARK

8800 Chardon Rd (I-90 to SR 306 S to SR 6 E). **Kirtland** 44094

- ❏ Phone: (800) 366-FARM, **Web: www.lakemetroparks.com**
- ❏ Hours: Daily 9:00am-5:00pm. Closed Mondays (January-March) and all major holidays.
- ❏ Admission: $6.00 adult, $5.00 senior (60+), $4.00 child (2-11)
- ❏ Miscellaneous: Gift Shop. Restaurant. Comfortable walking or tennis shoes are best to wear on the farm. Wagon rides throughout the park are included. Wagon rentals are available. Barnyard - ostriches, poultry, sheep petting. Pony rides are $2.00. Seasonal events are fantastic (see last chapter)!

Not really a farm - it's a park about farming (and the cleanest farm you'll ever visit!). Most of their focus is to discover where food and natural products come from. In the Dairy Parlor, you can milk a real cow and make ice cream from the cow's milk. Wander over to the Arena and watch the sheep show or a horse show. What products can be made with the help of sheep? - How about feta cheese from their milk and yarn from their wool coats. Use special brushes to clean their wool and then spin some by hand. Some of the cutest exhibits are the babies...look for them all around the Arena. Exhibits are ready to be played with all day in the Great Tomato Works. A giant tomato plant (6 feet wide with 12-ft. leaves) greets you and once inside the greenhouse, you can go down below the earth in the dirt to see where plants get their start. Sneak up on a real honeybee comb, but mind the words on the sign, "DO NOT DISTURB - HONEYBEES AT WORK". This visit generates lots of questions about the food you eat. Great learning!

LAKE MILTON STATE PARK

Lake Milton - *16801 Mahoning Avenue (1 mile South of I-76 off State Route 534), 44429. Phone: (330) 654-4989. **Web: www.dnr.state.oh.us/parks/parks/lkmilton.htm.*** Lake Milton's reservoir offers the best in water-related recreation. Boating, swimming and fishing are popular. The scenic shoreline provides a habitat for waterfowls and shorebirds for visitors to enjoy. 2,856 acres of boating, fishing, swimming and winter sports.

MAGICAL FARMS

Media (Litchfield) - *5280 Avon Lake Road (SR 83) (I-71 south to Rte. 18 west thru Medina. 9 miles past town, take SR 83 south), 44253. Phone: (330) 667-3233. Web: www.alpacafarm.com. Hours: 9:00am-4:30pm, best by appointment. Closed Christmas, New Year's Day and Thanksgiving. Tours: Daylight hours, daily, by appointment.* Second largest alpaca breeding farm in North America. With over 50 barns and sheds, a visit to Magical Farms is not only a learning experience...it's an adventure. It's an opportunity for hands-on training and lots of fun interacting with the animals. Picnic sites and gift shop, too.

ELM FARM - AMERICAS ICE CREAM & DAIRY MUSEUM & PARLOR

Medina - *1050 Lafayette Road (US 42, 2 mile south of the Square, near the water tower), 44258. Phone: (330) 722-3839. Web: www.elmfarm.com. Hours: Monday-Saturday 11:00am-6:00pm, Sunday Noon-5:00pm. Extended hours for parlor. Fewer hours in the winter. Admission: $2.00-3.50 (age 6+).* The dairy farm dates back to the early 1900's. They started manufacturing ice cream in the 50's. The parlor serves the treats and light lunch foods in a soda fountain theme. In the back, they have a museum that features displays showing the way dairies used to operate and lots of dairy inventions through the years (i.e.. Jack Frost freezer, 20's & 30's Popsicle molds). The interactive areas and collection of full-size rare trucks and milk bottles demonstrates a great deal about the history behind Elm Farm and the dairy industry.

LAWNFIELD - GARFIELD NATIONAL HISTORIC SITE, JAMES A.

8095 Mentor Avenue (I-90 exit Rte. 306, turn right 2 miles East on US 20), **Mentor** 44060

- ❑   Phone: (440) 255-8722, **Web: www.wrhs.org**
- ❑   Hours: Monday-Saturday 10:00am-5:00pm, Sunday Noon-5:00pm (May-October). Weekends only (November-April).
- ❑   Admission: $7.00 adult, $6.00 senior (60+), $5.00 child (6-12).

❑   Miscellaneous: Gift Shop. Summer Fun Programs (weekdays at 2:00pm) are recommended for hands-on. If touring with school-aged kids, ask for the Young People's club worksheet of puzzles & games. Not recommended for preschoolers. Garfield Birthplace Site & Monument east of Cleveland (440-248-1188 & 216-421-2665).

The Victorian farmhouse mansion was the home of President James A. Garfield. Notice the tiles in the dining room fireplace were painted by family as a craft project. The walk-in safe is neat (contains the wreath sent to his funeral by the Queen of England). Like to drape your legs over the side of a chair? Catch Garfield's office Reading Chair. Who killed him and why? A great museum explains his politics and death. Shortly after his election, an opponent at a railroad station in Washington D.C. assassinated him. See the video showing his life as a preacher (he strongly believed in Divine Providence), teacher and lawyer plus Garfield's campaign on the front porch of his home in 1880. Journalists standing on the lawn covering the campaign nicknamed the property "Lawnfield". Other structures on the 7.82 acre site include the carriage house (visitor center), the campaign office, the 75-foot tall pump house/windmill and barn. Be sure to spend as much time in the Visitors Center as on tour.

MIDDLEFIELD CHEESE HOUSE

Middlefield - *State Route 608 (north of Rte. 87), 44062. Phone: (440) 632-5228 or (800) 32-SWISS. www.middlefieldcheese.com. Hours: Monday – Saturday 8:00am – 5:30pm.* Over 20 million pounds of Swiss cheese are produced here each year. Your tour begins with the film "Faith and Teamwork" describing the cheese-making process. Then wander through the Cheese House Museum with Swiss cheese carvings, antique cheese-making equipment, and Amish memorabilia. Lastly, sample some cheese before you buy homemade cheese, sausage and bread.

PUNDERSON STATE PARK RESORT

Newbury - *(2 miles East of Newbury off State Route 87), 44065. Web: www.dnr.state.oh.us/parks/parks/punderson.htm or Web: www.pundersonmanorresort.com. Phone: (440) 564-2279.* Nature programs. Tennis. 996 acres of camping, hiking trails, boating and rentals, fishing, swimming and winter sports. Family cabins with A/C and fireplaces. Combine that with 15 miles of natural hiking trails (some are nature walks with signs) that wind past deer, squirrel, beaver, giant maples, and scented pine trees. When winter comes, you can snowmobile, cross-country ski, ice fish or race downhill on a giant grooved sled hill. And when it's time for sleep, you can hideaway in your room, the tower library or lounge by a fire. Lots of seasonal getaway packages are available.

WESTWOODS PARK

Newbury - *9465 Kinsman Road (Route 87) (I-90 to Route 306. Travel south on Route 306 for approximately 12.7 miles to Route 87. Turn east on Route 87), 44065. Phone: (440) 286-9516. Web: www.geaugaparkdistrict.org/nature/westwoods.htm. Miscellaneous: Geauga County Parks are nearby.* They had an excellent Ice Age exhibit that has left, but the Ice Age theme continues throughout the year through outdoor adventures. Take home a souvenir glacier rock. Other exhibits highlight the geology, hydrology, and diverse ecology of the county's lands. More than 5 miles of trails traverse through woodlands, across streams and past outcroppings of conglomerate sandstone. Other trails lead past "black swamp" pools, past Sunset Overlook, or to Ansel's Cave. This is a one-stop place for studying glaciers in northeast Ohio.

MCKINLEY BIRTHPLACE MEMORIAL AND MUSEUM

Niles - *40 North Main Street (SR 46 to downtown), 44446. Phone: (330) 652-1704. Web: www.mckinley.lib.oh.us. Hours: Monday-Thursday 9:00am-8:00pm. Friday and Saturday 9:00am - 5:30pm, Sunday 1:00 - 5:00pm (September - May Only).* The classic Greek structure with Georgian marble which houses a museum of McKinley memorabilia. Also see artifacts from the Civil War and Spanish-American War. McKinley was the 25th President and the first to use campaign buttons. He was assassinated in office.

HEADLANDS BEACH STATE PARK

Painesville - *State Route 44 (2 miles Northwest of Painesville), 44060.* ***Web: www.dnr.state.oh.us/parks/parks/headlnds.htm.*** *Phone: (440) 881-8141.* The trademark of Headlands Beach State Park is its mile-long natural sand beach, the largest in the state. In addition to its popularity during the summer season with picnickers and swimmers, the area is home to many plant species typically found only along the Atlantic Coast. 125 acres of hiking trails (adjacent nature preserve), fishing, swimming and winter sports.

CUYAHOGA VALLEY SCENIC RAILROAD

Cuyahoga Valley National Recreation Area (Independence Depot is off I-77 exit 155, follow signs), **Peninsula** 44264

- ❑   Phone: (330) 657-2000 or (800) 468-4070, **Web: www.cvsr.com**
- ❑   Hours: Departs Wednesday-Sunday, Morning and early Afternoon (June-October). Weekends, Morning and early Afternoon (Rest of the Year)
- ❑   Admission: $13.00-$20.00 adult, $11.00-$18.00 senior, $8.00-$12.00 child (3+). Reservations are highly recommended.
- ❑   Miscellaneous: Gift Shop Car/Concession Car, Park Ranger/Volunteer available for transportation or nature information. Main train trips depart from Independence, Peninsula & Akron. Bring a picnic lunch to eat in transit or at a stopover. Wheelchair car available. See Seasonal & Special Events Chapter for great holiday trains & Thomas the Tank Engine.

Ride in climate controlled coaches built between 1939 and 1940 on the very scenic 2 - 6½ hour ride to many exciting round trip destinations. Meadowlands, pinery, marsh, rivers, ravines, and woods pass by as you travel to Hale Farm and Village, Quaker Square, Inventor's Hall of Fame, Akron Zoo, Canal Visitor Center, Stan Hywet Hall or just a basic scenic tour (best if small kids take shorter trips or ones with layovers). Narration of views and history of changes in the area included. The Canal Limited is the only excursion which begins at the depot in Peninsula on a trip north to Canal Visitor Center. The center is a restored house on the Ohio & Erie Canal. Learn about the canal days in the museum and watch the canal lock demonstrations held every weekend during the summer and periodically in early fall. This is a fun way to spend the day family style (grandparents too!) and see one other attraction along the way. Be sure your little engineers get a blue or pink cap to wear along the trip as a memory of their first train ride! Preschoolers look forward to the summer special rides on the "Little Engine that Could".

DOVER LAKE WATERPARK

Peninsula (Sagamore Hills) - *7150 West Highland Road (access I-77, I-271, SR 303 or SR 82), 44067. Phone: (330) 467-SWIM or 655-SWIM (Akron).* **Web: *www.DoverLake.com.*** *Hours: Daily 11:00am-7:00pm (Mid-June thru mid-August). Admission: $18.00-$22.00 per person (40" and under are free). Parking $3.00.* 7 mountain slides, tube rides, speed slides, kiddie playland, wave pool, paddleboats and a nice small lake and beach.

TINKER'S CREEK STATE PARK

Portage - *10303 Aurora Hudson Rd. (2 miles West of State Route 43), 44266.* **Web: *www.dnr.state.oh.us/parks/parks/tinkers.htm.*** *Phone: (330) 296-3239.* Herons, ducks, geese and beaver can be found in the spring-fed waters, while cattail, buttonbush and swamp white oak line the shores of this beautiful park. Tinker's Creek State Nature Preserve is located adjacent to the state park and features extensive marshes. A 1.5-mile trail, known as the Seven Ponds Trail, features a boardwalk through the wetlands. An observation deck has been constructed to allow visitors excellent views of waterfowl. The preserve is open during daylight hours and is accessible only on foot. Parking is available on Old Mill Road in Aurora. 60 acres of fishing trails, swimming and winter sports.

WEST BRANCH STATE PARK

Ravenna - *5708 Esworthy Road (5 miles East of Ravenna off State Route 5), 44266.* **Web: *www.dnr.state.oh.us/parks/parks/westbrnc.htm.*** *Phone: (330) 296-3239.* West Branch State Park's large lake with its many forks and coves is extremely popular with fishermen, boaters and swimmers. The park's meadows and woodlots provide an excellent backdrop for camping, hiking and horseback riding. Nature programs. More than twelve miles of hiking trails provide access to a portion of the state's Buckeye Trail passing through the park and is linked to the campground by a two-mile spur trail. The park offers extensive snowmobile trails when conditions permit. Mountain biking is permitted on trails in the snowmobile area.

MILL CREEK PARK

(South of Mahoning Avenue off Glenwood Avenue)

Youngstown 44406

- ❑ Phone: (330) 740-7115 (Lanterman's Mill)
- ❑ (330) 740-7107 (Ford Nature Center) or 740-7109 (Winter)
  Web: www.millcreekmetroparks.com
- ❑ Hours: Tuesday-Friday 10:00am-5:00pm, Saturday and Sunday 11:00am-6:00pm (Center/Mill).
- ❑ Miscellaneous: Gift Shop. Lanterman's Mill (May - October), small admission.

This park has your basic scenic trails, lakes, falls, gorges, gardens and covered bridges but it also has more. The Ford Nature Center is a stone house with live reptiles and hands-on exhibits about nature. Recorded messages are available for the different stations along the trail beginning outside the Center. Lanterman's Mill is a restored 1845 water- powered gristmill with a 14-foot oak wheel. While in the mill, observe the pioneer ingenuity involved in the early production of meal and flour. Smell the aroma of freshly ground grains. Hear the gentle trickle of water as it flows toward the wheel. Feel the rumblings of the stones as they whirl, grinding the various grains. Later, if you would like, try baking some Johnny Cakes, a staple of an early American diet made with stone-ground corn meal. As you travel through the park, be on the look out for the Silver Bridge (reminiscent of Old England and Mary Poppins). Fellowship Riverside Gardens is a colorful mixture of greens and flowers. The best community park system (and very well kept) you'll find anywhere!

BUTLER INSTITUTE OF AMERICAN ART

Youngstown - *524 Wick Avenue, 44502. Phone: (330) 743-1711. Web: www.butlerart.com. Hours: Tuesday – Saturday 11:00am - 4:00pm, Sunday Noon - 4:00pm. Open Wednesday evenings until 8:00pm.* Showcases American art from colonial times to the present. Children's Gallery (hands on) and American Sports Art Gallery. FREE Sunday Family Programs and FEE paid "gift art" classes available.

YOUNGSTOWN HISTORICAL CENTER OF INDUSTRY & LABOR

151 West Wood Street (Wood Street is off of Market Street two blocks north of downtown), **Youngstown** 44503

❑ Phone: (330) 743-5934 or (800) 262-6137
   Web: www.ohiohistory.org/places/youngst/
❑ Hours: Wednesday-Saturday 9:30am-5:00pm, Sunday & Holidays Noon-5:00pm. Closed winter holidays.
❑ Admission: $7.00 adult, $3.00 student (all ages).

If your family has a heritage of steelworkers in the family, then this is the place to explain their hard work. The history of the iron and steel industry in the Mahoning Valley area can be viewed easily looking at the life-sized dioramas titled, "By the Sweat of Their Brow" or from the numerous videos shown throughout the building. Rooms are set up like typical steel mill locker rooms, company houses, and a blooming room. They certainly give you the "feel" of the treacherous work at the mill.

YOUNGSTOWN SYMPHONY

Youngstown - *260 Federal Plaza West, 44503. Phone: (330) 744-4264. Web: www.youngstownsymphony.com.* Performs Pops Concerts with guest artists in Powers Auditorium (tours). Community site Storytyme concerts provide opportunities for the Symphony to engage young people in programs on their common ground. Youngstown Symphony Youth Orchestra and Youngstown Symphony Symphonette programs.

GORANT CANDIES

Youngstown - *8301 Market Street (State Route 7, Boardman), 44512. Phone: (800) 572-4139 Ext.1236. Tours: Tuesday-Thursday until 1:30 p.m. (usually March only). Maximum 50 people. 1ˢᵗ grade and above. Miscellaneous: Candy store. Displays of chocolate history. Hair net (provided) must be worn.* Put on your paper hat and watch up to 375,000 pieces of chocolate candy being made each day. See the 2000-pound chocolate melting vats and color-coded rooms. The brown walls are the molding room where chocolate is poured and shook on vibrating tables (takes out the air bubbles). The yellow room is the coating room. A personalized hand dipper (only one) dips 3600 candies a day. Receive a free candy bar at the end of the tour.

WAGON TRAILS ANIMAL PARK

Youngstown (Vienna) - *907 Youngstown-Kingsville Road (SR 193), 44473. Phone: (330) 539-4494. Web: www.wagontrails.com. Hours: Daily, except Tuesday 10:00am-4:00pm (May-October). Admission: $13.00 adult, $10.00 senior (65+), $9.00 child (2-12). Tours: Include wagon ride, bucket of feed and petting zoo. Wagon and zoo are wheelchair and stroller accessible.* From horse-drawn wagons, you'll see and feed animals from the farm to the Outback. Your safari will now take you over a bridge where you will feed colorful koi fish in the pond. Then your safari will go to new heights as your safari truck takes you up the new "mountain" where you'll get a view of the animals. Knowledgeable safari guides narrate your tour through 60 acres of woods, ponds and animals. Zoo food included with your admission. Get up close and personal as you feed the animals. Don't forget your camera!

NATIONAL PACKARD MUSEUM

Youngstown (Warren) - *1899 Mahoning Avenue NW, 44482. Phone: (330) 394-1899. Web: www.packardmuseum.org. Hours: Tuesday-Saturday Noon-5:00pm, Sunday 1:00-5:00pm. Admission: $5.00 adult, $3.00 senior (65+), $3.00 child (7-12).* Watch a video about Packard's family of vehicles and personal family stories. See memorabilia about the manufacturer's history from 1899 – 1958. Also Packard Electric history display.

MOST MAGNIFICENT MCDONALD'S IN AMERICA

Youngstown (Warren) - *162 North Road SE, 44484. Phone: (330) 856-3611.* A 3-story building (mostly glass) complete with brass and marble fixtures, a glass elevator, an indoor waterfall, and even a baby grand piano! A must see...open daily, except Christmas.

SUGGESTED LODGING AND DINING

PUNDERSON MANOR HOUSE RESORT, Newbury. Punderson State Park, (440) 564-9144 or **www.atapark.com**. Become a royal guest in an English Tudor-style mansion. The charming rooms (not stuffy), modernized indoor and outdoor pools and cozy cabins combine enchantment with relaxation (Rooms run ~$100+ and Cabins run ~$120.00+). They have board games and videos to check out at the front desk. There are sport courts (including horseshoes and volleyball) and a playground or two. The restaurant is upscale English/American for dinner, but lunch offers a more casual, moderately-priced fare (ever tried Welsh Rarebit?). Weekly summer activities for kids include: playing tag, Storytime, sand art, chalk art, nature walks, and a variety show. The resort has indoor/outdoor pools, tennis, basketball, toboggan and winter chalet.

MAPLESIDE FARMS RESTAURANT, Brunswick. (330) 225-5576 or **www.mapleside.com**. Hours: Open daily for lunch and dinner, closed Mondays (November-August). Apple tree orchard view at the restaurant. Try yummy apple fritters and dishes with pork and apples. Even their side dishes are "apple-related" like: Waldorf Salad, homemade applesauce or escalloped apples.

COVERED BRIDGE PIZZA - **North Kingsville** or **Andover** - SR 85 or US 20. (440) 969-1000 or (440) 293-6776. Open daily for lunch and dinner. Casual. Actual covered bridge (late 1800s) was cut in two and rebuilt into pizza parlors! Located in the heart of Ashtabula County (Ohio's populous of covered bridges), historical pictures of the history of the bridge are displayed on the walls of the shop.

Chapter 6
North West Area

Our Favorites...

* Sauder Farm & Village - Archbold

* Fort Meigs - Perrysburg

* COSI - Toldeo

* SS Willis Boyer - Toledo

Front Porch Life - Sauder Homestead

SAUDER VILLAGE

22611 State Route 2 (off SR 66, 2 miles Northeast on State Route
2 or off turnpike exit 25), **Archbold** 43502

- ❑ Phone: (419) 446-2541 or (800) 590-9755
  Web: www.saudervillage.com
- ❑ Hours: Monday-Saturday 10:00am-5:00pm . Sunday & Holidays
  1:00 – 5:00pm (May – October). Closed one hour early in the
  spring and fall.
- ❑ Admission: $12.00 adult, $6.00 child (6-16). $1.00 Carriage, Train
  or Wagon rides-Group Rates available for 25+
- ❑ Miscellaneous: The Barn Restaurant serves wonderful home-style
  food with a children's menu ($3.00-5.00). Meals served buffet or
  family style. Gift Shop. Bakery. Country Inn.

Learn the history of Sauder Woodworking & Erie Sauder (his teenage woodworking shop is open for touring). He started from using wood scraps. Meet famous & very talented glass, pottery and wood crafters (you'll flip over the beautiful giant marbles!). Maybe get locked in jail, trade furs or take a lick from an old-fashioned ice cream cone. In the Homestead (1910), look for baby animals, an old baby walker, a Mother's Bench Rocker or a baby bottle warmer. Walk along the craft village where you can meet a weaver, broom maker, tinsmith or blacksmith all dressed in early 20th Century clothing. Natives & Newcomers: Ohio in Transition is a living-history experience telling the story of Northwest Ohio from 1803 to 1839. Covered with swamps and thick forests, this region of the state was one of the last to be settled by Europeans. The settlement depicts the family lives of the many Native American nations who called this area home. Workers here love what they do!

SNOOKS DREAM CARS MUSEUM

Bowling Green - *13920 County Home Road (adjacent to US 6), 43402. Phone: (419) 353-8338. **Web: www.snooksdreamcars.com.** Hours: Daily 11:00am-4:00pm.* Begin in a 1940's era Texaco filling station, featuring "automobilia" - everything from hood ornaments to backseat games to seat covers. Operational mechanics area leads to coin-operated amusement games (even a

Model T kiddie ride). Remember pedal cars? The showroom has dream cars showcased in themed rooms from the 30's-60's. $3.00-$5.00 admission.

AUGLAIZE VILLAGE FARM MUSEUM

Defiance - *Off US 24 (3 miles SW of Defiance - follow signs), 43512.* *Web: www.defiance-online.com/auglaise/index.html.* *Phone: (419) 784-0107. Hours: Event Weekends Only 11:00am-4:00pm (April-October).* A recreated late 19th Century village - 17 new, restored or reconstructed buildings that serve as museums. The Red Barn with the Street of Shops and Hall of Appliances is probably the most interesting - especially the old-fashioned appliances and authentic period food they serve. Best to visit during festivals or special events when there is an abundance of costumed guides. For example, they have an Old West Shoot-out the third Sunday of each month.

INDEPENDENCE DAM STATE PARK

Defiance - *State Route 424 (4 miles East of Defiance), 43512.* *Web: www.dnr.state.oh.us/parks/parks/indpndam.htm.* *Phone: (419) 784-3263.* Independence Dam State Park is situated along the banks of the beautiful Maumee River. The river is ideal for boating, fishing or a scenic canoe trip. A three-mile hiking trail, once the towpath of the Miami and Erie Canal, offers the hiker a glimpse into the colorful past of Ohio's canal era. The trail meanders between the canal and the river through a dense hardwood forest. The three-mile access road through the park offers a scenic ride for bicyclists. The park offers the perfect setting for a picnic or overnight camping experience.

MUSEUM OF POSTAL HISTORY

Delphos - *131 North Main Street (Lower Level of Post Office), 45833. Phone: (419) 695-2811. Hours: Monday, Wednesday, Friday 1:30-3:30pm.* 7000 square feet of displays plus media presentations that show development of American history and the influences of the U.S. Mail. See the progress of mail processing, development of the letter, stamps, postmarks and the idea of a post office. You can actually sit in a 1906 rural mail coach.

HARRISON LAKE STATE PARK

Fayette - *26246 Harrison Lake Road (4 miles South of Fayette off State Route 66), 43521. Phone: (419) 237-2593. **Web: www.dnr.state.oh.us/parks/parks/harrison.htm**.* A green island of scenic woodlands in a rich agricultural region. Harrison Lake is popular for swimming, fishing, camping and canoeing. 249 acres of camping, hiking trails, boating, fishing, swimming, and winter sports.

DIETSCH BROTHERS

Findlay - *400 W. Main Cross Street (State Route 12), 45839. Phone: (419) 422-4474. **Web: http://dietschs.com/**. Tours: Wednesday & Thursday mornings (1st grade & up). (Fall & Spring). Reservations please. ½ hour long, 20 people maximum. Reservations required.* Three brothers (2nd generation) run an original 1937's candy and ice cream shop. In the summer, see ice cream made with real cream. They make 1500 gallons per week. Fall, heading into the holidays, is the best time to see 500 pounds of chocolate treats made daily.

MAZZA COLLECTION MUSEUM

Findlay - *1000 North Main Street (University of Findlay Campus), 45840. **Web: www.mazzacollection.org**. Phone: (419) 424-4777 or (800) 472-9502. Hours:Wednesday-Friday Noon-5:00pm, Sunday 1:00-4:00pm. Closed all holidays. Admission: FREE. Tours: Tuesday-Thursday between 9:00am-2:00pm and Friday 9:00am-Noon. $2.00 per student, $1.00 extra for craft.* All the artwork here is based on children's storybooks and the teaching units include such exhibits as printmaking, the Mother Goose Corner, a borders section, the book-making process, an historical art gallery, and an art media exhibit. After a tour, some groups opt to have an art activity where the students get to use the ideas they saw in the galleria to produce their own artwork.

NORTHWEST OHIO RAILROAD PRESERVATION LIVE STEAM TRAIN RIDES

Findlay - *11600 County Rd. 99 (northeast corner of I-75 exit #161 east and County Rd. 99, north end of Findlay), 45840. Phone: (419) 423-2995.* **Web: www.nworrp.org.** *Hours: Generally weekends 1:00-4:00pm (April-December) plus evenings during peak seasonal excursions. Admission: $1.00 per person.* Experience the thrill of a coal-burning steam train ride on the nearly ½ mile of 15" gauge track layout. Special events, such as Tracks To The Past in September, the Pumpkin Train in October & Christmas' North Pole Express in December are best times to visit. Tours of their B&O caboose are the first Sunday of each month, April-September.

CANAL EXPERIENCE

Mill Rd. in Providence Park (US 24 & SR 578), **Grand Rapids** 43522

- ❑ Phone: (419) 535-3050 mill or (419) 407-9741 canal
  Web: www.metroparkstoledo.com/metroparks
- ❑ Hours: Wednesday-Friday 10:00am-2:00pm, Weekends & Holidays Noon-4:00pm (May-October). Extended weekday hours in the summer.
- ❑ Admission: FREE demonstrations of mill. Canal boat tickets: $5.00 adult, $4.00 senior (60 and over), $3.00 child (3 to 12).
- ❑ Tours: 45 minute mule drawn canal boat rides leave every hour until 4:00 p.m. Narrated.
- ❑ Miscellaneous: Fishing below the roller dam, hiking/biking on 8-mile towpath (once occupied by canal mules).

CANAL BOAT: It's always 1876 at Providence, where people and goods still travel by mule-drawn canal boat at 4 MPH. Grain is still ground in a gristmill and water still powers saws that slice logs. Visitors to the Metropark step back in time to become passengers on the Miami & Erie Canal aboard the "The Volunteer," with a crew of costumed interpreters in character for the first half of a 45-minute, narrated journey.

ISAAC LUDWIG MILL: At the mill, the saw whirs in the background as interpreters explain how people lived and worked in the former canal town of Providence, Ohio, on the Maumee River opposite the current canal town of Grand Rapids. One of the few mills left in Ohio, this 19th century mill sits on the Maumee River and demonstrates how a flour mill, sawmill and electric generator can be powered by water from the old canal below.

MARY JANE THURSTON STATE PARK

Grand Rapids - *State Route 65 (2 miles West of Grand Rapids), 43534. Web: www.dnr.state.oh.us/parks/parks/mjthrstn.htm. Phone: (419) 832-7662.* The Maumee is not only scenic, but also provides some of the best stream fishing in Ohio. Boaters have access to the river while history buffs may explore the remnants of the old canal. A one-mile portion of the Buckeye Trail passes through the park following the side cut canal. The trail continues on to the Village of Grand Rapids. A one-mile loop trail winds through the floodplain forest while an easy half-mile trail circles the day use area. Six miles of trails in the North Turkeyfoot Area may be used for backpacking, horseback riding or mountain biking.

ALLEN COUNTY MUSEUM

Lima - *620 West Market Street, 45801. Phone: (419) 222-9426. Web: www.allencountymuseum.org. Hours: Tuesday-Sunday 1:00-5:00pm. Closed holidays. Children's Museum only open in summer and by appointment in the school year. Admission: Suggested donation of $5.00 per adult. Miscellaneous: While in town, stop for lunch or dinner at the Old Barn Out Back (3175 W. Elm St - (419) 991-3075) serving country-style food in the "Chicken Coop" or "Pig Pen" - known for their fried chicken and cinnamon rolls.* Indian and pioneer artifacts. Antique automobiles and bicycles. Barber Shop, Doctor's office, country store, log house on grounds. Next door is MacDonell House (wall of purses). Lincoln Park Railroad exhibit locomotive and Shay Locomotive (huge train) is something the kids will love. The most unusual display is a collection of objects that people have swallowed (ex. Bolts, diaper pins). Try your hand at various trivia games and puzzles located throughout the Children's Museum. Each year, they present a new theme in the Children's Museum where kids can assemble and operate exhibit interactives based on relevant themes (ex. Railroads). Experiment with other means of communication.

Try your hand at sign language. Learn how to read and write Braille. Play checkers blindfolded. Send signals with flags. Write with hieroglyphs like an ancient Egyptian. Try to decipher a secret code. Make a craft or art project to take home with you.

BLUEBIRD PASSENGER TRAIN

Maumee (Waterville) - *49 North 6th Street (3rd and Mill Street - Grand Rapids Depot - departures), 43566. Phone: (419) 878-2177. Web: www.tlew.org. Hours: Wednesday & Thursday, Saturday, Sunday and Holidays- Afternoon Departures (Summer). Weekends and Holidays Only (May, September, October). Visit website for updated departure/arrival schedule. Admission: $9.00 adult, $8.00 senior (65+), $5.50 child (3-12). Round trip.* Can you guess why they call it "Bluebird"? Answer: The bluebirds come back to Ohio in the spring and leave in the early fall. That's when the train runs. The 45-minute trip (each way) on a 1930's era passenger train includes a spectacular view from a 900-foot long bridge over the Maumee River and Miami & Erie Canal (now the millrace for Isaac Ludwig Mill).

FORT MEIGS

29100 West River Road (1 mile Southwest of State Route 25, I-475 to exit 2), **Perrysburg** 43552

❑   Phone: (419) 874-4121or (800) 283-8916
    Web: www.ohiohistory.org/places/ftmeigs
❑   Hours: Wednesday-Saturday 9:30am-5:00pm. Sunday Noon-5:00pm (April-October).
❑   Admission: $7.00 adult, $3.00 student (all ages).
❑   Miscellaneous: Military History Center with Gift Shop at the stone shutterhouse describes role of Ohioans at War.

A War of 1812 era authentic castle-like log and earth fort with seven blockhouses that played an important role in guarding the Western frontier against the British. This newly remodeled museum with authentically restored fort is a child's dream! The museum has many unique artifacts, easily displayed with a large gift shop attached. But, the fort's blockhouses, earthen mounds and cannon holes are major "role-playing" spaces! Each blockhouse exhibits a "theme" and the re-enactors add flare to the scene. March like a soldier or try the Wheel of Disease. The walls of the blockhouses are 2 feet thick with 4-inch deep windows and cannon hole ports on the second floor. See actual cannons fired as the air fills with smoke. Notice how much manpower was needed to "run" a fort.

MAUMEE STATE FOREST

Swanton - *3390 County Road D, 43558. Phone: (419) 822-3052. www.dnr.state.oh.us/forestry/Forests/stateforests/maumee.htm* 3,068 acres in Fulton, Henry and Lucas counties. Bridle trails (15 miles), All-purpose vehicle area with 5 miles of trails (also snowmobile- weather permitting, Windbreak arboretum area. Open daily 6:00am - 11:00pm.

TOLEDO SPORTS

TOLEDO MUD HENS BASEBALL - Fifth Third Field, Warehouse District. (419) 725-HENS or **www.mudhens.com**. Semi-professional baseball (farm team for the Detroit Tigers) played in a newly built classic ballpark. See "Muddy" the mascot or sit in "The Roost" bleachers. Also, playground and picnic areas. Tickets $6.00-$8.00. (April-September).

TOLEDO STORM HOCKEY - Toledo Sports Arena. (419) 691-0200 or **www.toledostorm.com**. Semi-professional hockey part of the East Coast Hockey League (affiliate for the Detroit Red Wings). Season starts in October.

WOLCOTT HOUSE MUSEUM COMPLEX

Toledo - *1031 River Road, 43537. Phone: (419) 893-9602. Web: www.maumee.org/recreation/wolcott.htm.* Hours: *Wednesday-Sunday 1:00-4:00pm (April-December).* Life in the mid-1800's in the Maumee Valley. Costumed guides lead you through a building complex of a log home, depot, church and gift shop.

COSI TOLEDO

One Discovery Way (Downtown riverfront, corner of Summit and Adams Streets), **Toledo** 43604

- ❑ Phone: (419) 244-COSI, **Web: www.cositoledo.org**
- ❑ Hours: Tuesday-Saturday 10:00am-5:00pm, Sunday & Holidays Noon-5:00pm. Closed Thanksgiving, Christmas, New Years & Easter.
- ❑ Admission: $8.50 adult (13-64), $7.50 senior (65+), $6.50 child (3-12).
- ❑ Miscellaneous: Science 2 Go Gift Shop. Atomic Cafe - restaurant of food, "Science where you're encouraged to play with your food".

Eight learning worlds including Mind Zone (distorted Gravity Room, Animation, T-Rex), Sports (improve your game using science), Life Force (secrets of parts of the body like your skin, brain, and stomach), Water Works (water arcade, water travel, rainstorms), KidSpace, and BabySpace (18 months and under). The older kids will love Whiz-Bang Engineering and Power Force or Pit Stop Challenge (greeted by Ed the animatronic security guard, feel hydraulics with motion simulator, take the Science on the Go Challenge!). New BOYO – human Yo-Yo's!

TOLEDO SYMPHONY ORCHESTRA

Toledo - *2 Maritime Plaza, 43604. Phone: (800) 348-1253 or (419) 246-8000. Web: www.toledosymphony.com.* Regional symphony performs orchestral masterpieces with guest artists, chamber, contemporary, pops, youth and summer concerts. Their Young People's concerts combine other forms of art with classical music (September-May)

SS WILLIS B BOYER MARITIME MUSEUM

26 Main Street, International Park (East side of Maumee River – Downtown, **Toledo** 43605

- ❑ Phone: (419) 936-3070
  Web: www.internationalpark.org/boyermain.html
- ❑ Hours: Monday-Saturday 10:00am-5:00pm, Sunday Noon-5:00pm (May-October). Wednesday-Sunday by appointment (November-April).

❑   Admission: $6.00 adult, $5.50 senior, $4.00 student.

The 617-foot freighter depicts how ships of the Great Lakes worked in the early to mid-1900's. It was the biggest, most modern ship on the Great Lakes (in its day) and as you drive up, it takes up your whole panoramic view. A nautical museum of Lake Erie resides inside with photographs, artifacts and best of all for kids, hands-on exhibits. Have your picture taken "at the wheel". Ask for the "child-oriented" tours.

SANDPIPER CANAL BOAT

Toledo - *2144 Fordway, Riverfront (Jefferson Street Docks), 43606. Phone: (419) 537-1212. Web: www.sandpiperboat.com. Admission: Range of $6.00-$12.00. Basically double the price for lunch cruises.* Replica of a Miami and Erie Canal boat. Educational or historical Cruise up river past riverside estates, downtown or down river. See busy ports, shipyards and dry docks. Public and group tours average 2-4 hours. Mostly weekends (morning/lunchtime). Some evening cruises. Seasonal Fireworks and Fall Cruises. Bring a picnic. Reservations suggested. (May-October)

TOLEDO ZOO

2700 Broadway (I-75 to US 25 - 3 miles South of downtown),

Toledo 43609

❑   Phone: (419) 385-5721, **Web: www.toledozoo.org**
❑   Hours: Daily 10:00am-5:00pm (May-Labor Day). Daily, 10:00am-4:00 pm (Rest of the Year)
❑   Admission: $10.00 adult, $7.00 senior (60+) and child (2-11). Parking fee $5.00. Lucas County residents may receive free admission on set mornings (usually Mondays).
❑   Miscellaneous: Carnivore Cafe (dine in actual cages once used to house big cats!). Children's Zoo - petting zoo and hands on exhibits.

They have areas typical of a zoo but they are known for their Hippoquarium (the world's first underwater viewing of the hippopotamus) along with a well-defined interpretive center and hands- on exhibits. The Kingdom of Apes and African Savanna are other popular exhibits. The renovated Aviary, new Primate

Forest and Arctic Encounter (a nose-to-nose view thru a cabin window to observe gray wolves and an underwater view of seals) are hot spots too.

TOLEDO FIREFIGHTERS MUSEUM

Toledo - *918 Sylvania Avenue, 43612. Phone: (419) 478-FIRE. Web: www.toledofiremuseum.com. Hours: Saturday Noon-4:00pm.* Feel what 150 years of history of fire-fighting must have meant to the fireman. Learn fire safety tips. In Jed's Bedroom, children are taught how to roll out of bed, keep low in case of smoke, and feel the door for heat with the back of their hand. See actual vintage pumpers, uniforms, and equipment used that trace the growth of the Toledo Fire Department. Located in the former No. 18 Fire Station.

TOLEDO BOTANICAL GARDENS

Toledo - *5403 Elmer Drive (off North Reynolds Road), 43615. Phone: (419) 936-2986. Web: www.toledogarden.org. Hours: Open 8:30am-5:30pm.* Fifty-seven acres of meadows and gardens. Outdoor sculpture and storybook garden appeal to kids. Gallery and gift store. FREE except for special events. Family Nights are held each season (fee).

TOLEDO MUSEUM OF ART

Toledo - *2445 Monroe at Scottwood (off I-75), 43620. Phone: (419) 255-8000. Web: www.toledomuseum.org. Hours: Tuesday-Saturday 10:00am-4:00pm, Sunday 11:00am-5:00pm. Open Friday evening til 10:00pm.* Discover treasures from the riches of the medieval, the splendors of a French chateau and the tombs of Egypt. Also glass, sculpture, paintings.

MAUMEE BAY STATE PARK

Toledo (Oregon) - *1400 Park Road #1 (8 miles East of Toledo, then 3 miles North off State Route 2), 43618. Phone: (419) 836-7758 park, 836-1466 Lodge or 836-9117 Nature Center. Web: www.dnr.state.oh.us/parks/parks/maumebay.htm or Web: www.maumeebayresort.com.* Resort cottages and rooms, golf, racquetball, sauna, whirlpool, fitness, tennis, volleyball and basketball are available. The lodge, cottages and golf course are nestled among the scenic meadows, wet woods and lush marshes teeming with wildlife. Developed hiking trails in the park include the Mouse Trail, a 3-mile diverse trail winding through meadows and young woodlands, and several miles of paved combination trails for bicycling and cross-country skiing. Hikers will discover acres of meadow, marshland and woodland. A 2-mile boardwalk traversing swamp and marsh wetlands has interpretive signs, an observation blind and tower, and wheelchair accessible loop. 1,845 acres of camping, hiking trails, boating, fishing, swimming and winter sports.

VAN BUREN LAKE STATE PARK

Van Buren - *State Route 613 (1 mile East of Van Buren), 45889. Web: www.dnr.state.oh.us/parks/parks/vanburen.htm. Phone: (419) 832-7662.* Hiking trails circle the lake. Hikers, horseback riders, and mountain bikers are welcome on 6 miles of multiple-use trails traversing steep ravines and gentler terrain in scenic woodlands. 296 acres of camping, hiking trails, boating, fishing, and winter sports.

SUGGESTED LODGING AND DINING

TONY PACKO'S CAFÉ – **Toledo**. (1902 Front Street, 419-691-6054 or **www.tonypackos.com**). After seeing the "macho" life of "shipsmen" near the Toledo port, try some fiery or authentic ethnic Hungarian food at Tony Packo's Café. Be sure to look for the thousands of hot dog buns signed by TV & Movie stars that have visited the café.

Chapter 7
South Area

Our Favorites...

* 7 Caves - Bainbridge

* Lee Middleton Doll Factory - Belpre

* Adena State Memorial - Chillicothe

* Hopewell Culture Nat'l Hist'l Park - Chillicothe

* Ross County Historical Museum - Chillicothe

* Hocking Hills Area - Logan

* Campus Martius Museum - Marietta

* Portsmouth Murals - Portsmouth

Discovering the Seven Caves - Too Cool!

STROUD'S RUN STATE PARK

Athens - *11661 State Park Road (8 miles Northeast of Athens off US 50A, Cty Road 20), 45701. Phone: (740) 592-2302. **Web: www.dnr.state.oh.us/parks/parks/strouds.htm.*** The first settlers arrived in the Athens County region in 1796. Two townships of land in the area had been apportioned by the Ohio Company in 1795 for the benefit of a university. Settlers were encouraged to settle on these college lands so as to make them attractive, productive and to form a fund for the institution. The park derives its name from the Strouds family who settled in the area in the early 1800s. Fifteen miles of hiking trails meander through the wooded hills of Strouds Run leading to scenic vistas throughout the park. Excellent bird-watching and nature study can be done along the trail. An 8½ mile bridle trail has been constructed. 2,767 acres of camping, hiking trails, boating and rentals, fishing, swimming and winter sports.

7 CAVES NATURE PRESERVE

7660 Cave Road (US 50, 4 miles Northwest, follow signs)

Bainbridge 45612

❑ Phone: (937) 365-1935, **Web: www.highlandssanctuary.org**
❑ Hours: Friday, Saturday, Sunday 10:00am-4:00pm (May-October).
❑ Admission: Free admission fee to Etawah Woods Self-guided trail & Appalachian Forest Museum.
❑ Tours: Guided Nature Tours: 11:00am & 2:00pm. $10.00 adult, $5.00 child. Group reservation are possible throughout the week by appointment (April-November).
❑ Miscellaneous: Many stairs. Shelter house. They have plans to create a Natural History Center in the Gift Shop Welcome Center area.

Wear layered clothing and comfortable walking shoes because your family is going on an adventure! An absolutely wonderful way to spend almost the entire day in nature as you explore a series of small caves you actually walk into. Naturalist-led tours include a forest walk and candle-lit cave tours (led Tom Sawyer style - with old-fashioned candle lanterns). Guided tours allow for the kids to learn about the unusual structures as they walk along. Cute, clever names are given to each naturally carved figure. Some areas require following "corkscrew" paths to deep dungeons or grottos. Three different trails lead to caves with cemented walkways, handrails, and lighting showing specific formations. See cliffs, canyons, and waterfalls. About a hundred kinds of birds inhabit The Seven Caves, the Pileated Woodpecker is the rarest. It's a beautiful and humbling experience. A hidden treasure here!

MAGIC WATERS AMPHITHEATRE

Bainbridge - *7757 Cave Road, 45612. Phone: (937) 365-1388.* ***Web:*** *www.highlandcounty.com/magic.htm. Performances: Friday-Saturday 8:00pm, Sunday 7:00pm (mid-June through Labor Day). Pre show picnics available with reservations and additional fee. Admission: $7.00 adult, $4.00 senior, $3.50 child.* Live outdoor drama in a rustic amphitheater featuring magic shows and kid's theatre (i.e. The Wizard of Oz).

PAINT CREEK STATE PARK

Bainbridge - *14265 US 50 (17 miles East of Hillsboro on US 50), 45612. **Web:** www.dnr.state.oh.us/parks/parks/paintcrk.htm. Phone: (937) 365-1401.* Located amid the scenery of the Paint Creek Valley, Paint Creek State Park features a large lake with fine fishing, boating and swimming opportunities. A modern campground and meandering hiking trails invite outdoor enthusiasts to explore the rolling hills and streams of this area. Nature programs. On the west side of the lake is Paint Creek Pioneer Farm. The pioneer farm includes a log house, collection of log buildings, livestock, gardens and fields which represent a typical farm of the early 1800's. A walk through Pioneer Farm provides further insight into the settlers' lives. Boating rentals and winter sports. Bicycle rental is available and miniature golf can be enjoyed for a small fee.

PIKE LAKE STATE PARK

Bainbridge - *1847 Pike Lake Road (6 miles Southeast of Bainbridge), 45612. www.dnr.state.oh.us/parks/parks/pikelake.htm. Phone: (740) 493-2212.* The surrounding state forest is known for its variety of ferns, mosses, lichens and fungi. The wildflowers are diverse, creating spectacular displays--spring through autumn. The park features 12 standard cottages and 12 family cottages. Six miles of hiking trails provide strenuous and/or casual walks to scenic locations. The adjacent state forest has several miles of bridle trails. Horses are not provided by the park or forest. Nature programs. 613 acres of camping, hiking trails, boating and rentals, fishing, swimming and winter sports.

LEE MIDDLETON ORIGINAL DOLL FACTORY

1301 Washington Boulevard (I-77 to SR 50/618), **Belpre** 45714

❑ Phone: (740) 423-1481 or (800) 233-7479
   Web: www.leemiddleton.com
❑ Tours: Monday – Friday 9:00am – 2:00pm (Hourly). February – December. Approximately 20 minutes. Reservations Suggested. FREE.
❑ Miscellaneous: Factory Store with bargain buys and Nursery where you can adopt a life-sized Middleton infant baby doll complete with papers, promises and pictures. You can also visit a Newborn Nursery at many locations in the nation to adopt a baby.

Hopefully during your visit you'll get to experience a little girl adopting her first Middleton baby. It's so real, you'll swell with emotion as you see the new "Mom" promise the nursery worker to care for her baby properly. Lee Middleton started making dolls at her kitchen table in 1978 and modeled them after her children and children she knew. On tour a guide shows you techniques critical to the distinctiveness of these high-quality collectable dolls that look and feel almost real. One machine makes feet, hands and heads out of liquid vinyl cured in molds. Watch them put eyes in by blowing up the mold head like a balloon (with an air compressor) and popping in the eyes. Then, they release the air and the eye is set in place (this is the part the guys like!). See the artist's hand paint each doll's face using stencils and paint makeup. What a fun "girl's place" to visit. Prepare to fall in love with a doll and want one for your own!

TAR HOLLOW STATE FOREST

Chillicothe - *(northeast of Chillicothe, south of Adelphi), 43101.* *www.dnr.state.oh.us/forestry/Forests/stateforests/tarhollow.htm.* *Phone: (740) 663-2523 (Waverly office). Hours: Open daily 6:00am -* *11:00pm.* 16,120 acres in Ross, Vinton and Hocking counties. Bridle trails (33 miles), horse campground, hiking trails (22 miles), grouse management area. Tar Hollow State Park is adjacent.

ADENA STATE MEMORIAL

(West of State Route 104 off Adena Road)

Chillicothe 45601

- ❏ Phone: (740) 772-1500 or (800) 319-7249
  Web: www.ohiohistory.org/places/adena
- ❏ Hours: Wednesday-Saturday 9:30am-5:00pm, Sundays and Holidays Noon-5:00pm (Summer). Weekends Only (September & October).
- ❏ Admission: $7.00 adult, $3.00 student (all ages).
- ❏ Tours: Tours of the mansion begin on the hour, from 10:00am-4:00pm, with no tour at noon.

View the overlook of the hillside that was used to paint the picture for the Ohio State Seal. Looking east from the north lawn, one can see across the Scioto River Valley to the Mount Logan range of hills (the Seal view). Adena was the 2000-acre estate of Thomas Worthington (1773-1827), sixth governor of Ohio and one of the state's first United States Senators. The mansion house, completed in 1806-1807, has been restored to look much as it did when the Worthington family lived there, including many original Worthington family furnishings. Look for Thomas Jefferson's invention, a giant dumb waiter - why was it called that? Adena is an important site for many reasons. It is the only plantation-type complex of its kind in the state and the stone mansion was built by the Father of our Statehood. Also visit a tenant house, smoke house, wash house, barn and spring house. Begin at the Visitors Center for an overview. Then, play games in two interactive areas, one dress-up, the other running a supply boat successfully in the early 1800s computer game area. A good area to study early Ohio statehood.

GREAT SEAL STATE PARK

Chillicothe - *Marietta Pike (3 miles Northeast of Chillicothe), 45601. Web: www.dnr.state.oh.us/parks/parks/grtseal.htm. Phone: (740) 773-2726.* Great Seal State Park is dedicated to the wilderness spirit of Ohio. The history of the Shawnee nation and Ohio's early statehood is in these hills. Rugged trails take visitors to scenic vistas of distant ridge tops and the Scioto Valley below. The Sugarloaf Mountain Trail (yellow), 2.1 miles, climbs through dense maple-dominated forests to the crest of Sugarloaf. This loop is short and rises almost 500 feet in less than a quarter mile. These very hills are depicted on the Great Seal of the State of Ohio, from which the park gets its name.

HOPEWELL CULTURE NATIONAL HISTORICAL PARK

16062 State Route 104 (two miles north of the intersection of US 35 and SR 104), **Chillicothe** 45601

- ❑ Phone: (740) 774-1126, **Web: www.nps.gov/hocu**
- ❑ Hours: Daily 8:30am-5:00pm. Extended closing at 6:00pm in the summer. Closed Thanksgiving, Christmas and New Year's Day, and on Monday/Tuesday during December-February. Grounds open daily dawn til dusk.
- ❑ Admission: $3.00 per adult. Maximum charge per vehicle $5.00.
- ❑ Miscellaneous: There is popular activity booklet for kids that come to the park. Along with this they also offer Native American games and pottery making for kids.

The 120-acre park with 13-acre earthwall enclosure is home to 23 prehistoric burial and ceremonial mounds of the Hopewell Indians. The center presents the story of the prehistoric Hopewell culture with exhibits, brochures and the 17-minute video "Legacy of the Mound Builders." Question: How did they make so many trinkets from materials like copper, seashells and mica (materials not found in Ohio)? After viewing many effigy (animal-shaped) pipes, maybe purchase a reproduction (inexpensively) as a souvenir.

LUCY HAYES HERITAGE CENTER

Chillicothe - *90 West Sixth Street, 45601. Phone: (740) 775-5829 or (740) 775-1780. Hours: Friday & Saturday 1:00-4:00pm (April-October) and by appointment. Admission: $2.00 general.* They provide guided tours through the former home of Lucy Ware Webb Hayes, the wife and "First Lady" of the 19th President of the United States, Rutherford B. Hayes. She is actually considered to be the first, First Lady. They especially welcome students.

PUMP HOUSE CENTER FOR THE ARTS

Chillicothe - *Enderlin Circle, Yoctangee Park, 45601. Phone: (740) 772-5783. Web: www.bright.net/~pumpart. Hours: Tuesday-Friday 11:00am-4:00pm, Saturday-Sunday 1:00-4:00pm. Admission: FREE.* Visit art gallery and cultural center in restored water pumping station. It features regional artists including school children (i.e. Trash can art & historical themes).

ROSS COUNTY HISTORICAL SOCIETY MUSEUMS

45 W. Fifth Street (near Paint St., downtown), **Chillicothe** 45601

❑   Phone: (740) 772-1936 **Web:** www.rosscountyhistorical.org

❑   Hours: Tuesday-Sunday Noon-5:00pm (April-December). Friday & Saturday 1:00-5:00pm (January-March).

❑   Admission: $4.00 adult, $2.00 senior & student.

See the table upon which Ohio's Constitution was signed and Thomas Worthington's sea chest! See exhibits on early Chillicothe (diorama of town in 1803) and Ohio, Civil War (Camp Sherman -- "Ohio's World War I Soldier Factory,"), World War I and the Mound Builders. Also the McKell Library, the Knoles Log House Museum (everyday life in early 1800's Chillicothe) and Franklin House Women's Museum. Kids will be intrigued by the stories of olden times like: No garbage pickup? Just throw it in the streets and let roving animals eat the "slop". Or, how did the saying: Peas, Porridge Hot...Peas, Porridge Cold...Nine Days Old" come about (something to do with leftovers!). And, why didn't they use forks? Learn the real "scoop" about Conestoga wagons and how kids used miniature wagons to train their "pets". Look through an authentic old-fashioned ViewMaster (Megalethoscope). Because this complex showcases the first capital of Ohio, it has early Ohio historical value hidden in every corner!

SCIOTO TRAIL STATE PARK

Chillicothe - *144 Lake Road (10 miles South of Chillicothe off US 23), 45601. Web: www.dnr.state.oh.us/parks/parks/sciototr.htm. Phone: (740) 663-2125.* A small, quiet park nestled in beautiful 9,000-acre Scioto Trail State Forest, this state park is an undisturbed wooded refuge. Twelve miles of hiking trails and 17 miles of bridle trails lead to scenic overlooks and breathtaking vistas. 248 acres of camping, hiking, boating, fishing & winter sports.

TECUMSEH

Sugarloaf Mountain Amphitheater (US 23 to Bridge St. exit, left on SR 159, right on Delano Road), **Chillicothe** 45601

- ❏ Phone: (740) 775-0700 or (866) 775-0700
  Web: www.tecumsehdrama.com
- ❏ Hours: Monday-Saturday, Show time 8:00pm. Show ends around 10:45pm. Reservations please. (Mid-June to Labor Day)
- ❏ Admission: $18.00 General (slightly reduced Monday-Thursday), Half Price for children (10 and under).
- ❏ Tours: Backstage Tours 4:00 or 5:00pm ($2.50-$3.50). FREE! Prehistoric Indian Mini-Museum. Backstage Tour - HIGHLY RECOMMENDED for all ages. The stuntmen of TECUMSEH! give a dazzling display of stage-combat and flintlock firing, then pitch headfirst from a twenty-one foot cliff, get up, and explain how they did it. Tours last approximately one hour and also includes make-up demonstrations (including mock "yummy" blood bags & Native "tanning" products) and detailed historical information on the drama and area. Necessary to understand storyline and not be frightened by savage conflicts.
- ❏ Miscellaneous: Gift Shop & Restaurant with buffet (good food & entertainment - $6-$9 per person) served a few hours before the show. Warning: We recommend the Drama for 4th graders and older who have studied Ohio History and understand the savage, violent conflicts.

Tecumseh (*cont.*)

This production has received national attention. Witness the epic life story of the legendary Shawnee leader as he struggles to defend his sacred homelands in the Ohio country during the late 1700's (before Ohio was a state). Fast action horses, loud firearms and speeding arrows make the audience part of the action especially when costumed actors enter the scene from right, left and behind. Lots of lessons learned about courage, honor, wisdom and greed...for kids and adults. We left quietly sobbing. As the actor playing Tecumseh said to us afterwards, "we got it."

TELEPHONE MUSEUM, JAMES M. THOMAS

Chillicothe - *68 East Main Street, 45601. Phone: (740) 772-8200. Hours: Monday-Friday 8:30am-4:30pm. Closed holidays.* Run by the Chillicothe Telephone Company, it shows the telephone from its invention stages to modern times. The museum features telephone equipment and paraphernalia dating back to 1895. Included are telephone instruments, early local directories, wooden underground conduit and a working section of electro-mechanical "step-by-step" switching equipment. Free tours by appointment.

OUR HOUSE MUSEUM

Gallipolis - *434 1st Avenue (off State Route 7), 45631. Phone: (740) 446-0586.* **Web: *www.ohiohistory.org/places/ourhouse.*** *Hours: Wednesday-Saturday 10:00am-4:00pm, Sunday 1:00-4:00pm (Summer). Weekends only (September, October). Admission: $4.00 adult, $3.00 senior, $1.00 child/student.* A restored river inn with furnishings of early Americana. On 22 May 1825, General Lafayette visited Gallipolis and was entertained at Our House Tavern. The town celebrates this visit each spring (good time to visit for festivities).

BURR OAK STATE PARK

Glouster - *10220 Burr Oak Lodge Road (6 miles Northeast of Glouster off State Route 13), 45732. Phone: (740) 767-3570 or (740) 767-2112 Lodge. www.dnr.state.oh.us/parks/parks/burroak.htm or www.burroakresort.com.* Located in southeast Ohio, quiet and remote Burr Oak State Park has a rustic country charm in its scenery of wooded hills and valley farms. Twenty-eight miles of hiking trails, including a portion of the state's Buckeye Trail, take hikers to scenic vistas and unique rock outcroppings. There are 30 family cottages with air conditioning and cable TV situated near the lodge in the wooded hills overlooking the lake. Nature programs, Bridle trails, Guest rooms in the Lodge with an indoor pool, tennis and basketball courts are highlights of this park. Also camping, hiking trails, boating and rentals, fishing, swimming, and winter sports.

NOAH'S ARK ANIMAL FARM

Jackson - *1527 McGiffins Road (5 miles East on State Route 32), 45640. Phone: (740) 384-3060 or (800) 282-2167.* **Web:** *www.placesohio.com/noahsark/index.htm. Hours: Monday-Saturday 10:00am-5:00pm, Sunday Noon-5:00pm (April-October). Admission: $5.50-$6.50 (age 3+).* You will enjoy miniature golf, playground equipment, and fairy-book characters. They also have a train that travels 3/4th of a mile around the farm. Exotic animals and birds (more than 150) including lemurs. Pay Fishing lake and train ride (additional $1.00). Most love the black bears & their cubs best.

SPLASH DOWN

Jackson - *6173 SR 327, 45640. Phone: (888) SPLASH-1 or (740) 384-5113.* **Web:** *www.splashdownohio.com. Hours: Monday-Saturday 10:00am-7:00pm, Sunday 11:00am-6:00pm (Memorial Day-Labor Day). Admission: $16.95 adult, $11.95 child (3-11). $7.95 twilight (after 4:00pm).* The water adventure theme park and campgrounds have log cabins, 850 foot Lazy River, 2 Thrill Slides, Kids Water Activity Pools, Putt-Putt, concessions, Paddle Boats/Kayaks, Game Room, Fishing and Sand Volleyball.

PIKE STATE FOREST

Latham - *334 Lapperrel Road (on SR-124, just west of Latham), 45646. www.dnr.state.oh.us/forestry/Forests/stateforests/pike.htm. Phone: (740) 493-2441. Hours: Open daily 6:00am - 11:00pm.* 11,961 acres in Pike and Highland counties. Hiking/Bridle trails (33 miles), APV trails (15 miles), Pike Lake State Park is adjacent.

TAR HOLLOW STATE PARK

Laurelville - *16396 Tar Hollow Road (10 miles South of Adelphi off State Route 540), 43135. Phone: (740) 887-4818. **Web:** www.dnr.state.oh.us/parks/parks/tarhollw.htm.* Dense woodlands of scattered shortleaf and pitch pines growing on the ridges were once a source of pine tar for early settlers, hence the name Tar Hollow. Dogwoods, redbuds and a variety of wildflowers color the hillsides in the springtime. The 2-mile Pine Run mountain bike trail begins at the general store. 634 acres of camping, hiking trails, boating, fishing, swimming.

HOCKING HILLS STATE PARK

19852 St. Rt. 664 South (Route 33 south to Route 664, follow signs), **Logan** 43138

❑   Phone: (740) 385-6841 or (800) HOCKING
     Web: www.dnr.state.oh.us/parks/parks/hocking.htm
❑   Hours: 6:00am-Sunset (Summer), 8:00am (Winter)

In the mid 1700's, several Indian tribes traveled through or lived here including the Wyandot, Delaware and Shawnee. Their name for the river, from which the park gets its name, was Hockhocking or "bottle river." Nature trails are found throughout the park, many of them lead to obscure, out-of-the-way natural creations. The park includes: Ash Cave (an 80 acre cave and stream), Cantwell Cliffs, Cedar Falls, Conkle's Hollow, Rock House, and the most popular, Old Man's Cave (a wooded, winding ravine of waterfalls and caves). The recess caves at Ash Cave, Old Man's Cave and Cantwell Cliffs are all carved in the softer middle rock. Weathering and erosion widened cracks found in the middle layer of sandstone at the Rock House to create that unusual formation. Overnight accommodations, bed and breakfasts, camping, cabins with A/C, heat and fireplaces, recreation, picnic grounds, and hiking. Your children's sense of adventure will soar! Concessions available at Old Man's Cave or dining in the Lodge, seasonally (with outdoor pool). We recommend close supervision on the hiking trails for your child's safety.

LAKE LOGAN STATE PARK

Logan - *30443 Lake Logan Road (4 miles West of Logan off State Route 664), 43138. Phone: (740) 385-3444. Web: www.dnr.state.oh.us/parks/parks/lklogan.htm.* One of the best fishing lakes in Ohio, the lake sports northern pike, bass, bluegill, crappie, catfish and saugeye. 717 acres of hiking, boating and rentals, fishing, swimming and winter sports for day-use only.

CAMPUS MARTIUS: MUSEUM OF NORTHWEST TERRITORY

601 2nd Street (2nd and Washington Street ,Downtown)

Marietta 45750

- ❑ Phone: (740) 373-3750 or (800) 860-0145
  Web: www.ohiohistory.org/places/campus
- ❑ Hours: Wednesday-Saturday 9:30am-5:00pm and Sundays and Holidays Noon-5:00pm (March-October)
- ❑ Admission: $7.00 adult, $3.00 student (all ages).

Campus recreates early development of Marietta as the first settlement in the Northwest Territory. The Putnam House is the oldest residence in Ohio. The home and land office display replicas of the hardships of early pioneer life including old surgical and musical instruments. An exhibit titled "Paradise Found and Lost: Migration in the Ohio Valley" highlights migration from farms to cities and from Appalachia to industry. See the stage jacket worn by Appalachian born Country Singer, Dwight Yoakum. Videos and interactive computer games on migration. You can actually create a feeling of being taken back in time by walking through the train passenger car and listening to actual stories of passengers taking a trip to the "big city" for business or jobs (Stories are told on telephone handsets). See actual huge photographs of downtown Columbus and Marietta in the early 1900's that take up an entire wall - you'll feel as if you're walking into them!

CASTLE, (THE)

Marietta - *418 Fourth Street, 45750. Phone: (740) 373-4180.* **Web: www.mariettacastle.org.** *Hours: Monday-Friday (Summer), Thursday, Friday & Monday (April, May, September-December). Weekdays 10:00am-4:00pm. Admission: $2.50-$4.00 (age 6+).* Historic area furnishings. Impressive parlor and chandelier. Be a Victorian child for a day with their interactive group programs.

MARIETTA SODA MUSEUM

109-111 Maple Street, Harmar Village (across the pedestrian bridge from downtown), **Marietta** 45750

❑   Phone: (740) 376-COKE

  Web: www.mariettasodamuseum.com

❑   Hours: Thursday–Saturday 11:00am–3:00pm, Sunday Noon-5:00pm (Spring-Fall). Friday and Saturday 10:00am-4:30pm (Winter).

❑   Admission: FREE

❑   Miscellaneous: Down the street is the Children's Toy & Doll Museum open Saturday afternoons (740-373-0799).

Memorabilia from 1900 to the present traces the history of this beverage and its marketing. Buy a bottle of COKE or Sarsaparilla (vanilla Root Beer) and sip it while you browse. Although it's rusted, you can still see the COCA-COLA logo on the front of many old dispensers and metal signs. The soda fountain features 10 cent cokes and serves lunch items. The building has hundreds of soda collectibles (both on display and for sale).

MARIETTA TROLLEY TOURS

Marietta - *127 Ohio Street (Levee House Café), 45750. www.mariettaonline.com/thingstodo/attractions/tours.php. Phone: (740) 374-2233. Hours: Afternoon 12:30 and 2:30 pm (April – November). Schedule can vary. Call or visit website for details. Admission: $5.00-$8.00 (ages 5+).* Narrated one-hour tours describing and viewing historic architecture, shops along Front Street, Marietta College and more.

OHIO RIVER MUSEUM

601 Second St (St. Clair & Front St, Downtown), **Marietta** 45750

- ❑   Phone: (740) 373-3717 or (800) 860-0145
    Web: www.ohiohistory.org/places/ohriver
- ❑   Hours: Saturday 9:30am-5:00pm. Sunday Noon-5:00pm
    (Memorial Day weekend - Labor Day).
- ❑   Admission: $7.00 adult, $3.00 student (all ages).

The Ohio River Museum consists of three exhibit buildings, the first of which houses displays depicting the origins and natural history of the Ohio River. The golden age of the steamboat is featured in the second building, along with a video presentation on river steamboats. The last building features displays about boat building, mussels inn the Ohio River system, and tool and equipment from the steamboat era. The WP Snyder, Jr. moored along the museum is the last surviving stern-wheeled towboat in America. Also, see a model of a flat boat and other scale models of many riverboats. A video titled, "Fire on the Water" describes dangerous early times when boilers might explode, killing many. Diorama (full scale) of wildlife along the Ohio River.

ROSSI PASTA

Marietta - *114 Greene Street (Downtown), 45750. Phone: (740) 376-2065 or (800) 227-6774. **Web: www.rossipasta.com**. Hours: Monday - Friday 9:00 am - 6:00pm, Saturday 9:00am-5:00pm, Sunday Noon - 5:00pm. Pasta making times vary. Call ahead for best times to maybe view production.* A retail store where they show a production video and have many archived pictures about Rossi Pasta. They hand roll dough adding fresh flavor ingredients as they "turn" the dough. Their secret is using spring wheat flour instead of highly manufactured semoline flour. A machine cuts the pasta into very long and wide strips (linguini) or thin soup noodles. Teardrop shapes are stamped out. Next, the cut pasta goes into one of two large drying chambers which are precisely regulated to insure even temperatures. Finally, the pasta is packaged in clear Rossi-labeled bags. Be sure you invite your favorite gourmet cook along for this visit - it's a new level of pasta to experience.

VALLEY GEM STERNWHEELER

Marietta - *601 Front Street (State Route 60 and State Route 7) (Docks next to the Ohio River Museum under the Washington Street Bridge), 45750. Phone: (740) 373-7862.* **Web:** *www.valleygemsternwheeler.com. Hours: Tuesday – Sunday. Departs every hour from 1:00 – 4:00pm (Summer). Rest of Year and Holidays, call for schedule. Admission: $3.00-$5.50 (ages 2+). Saturday dinner cruises $13.00-$27.00 (2 hours). Fall Foliage 3-4 hour tours $9.00-$15.00. Miscellaneous: Gift and snack area on board. Fall foliage cruises very popular in October. Heated or A/C main cabin.* Take the 300 passenger, 60 minute cruise on the Valley Gem where the captain points out historic interests. See who can find the large stone blocks spelling "Marietta" on the landing welcoming steamboats. Why was the boat named after a piano company?

LAKE HOPE STATE PARK

McArthur - *27331 SR 278 (12 miles Northeast of McArthur on State Route 278), 45651. Phone: (740) 596-5253 or (740) 596-0400 restaurant.* **www.dnr.state.oh.us/parks/parks/lakehope.htm**. Lake Hope State Park lies entirely within the 24,000-acre Zaleski State Forest in the valley of Big Sandy Run. It is a rugged, heavily forested region traversed by steep gorges, narrow ridges, abandoned mines, ancient mounds and beautiful scenery. The dining lodge features The Stone Terrace Restaurant, meeting room, General Store, as well as lodge and cottage reservation office. A fine swimming beach is located near the dam. Nature programs. 3,223 acres of camping, family cabins, hiking, boating and rentals, fishing, swimming.

SMOKE RISE RANCH RESORT

Murray City - *6751 Hunterdon Road (US 33 to SR 78 to CR 92), 45732. Phone: (740) 767-2624 or (800) 292-1732.* **Web:** *www.smokeriseranch.com.* Full service campground or cabins. Working Cattle Ranch (Ridin' & Ropin'), Riding Arenas, Trail riding. Activities Include: Round Up Rides , Pool and Hot Tub Parties, Hay Rides, BBQ's , Team Ropings and Team Pennings, Music Events and Dances.

HOCKING VALLEY SCENIC RAILWAY

Nelsonville - *33 Canal Street (Off US 33), 45764. Phone: (740) 470-1300 or (800) HOCKING. (513) 753-9531. (Saturday and Sunday).* **Web: www.hvsry.com**. *Hours: Weekends Noon and 2:30 pm, (June – October). Special Holiday Schedule. Admission: $10.00-$14.00 adult, $7.00-$9.00 child (2-11).* Ride through the hills of scenic Hocking Valley on an authentic 1916 steam locomotive or a 1950 diesel locomotive (trips are 14 & 22 miles roundtrip). Both rides include a 30-minute stop over at Robbins Crossing Visitor's Center (small 1850's settler village). Enjoy the blooming dogwood trees in the spring, summertime fun, nature's spectacular fall foliage or a special winter ride with Santa (heated cars). No A/C or restrooms on train.

JACKSON LAKE STATE PARK

Oak Hill - *35 Tommy Been Road (2 miles West of Oak Hill on State Route 279), 45656. Phone: (740) 682-6197.* **Web: www.dnr.state.oh.us/parks/parks/jacksonl.htm**. The park's serene lake is a focal point for excellent fishing and provides the ideal setting for a peaceful walks. 335 acres of camping, boating, fishing, swimming and winter sports.

DEAN STATE FOREST

Pedro - *149 Dean Forest Road, Rte. 1, 43558. Phone: (740) 532-7228. www.dnr.state.oh.us/forestry/Forests/stateforests/dean.htm. Hours: Open daily 6:00am - 11:00pm.* Located in the un-glaciated hill country of extreme south central Ohio, the early history of the region centered around Dutch and Irish farmers who emigrated from Pennsylvania. From the early 1800's to about 1900, most of the timber in the area was cut for charcoal to supply blast furnaces for the smelting of locally mined iron ore. Reforestation has created 2,745 acres in Lawrence County of 20 miles of bridle/hiking trails. Wayne National Forest is adjacent.

SERPENT MOUND STATE MEMORIAL

Peebles - *3850 State Route 73 (six miles north of State Route 32), 45660. Phone: (937) 587-2796 or (800) 752-2757.* **Web:** *www.ohiohistory.org/places/serpent.* Hours: Museum open Wednesday-Sunday 10:00am-5:00pm (summer). Weekends only (April, May, September, October). Park open year-round 10:00am-5:00pm, except Mondays and winter holidays. Admission: $7.00 per car. Miscellaneous: Profile of the "cyptoexplosion" doughnut shape can be seen off State Route 770 - East of Serpent Mound. The largest earthwork in the United States, it measures 1335 feet from head to tail and is about 15 feet high. The mound appears as a giant serpent uncoiling in seven deep curves. The oval doughnut at one end probably represents the open mouth of the snake as it strikes. The museum contains exhibits on the effigy mound and the geology of the surrounding area.

MITCHELLACE SHOESTRING FACTORY

830 Murray St. (Corner of Gallia St. off US-52), **Portsmouth** 45662

- ❑   Phone: (740) 354-2813 or (800) 848-8696
   Web: www.mitchellace.com (to see product line)
- ❑   Tours: Groups of 10 (no more than 50). One hour tour. Age 8+
- ❑   Miscellaneous: All guests receive a free pair of laces.

The former shoe factory works 2-3 shifts per day to make more than 4,000,000 pairs of shoelaces per week. They are the world's biggest shoelace manufacturers for shoes and skates (especially RollerBlades). Family descendants still run the company started in 1902. Start the tour by watching weaving and braiding machines (over 1300) producing strands of fabric. This process takes up an entire floor and when you step onto the floor, all you see are flashes of color. The tipping department takes long strands and cuts them into different lengths and then they are tipped with aglets of nylon or metal. Automatic machines band, fold, label and seal. Other laces are blister packed (plastic pouch over laces is melted onto backing card). The shortest lace is 10 inches. The longest made is 120 inches (for ice skates). What new products might they be making based on shoelaces?

PORTSMOUTH MURALS

State Route 23 South (Washington Street to Ohio River - follow green mural signs), **Portsmouth** 45662

❑   **Web: www.portsmouth.org**

Artist Robert Dafford (internationally known muralist) can be seen working on new murals in the months of May – September. Look for the paint dotted scaffold and the artist dressed in paint- dotted white painter's pants and shirt. Our two favorites were Chillicothe Street 1940's (a very colorful, tremendously detailed, cartoon-like mural) and Twilight (a modern day view of the bridge over the river, looks like a photograph).

FORKED RUN STATE PARK

Reedsville - *63300 State Route 124 (3 miles Southwest of Reedsville off State Route 124), 45772. Phone: (740) 378-6206. Web: www.dnr.state.oh.us/parks/parks/forkedrn.htm.* Located in the heart of Appalachia, colorful history, riverboats, scenic vistas and abundant wildlife give the park its rural charm. 817 acres of camping, hiking, boating and rentals, fishing, swimming, winter sports and food service. Shade River State Forest (hiking trails) is adjacent (740) 554-3177.

BOB EVAN'S FARM

Rio Grande - *State Route 588 (off US 35 to State Route 325 South), 45674. Web: www.bobevans.com. Phone: (800) 944-FARM. Hours: Daily 9:00am-5:00pm (Summer). Admission: FREE for tour - Activities additional.* Begin or end your visit at the restaurant, once named "The Sausage Shop" - Bob's first restaurant. Then, wander round to visit the Farm (implements of yesteryear farms) and small animal barn yard, plus the Homestead (an old stagecoach stop and former home of Bob and Jewel Evans). At the Homestead Museum, sit at the reconstructed counter of the original Steak House owned by Bob Evans, view on an old television console commercials that were hosted by Bob and Jewell Evans in their own kitchen, see through the lens of an actual television camera of the era a setting of Bob and Jewell "at work" filming the ads and tour many other displays which form a life-sized "scrapbook of the business." Nearby in Bedwell (State Route 50/35) is Jewel Evan's Mill where you can view millstones grinding flour. Also in the area are good horseback riding stables and canoe liveries.

HOCKING STATE FOREST

Rockbridge - *19275 SR-374 (off SR 374 and 664, northeast of Laurelville), 43149. Phone: (740) 385-4402. Web: www.dnr.state.oh.us/forestry/Forests/stateforests/hocking.htm. Hours: Open daily, 30 minutes before sunrise - 30 minutes after sunset.* 9,267 acres in Hocking County. Hiking trails (9 miles), Bridle trails (40 miles), horse campground, see a former fire lookout tower, rock climbing a rappelling area, and state nature preserves. Hocking Hills State Park is adjacent.

BARN, THE

Stockport - *State Route 78, 43787. Phone: (740) 962-4284. Web: www.chuckglass.com.* 1904 stained glass studio used by nationally known artist, Chuck Borsari. Sunday-Thursday 1:00-5:00pm.

LAKE WHITE STATE PARK

Waverly - *2767 State Route 551 (4 miles Southwest of Waverly on State Route 104), 45690. Phone: (740) 947-4059. Web: www.dnr.state.oh.us/parks/parks/lkwhitew.htm.* Part of Lake White State Park includes the remains of the old canal channel. 358 acres of camping, boating, fishing, swimming and wintersports.

BUCKEYE FURNACE MUSEUM

123 Buckeye Park Road (two miles south of SR 124 on Buckeye Furnace Road in Jackson County), **Wellston** 45692

❑ Phone: (740) 384-3537

   Web: www.ohiohistory.org/places/buckeye

❑ Hours: Park is open daylight hours. Museum is closed except to group tours.

❑ Admission: Donations.

❑   Miscellaneous: The stone remnant of the old Richland iron
     furnace still stands on private property just north of Richland
     Furnace State Forest and is adjacent to Vinton Township Road 6.
     The required iron ore was mined by oxen from the underlying
     sandstone and limestone. The trees were cut and burned to
     produce charcoal to fire the furnace. The old ore pits are still
     noticeable near the ridges throughout the state forest. With the
     development of the ore fields in Missouri and the Lake Superior
     region at the end of the 19th century, the Hanging Rock iron
     industry quickly faded away. 2,448 acres in Jackson and Vinton
     counties. APV trails (7 miles).

Visit Ohio's only restored charcoal furnace which remains from
the original 80 furnaces in Ohio. In the mid – 1800's, this
industry took root as large trees were converted into charcoal to
make iron for railroads and ammunition. The self-guided tour of
the furnace shows you where raw materials (charcoal, iron ore,
etc.) were brought to the top of the hill and poured into the furnace
to be heated to 600 degrees F. Impurities (slag) stayed on the top
while liquid iron (which is heavier) flowed to the base. The
reconstructed company store serves as a visitor orientation area.
There are two nature trails.

LAKE ALMA STATE PARK

Wellston - *Rte. 1 (3 miles Northeast of Wellston on SR 349),
45692. www.dnr.state.oh.us/parks/parks/lakealma.htm. Phone:
(740) 384-4474.* A quiet lake and a gentle creek meandering
through a wooded valley provide a restful setting for park visitors.
Approximately 3.5 miles of trail traverse hilltops and valleys
offering hikers a scenic view of the park. A 1-mile paved
walkway/bicycle path begins at the park entrance and ends at the
park exit. 279 acres of camping, hiking, boating, fishing and
swimming.

BRUSH CREEK STATE FOREST

West Portsmouth - *(off State Route 73, about one mile west of the village of Rarden), 45663. Phone: (740) 858-6685. Web: www.dnr.state.oh.us/forestry/Forests/stateforests/brushcreek.htm Hours: Open daily 6:00am - 11:00pm.* The vast majority of these 12,000+ acres is made up of steep hillsides, deep hollows, and narrow ridge tops. Combined with the climate in the region, this land is ideally suited to the growth of deciduous hardwood forests. 12 miles bridle trails, 3 miles hiking trails.

SHAWNEE STATE FOREST

West Portsmouth - *13291 US-52, 45663. Phone: (740) 858-6685. www.dnr.state.oh.us/forestry/Forests/stateforests/shawnee.htm Hours: Open daily 6:00am - 11:00pm.* 62,583 acres in Scioto and Adams counties. Ohio's largest state forest. Backpack trails (60 miles) with 8 walk-in camp areas (self-registration permit - no fee), Bridle trails (75 miles), horse campground (no fee), 5 small forest lakes, 8000 acre wilderness area. Shawnee State Park is adjacent.

SHAWNEE STATE PARK

4404 State Route 125 (8 miles West of Portsmouth on State Route 125), **West Portsmouth** 45663

- ❑ Phone: (740) 858-6652, Web: www.ShawneeLodgeResort.com
- ❑ Miscellaneous: Watch out for 1000's of ladybugs visiting each mid-October.

Lodge rooms are furnished with American Indian and Appalachian furnishings and the restaurant serves an extensive children's menu (even steak), plus many good sandwiches and entrees (good food, slower service). Weekends, the restaurant has a guitar player. Many seasonal events include hayrides, hikes, campouts and cookouts (Autumn: Cornbread and Beans Black Pot Supper Days). Their one mile hiking trails are unpaved and just right for families. Nature programs, acres of camping, boating and rentals, fishing, swimming, winter sports and food service. Family cabins, lodge with indoor/outdoor pools, sauna, whirlpool, fitness center, tennis and basketball.

ZALESKI STATE FOREST

Zaleski - *State Route 278 (south of Logan), 45698. www.hcs.ohio-state.edu/ODNR/Forests/stateforests/zaleski.htm* Phone: *(740) 596-5781. Hours: Open daily 6:00 am -11:00 pm.* The Zaleski State Forest Sawmill is Ohio's only publicly owned and operated sawmill. It began operation in 1967. The "low-tech" approach taken at Zaleski gives the mill an almost historical significance. It is an efficient functioning mill that turns out specialty orders for many public works projects. Additionally, demonstrations and training activities (for example, grading workshops) are held every year at Zaleski. 26,827 acres in Vinton and Athens counties. Bridle trails (50 miles), 3 walk-in camp areas (self-registration permit - no fee) and sawmill. Lake Hope State Park is adjacent.

SUGGESTED LODGING AND DINING

SUMBURGER RESTAURANT, **Chillicothe.** To add to your "telephone" experience in town (Telephone Museum listing), eat a casual lunch or dinner *(ordered from table telephones)* at Sumburger Restaurant (740-772-1055) at 1487 North Bridge Street on the retail strip.

Chapter 8
South West Area

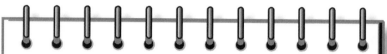

Our Favorites...

* Cincinnati Fire Museum
* Cincinnati History Museum
* Cincinnati Museum of Natural History / Science
* Cinergy Children's Museum - Cincinnati
* United Dairy Farmer's Factory - Cincinnati
* Jungle Jim's - Cincinnati (Fairfield)
* Loveland Castle - Cincinnati (Loveland)
* Heritage Village - Cinncinnati (Sharonville)
* Hueston Wood State Park - Oxford

This castle is in Ohio? Amazing!

EAST FORK STATE PARK

Amelia - *3294 Elklick Road (4 miles Southeast of Amelia off SR 125, I-275 exit 63 or 65), 45106. Phone: (513) 734-4323. Web: www.dnr.state.oh.us/parks/parks/eastfork.htm.* East Fork offers a great diversity of recreational opportunities and natural history only 25 miles from Cincinnati. The park's terrain includes both rugged hills and open meadows. Bridle trails. 10,580 acres of camping, hiking, boating, fishing, swimming and winter sports.

CINCINNATI SPORTS

CINCINNATI BENGALS - (513) 621-3550 or **www.bengals.com**. Professional football at Paul Brown Stadium (downtown, riverfront). Join the Bengals Kids Club for great novelty items (August – December).

CINCINNATI REDS - (513) 421-REDS or (877) 647-REDS or **www.cincinnatireds.com**. Professional Major League baseball at downtown riverfront Stadium. First professional baseball team. Several family-friendly ticket days and fun promotions for kids on game days. ($5.00 - $25.00+) (April – September)

CAREW TOWER

Cincinnati - *441 Vine Street (5th and Vine, across from Fountain Square, Downtown), 45202. Phone: (513) 241-3888. Hours: Monday-Thursday 9:30am-5:30pm, Friday 9:30am-7:00pm, Saturday/Sunday 10:00am - 7:00pm.* An 1930's Art Deco building that is the tallest building downtown. The building itself is a study in old and new. Modern elevators passing renovated plush office floors transport guests only as high as the 45th floor. A trip to the observation deck requires a ride in a rickety, phone booth-sized elevator to the 48th floor. The Observation deck has a panoramic view. Small admission fee per person ($2.00).

CINCINNATI ART MUSEUM

Cincinnati - *953 Eden Park Drive, 45202. Phone: (513) 721-ARTS. Web: www.cincinnatiartmuseum.org. Hours: Tuesday-Sunday 11:00am-5:00pm. Extended Wednesday evening hours. Closed Thanksgiving, Christmas and New Years. Admission:*

FREE admission daily except during special exhibits. Art collection presents 5000 years of visual arts. Favorites include the Syrian Damascus Room, Blue glass chandelier, old musical instruments, Andy Warhol's Pete Rose and the futuristic robot (good size Contemporary Art Section). Family First Saturdays. Museum shop and café.

CINCINNATI FIRE MUSEUM

315 West Court Street, near Plum, Downtown, **Cincinnati** 45202

- ❑   Phone: (513) 621-5553 **Web: www.cincyfiremuseum.com**
- ❑   Hours: Monday-Friday 10:00am-4:00pm, Weekends Noon-4:00pm. Closed holidays.
- ❑   Admission: $6.00 adult, $5.00 senior (55+), $4.00 child (2-12).

From the minute you walk in the restored fire station, the kids will be intrigued by the nation's first professional fire department exhibits. Displays chronicle fire fighting history from antique equipment to the cab of a newer fire truck where you can actually pull levers, push buttons, ring bells, operate the siren and flash emergency lights. The history of Cincinnati in frontier days comes to life as the children participate in a "hands-on" bucket brigade and take a turn on an old style hand pumper. Three interactive computers are fun and tell you all about today's firefighting and fire safety. The museum has an emphasis on fire safety with "Safe House" models (touch and demo area) and a video about fire fighting dangers. Before you leave be sure you slide down the 5-foot fire pole or ring the old fire bell. Let's Stop, Drop and Roll. Everyone can do it! This is the most kid-friendly fire museum in the Midwest!

KROHN CONSERVATORY

Cincinnati - *950 Eden Park Drive (I-71 North to the Reading Road exit #2. Turn right at the end of the exit/traffic light onto Eden Park Drive), 45202. Phone: (513) 421-4086. **Web: www.cinci-parks.org**. Hours: Daily 10:00am-5:00pm.* A rainforest full of 5000 varieties of exotic desert and tropical plants. One of the nation's largest - check out their seasonal displays. FREE, Small admission for special exhibits.

NATIONAL UNDERGROUND RAILROAD FREEDOM CENTER

50 East Freedom Way (Cincinnati waterfront), **Cincinnati** 45202

❑   Phone: (513) 412-6900, **Web: www.freedomcenter.org**
❑   Hours: Tuesday-Sunday 11:00am-5:00pm. Freedom Center
      Closed During Bengals Home Games & most winter Sundays.
❑   Admission: $12.00 adult, $10.00 senior (60+) and students with
      ID, $8.00 child (6-12).

The Center is made up of three buildings that symbolize the cornerstones of freedom - it's an warm art museum with an historical twist. In the 1800's the city served as a major hub of activity on the Underground Railroad. A dynamic presentation, the "moving painting" titled "Suite for Freedom" takes visitors on an emotional journey from freedom to un-freedom. Next, move on to the Slave Pen - used to "warehouse" slaves being moved further south for sale. ESCAPE! This child-friendly gallery uses storytelling and hands-on interaction. Probably the only area designed for kids, time can be spent listening to choices slaves must make, then testing YOUR decisions as a computer-interactive slave yourself. Your choices reveal a lot about your character. From Slavery to Freedom takes the visitor on a journey from the slaves' arrival in the New World through the Colonial period to the Civil War. The Concluding Experience area is designed to help each visitor put into personal perspective all that he or she has just experienced. What does freedom mean today? To you? To all of us? Visitors can participate in individual polling based on "what would you do" scenarios. This is serious stuff, be sure your children are prepared to think about their reactions to the material. The site would be an excellent student post-study of Pre-and-Post Civil War era history would be helpful. Some pre-study of the Underground Railroad is helpful.

TAFT MUSEUM OF ART

Cincinnati - *316 Pike Street (Broadway to Fifth to Pike Sts), 45202. Phone: (513) 241-0343. Web: www.taftmuseum.org. Hours: Tuesday-Friday 11:00am-5:00pm, Saturday 10:00am-5:00pm, Sunday Noon-5:00pm. Admission: $5.00-$7.00 (age 18+).* See works of European and American painters, Chinese porcelains, Limoges enamels displayed in a federal period mansion. Select Saturdays "Families Create!" programs combine storytelling and games with art-making activities.

CINCINNATI HISTORY MUSEUM

1301 Western Avenue, Cincinnati Museum Center (I-71 south to I-275 west to I-75 south exit 2A; I-75 north exit 1), **Cincinnati** 45203

❑   Phone: (513) 287-7000 or (800) 733-2077

      Web: www.cincymuseum.org

❑   Hours: Monday-Saturday (& Holidays) 10:00am-5:00pm, Sunday
      11:00am-6:00pm. Closed Thanksgiving and Christmas.

❑   Admission: $5.25-$7.25 per person. Toddler (age 1-2) rates are
      slightly lower. Combo prices with other museums in the Center.
      Parking fee.

❑   Miscellaneous: Gift Shops - Worth a good look! OmniMax
      Theatre on premises has several shows daily (a movie fee is
      charged per person).

As you enter the museum, your eyes will race around the Cincinnati in Motion model of the city (from 1900-1940) with interactive computer booths and most of the transportation moving (planes, trains, cars, etc). Such an easy and fun way to learn about historical buildings in town or, just reminisce or admire the fascinating layout. Next, you'll visit with The Flynns (ring the doorbell first) talking about life at home during World War II. Hop on board a streetcar with the conductor telling news of the war. Moms and grandmothers will have to check out the "Leg Makeup Bar" (clue: there was a stocking shortage during the war). Now, walk through a life-like forest with shadows and birds wrestling and singing. Then, walk through re-created streets of Cincinnati. Visit the Fifth Street Market and Millcreek Millery - try on hats of the early 1900's and then shop next door at the pretend open air market. The kids can play in a miniature cabin and flat boat, then actually board a steamboat and pretend you're the captain. Very authentically presented, clever displays throughout the whole museum. Cincinnati folks should be proud.

CINCINNATI MUSEUM OF NATURAL HISTORY AND SCIENCE

1301 Western Avenue, Cincinnati Museum Center (I-71 south to I-275 west to I-75 south exit 2A; I-75 north exit 1), **Cincinnati** 45203

- ❏ Phone: (513) 287-7000 or (800) 733-2077
  Web: www.cincymuseum.org
- ❏ Hours: Monday-Saturday (& Holidays) 10:00am-5:00pm, Sunday 11:00am-6:00pm. Closed Thanksgiving and Christmas.
- ❏ Admission: $5.25-$7.25 per person. Toddler (age 1-2) rates are slightly lower. Combo prices with other museums in the Center. Parking fee.
- ❏ Miscellaneous: Gift shops. All are worth a visit. Many science projects to do at home.

Want to know a lot about the Ohio Valley's Natural and Geological history? The Glacier and Cavern simulated areas are both wonderful walk-thru reproductions that are so real, it's almost spooky. Start at the Ice Age of fossils and re-created walk-through glaciers. Maybe try to solve the Ice Age mystery or change the landscape of glaciers. The Paleo Lab (within the Ice Cave) is the place to watch actual scientists at work on lots of fossils. On to the simulated Limestone Cavern with underground waterfalls and a live bat colony (behind glass!). (There are two routes - one that is challenging and involves much climbing and navigating, and the other that is wheelchair or stroller accessible). Look for lots of dino skeletons in Dinosaur Hall. Find out "All About You" as you explore inside, outside and beneath your great body. Brush a huge tooth, see under the skin of your hand, pretend in the office of doctors and dentists, or maybe play pinball as your "food ball" goes through the digestive system. Plan a few hours at this extremely well done museum - we promise it will engage you and you'll learn many new things…easily!

CINERGY CHILDREN'S MUSEUM

Cincinnati Museum Center, 1301 Western Avenue (I-71 south to I-275 west to I-75 south exit 2A; I-75 north exit 1), **Cincinnati** 45203

- ❑   Phone: (800) 733-2077 or (513) 287-7000
     Web: www.cincymuseum.org
- ❑   Hours: Monday-Saturday (& Holidays) 10:00am-5:00pm, Sunday 11:00am-6:00pm. Closed Thanksgiving and Christmas.
- ❑   Admission: $5.25-$7.25 per person. Toddler (age 1-2) rates are slightly lower. Combo prices with other museums in the Center. Parking fee.
- ❑   Miscellaneous: Museum stores (great kids gift ideas). Snack Bar.

Start in the Woods, kiddies. The dim lighting adds mystery to the slides, tunnels, rope climbing mazes and walls, and treehouses. The Energy Zone has kids move plastic balls along a conveyor to a gigantic dump bucket. It's actually a gigantic physics experiment in this Zone - lots of machines and tubes to move balls. Kids At Work lets them make real-life and pretend structures from blocks, pebbles and Legos. They can even use a 12 foot crane to move and lift blocks. Other highlights are the Little Sprouts Farm (age 4 and under), Water Works, Kids Town (pretend town), or Animal Spot (lots of unusual skeletons). Each area is so interactive and so different from the other. Each exhibit had activities for toddlers up to pre-teens. We liked how most areas required friend's/parent's participation to complete a task. Make a new friend each visit!

FRISCH'S COMMISSARY

Cincinnati - *3011 Stanton Avenue (I-71 to Taft Road West Exit), 45206. Phone: (513) 559-5288. Tours: Wednesday 9:00am. Ages 8 and above. Maximum 15 people. One hour. Reservations required.* This commissary supplies 85 Big Boy Restaurants in Ohio, Indiana, and Kentucky (and they're still family owned). They prepare cooked soups, salad dressings, raw meats, vegetables, and baked goods. Children will marvel at large-scale production, especially when the tour guide describes the quantities of ingredients used for each product. For example, two people peel 600 pounds of carrots by hand each day. The bakery ovens can hold 24 pies at one time. They save the restaurants time by pre-slicing or shredding vegetables and bagging them. We understand they use an air compressor to blow the skins off onions!

CINCINNATI SYMPHONY ORCHESTRA

Cincinnati - *1241 Elm Street, 45210. Phone: (513) 381-3300.* *Web: www.cincinnatisymphony.org.* The CSO presents soloists, pops concerts and an artist series in Music Hall. Parties of 1/2 Note are parties designed especially for children ages 3–14. The purpose of these fun theme parties is to create awareness of, and cultivate future audiences for, the Cincinnati Symphony Orchestra. Lollipop Concerts are themed concerts with instrument demos and hands-on activities. CSO RiverBend Music Center hosts Symphony/Pops Orchestra, plus contemporary artists (May-September).

UNITED DAIRY FARMERS

3955 Montgomery Road, **Cincinnati** 45212

- ❑   Phone: (513) 396-8700 - Ask for Consumer Relations
- ❑   Admission: FREE
- ❑   Tours: Mondays and Fridays, 9:30 a.m. - 1 ½ hours, Ages 6+. Maximum 25 persons.

As a group, weigh yourselves on their giant truck scale! See milk being filled in containers (and the large vats where they store raw and treated milk). The plastic bottles are also made on the premises from tiny pellets of plastic melted, blown up and compressed (see it up close). Stop in and visit with the Food Scientists in the Flavor Lab (maybe help pick a new flavor). Best of all, watch ice cream packed and frozen (you even get to step inside the deep-freeze room). Get a free ice cream sundae (flavor of the day - right off the production line!) as a souvenir. We have found this to be one of the best organized, interesting and fun factory tours around!

HARRIET BEECHER STOWE HOUSE

Cincinnati - *2950 Gilbert Avenue (SR 3 and US 22), 45214. Phone: (513) 632-5120. Web: www.ohiohistory.org/places/stowe. Hours: Tuesday-Thursday 10:00am-2:00pm, Saturday 1:00-4:00pm. Admission: Donations.* The home of the author of "Uncle

Tom's Cabin" novel that brought attention to the evils of slavery. Displays describe the Beecher family, the abolitionist movement and the history of African-Americans. Request the video about the story of the book. Mrs. Stowe's journal is available for viewing, as are photo quilts of slave faces. This museum is best visited after some study of the anti-slavery roots along the Ohio River. The videos are long, but helpful.

TAFT NATIONAL HISTORIC SITE, WILLIAM HOWARD

2038 Auburn Ave. (I-71S, take Exit 3 (Taft Road). Go 3/4 mile to Auburn Ave. Turn left and go 1/2 mile to the home), **Cincinnati** 45219

- ❑ Phone: (513) 684-3262, **Web: www.nps.gov/wiho**
- ❑ Hours: Daily 8:00am-4:00pm. Closed Thanksgiving, Christmas & New Year's.
- ❑ Admission: Donations
- ❑ Miscellaneous: Check out the orientation video first in the Education Center. Tours every 30 minutes on hour & half hour.

Visit the birthplace and boyhood home of a US President and Chief Justice. Four of the rooms are furnished to reflect Taft's family life 1857-77. Other exhibits depict his public service career. The signature exhibit of the center is an animatronic figure of the President's Son, Charlie Taft. Charlie tells stories about different family members. Children's group tours give kids the opportunity to dress up from a trunk of period hats and over-garments and play with old fashioned toys. This really helps the children understand life for a young person in the mid-1800's.

CINCINNATI ZOO & BOTANICAL GARDENS

3400 Vine Street (I-75 to exit 6, Mitchell Ave), **Cincinnati** 45220

- ❑ Phone: (513) 281-(800) 94-HIPPO, **Web: www.cincyzoo.org**
- ❑ Hours: Daily 9:00am-6:00pm (Summer); 9:00am-5:00pm (Winter), 9:00am-8:30pm (Summer Saturdays). Closed Thanksgiving and Christmas

❑   Admission: $12.95 adult, $10.95 senior, $7.95 child (2-12).
       Children's Zoo and rides are $1-2 additional. Parking Fee.
       Advance online tickets save $1.00-$3.00 per person.
❑   Miscellaneous: Safari Restaurant. Concessions. Tram and train
       rides. Children's Zoo & Animal Nursery. Wildlife Theatre.
       Stroller rentals.

Ranked one of the top 5 zoos in the United States, its highlight is the successes in breeding white Bengal tigers and other rare wild animals. Komodo dragons (10 feet long and 300 lbs!) and endangered Florida Manatees are some of the large, unusual animals there. Visitors can pass into the underwater world of the manatee in a freshwater spring habitat. Cameras positioned above and behind the manatee tank provide a behind-the-scenes experience for visitors. The Lords of the Artic area features polar bears on land and nose-to-nose through underwater glass panels, too. Dramatic waterfalls and a polar bear cave, with educational interactives complement the exhibit. Their landscaped gardens duplicate the animals' world and the Jungle Trails exhibit even has a tropical rainforest. The first Insectarium (you guessed it!) in the nation is also here.

CONEY ISLAND

Cincinnati - *6201 Kellogg Avenue (Off I-275 East), 45228. Phone: (513) 232-8230.* **Web: www.coneyislandpark.com.** *Hours: Daily: Pool 10:00am-8:00pm, Rides 11:00am-9:00pm (Memorial Weekend-Labor Day). Admission: $9.95 for pool or rides day pass. Discount combo park passes (Ages 4+). Tikes pricing around $3.00. Half price after 4pm. Parking $6.00.* Sunlite, the world's largest re-circulating pool (200' x 401' and holding more than three million gallons of water!) with a huge slide and 6 diving boards, is one of the many fun attractions. Also, Zoom Flume water toboggan, Pipeline Plunge tube water slide, Giant Slide, kiddie rides, classic rides (Scrambler, Ferris Wheel, Tilt-a-whirl, etc) miniature golf, bumper boats, pedal boats and picnic areas.

COVEDALE CENTER FOR THE PERFORMING ARTS

Cincinnati - *4990 Glenway Avenue (I-75 to Harrison Ave exit. Follow signs to Queen City Ave, take that 2 miles. Left on Sunset Ave. Right on Glenway), 45238. Phone: (513) 241-6550.* **Web:**

www.cincinnatilandmarkproductions.com/ccpa/. Hours: Thursday-Saturday 8:00pm, Sunday 2:00pm (mid-April-mid-October). Additional shows on Wednesdays and Sundays on the Majestic. Weekends (November,December seasonal shows). Contemporary and classic musicals, comedies and dramas. Choose venues from the Showboat Majestic - live riverfront shows (moored at Broadway St landing); Cincinnati Young Peoples Theatre - end of summer drama; or the Covedale Center Performances - including a Christmas Carol. $14.00-$20.00 for tickets.

PARKY'S FARM

Cincinnati - *1515 West Sharon Road (Winton Woods Park) (Winton Road & Lake Forest Drive), 45240. Phone: (513) 521-PARK.* **Web:** *www.hamiltoncountyparks.org/parks/parkys.htm. Hours: Winton Park open daily during daylight hours. Farm open daily but activities only open during the summer and weekends (including Fridays) in the Spring and Fall.* The park has a 3-mile paved hike-bike trail (bike rental is available), bridle trail and riding center on the south side of Winton Lake. The park also has picnic areas, a 1-mile fitness trail, a boathouse, nine shelters and an 18-hole Frisbee golf course and a regular golf course. At Parky's Farm explore orchards and crops plus farm animals. Pony rides, Wagon Rides and PlayBarn (farm theme play pits with plastic apples and eggs to jump in) cost $2.00 each. Note, some parts of farm are open only in the summer.

BB RIVERBOATS

Cincinnati (Covington, KY) - *Covington Crossing, just over the blue suspension bridge, 45202. Phone: (800) 261-8586.* **Web:** *www.bbriverboats.com. Admission: $14.00 and up. Basically, double the cost if meal served. Children nearly half price. Tours: 1 hour sightseeing cruises on the Ohio River. Several times daily (best to call for schedule). Reservations Required (May-October).* Docked at the foot of Madison Street see the Modern "Funliner", "Mark Twain" sternwheeler or steamboat "Becky Thatcher". Also theme cruises like ice cream social, Lock and Dam, or holiday. Many cruises offer additional lunch, brunch and dinner cruise options with live entertainment.

JUNGLE JIM'S INT'L FARMERS MARKET

5440 Dixie Highway, **Cincinnati (Fairfield)** 45014

❑ Phone: (513) 674-6000, **Web: www.junglejims.com**

❑ Hours: Open daily 8:00am-10:00pm.

A grocery store is an adventure? This store, selling exotic and even normal foods, is! This Fairfield, Ohio landmark is as popular a supermarket as it is a tourist attraction. Ohio's Famous Playground for Food Lovers (Foodies) allows customers to shop in four acres of food from all around the world all under one roof. Plastic animals and giant fruits greet you. Once inside, the store is divided into theme areas. Visit Amish Country, The Ocean, Europe, South America, India and the Middle East. Does the Big Cheese ever change? Try some new food like medallions of alligator! Their fish are so fresh, they keep them in holding ponds and tanks in the store until they are ready to be purchased. You can view this tanks and a mezzanine walkway near the indoor ponds. Spicy food is inside a walk-thru firetruck - hot. Food from England lies under a moving display of Robinhood and friends in the Sherwood Forest. Tea and crumpets, anyone? Even Elvis is here and will occasionally sing a tune while you choose pastries.

CINCINNATI RAILWAY COMPANY

(2 depots: Cincinnati Riverfront - 1901 River Rd (west of downtown) & Lebanon - 198 S. Broadway/US 42), **Cincinnati (Lebanon)** 45204

❑ Phone: (513) 398-8584 or (513) 933-8022 info line
   Web: www.cincinnatirailway.com

❑ Departures: Late Morning, Noon, Early Afternoon. Wednesday, Friday, Saturday, Sunday (June-August). Saturday, Sunday (May, September, December)

❑ Admission: $12.00 adult, $10.00 child (1-12). Special rates for theme train rides for the holidays and Day Out with Thomas. $15.00-$20.00 for excursion trains.

❑ Miscellaneous: Station Depot with Gift Shop. The passenger cars do not have restrooms and are not heated or air-conditioned. You are permitted to bring snacks and beverages on the trains. Refreshments are also available for purchase on specific rides.

Cincinnati Railway Company (*cont.*)

<u>LEBANON:</u> The one-hour rides depart from Historic downtown Lebanon and travel along the original CL&N line. Trains operate with a restored 1950s-era GP-7 diesel-electric locomotive, open window commuter coaches built in 1930 and a popular open-air gondola car on the rear of the train allows you to enjoy a panoramic view of the countryside.

<u>CINCINNATI:</u> Climb aboard their 1950's / 1960's vintage stainless steel High-Level streamliner coaches and settle back for a nostalgic journey. You'll be treated to a unique High Level experience as you ride up above the surrounding terrain. Most excursions are half or whole day long.

HERITAGE VILLAGE MUSEUM

11450 Lebanon Pike, Sharon Woods Park (US 42, 1 mile south of I-275 exit 46), **Cincinnati (Sharonville)** 45241

- ❑   Phone: (513) 563-9484, **www.heritagevillagecincinnati.org**
- ❑   Hours: Wednesday-Saturday Noon-4:00pm, Sunday 1:00-5:00pm. (May-October). Weekends only (April, November, & December)
- ❑   Admission: $7.00 adult, $6.00 senior (62+), $5.00 child (6-11)
- ❑   Miscellaneous: Dressed interpreters. Bicycle rental, hiking trails. $2.00 entry into Sharon Woods park (per vehicle). Many picnic and shelter areas, mostly wooded for shade. General Store with many pioneer hand-make items and lots of American Girl clothes and books for sale.

See 18th Century Ohio. Nine actual buildings from Southwest Ohio including: The Elk Lick House - "fancy house", learn about the gothic Ohio clock and why the "mouse ran up the clock"; the Train Station - with its treasure trunk hands-on pieces to play with; Kemper Log House - look for Isabella's sampler (Little House on the Prairie theme here) and the "Y" staircase; the kitchen and smokehouse - during festivals they cook here; and the medical office - see Civil War medical and pharmaceutical equipment-amputation city! Their Kids History Camps are wonderfully organized and a great way to "participate" in history.

LITTLE MIAMI STATE PARK

Corwin - *(North of Corwin), 45068. Phone: (513) 897-3055. Web: www.dnr.state.oh.us/parks/parks/lilmiami.htm.* As the river twists and bends, visitors will discover many natural wonders such as steep rocky cliffs, towering sycamores and elegant great blue herons on the wing. Little Miami State Park introduces a new concept to the state park system--a trail corridor. This non-traditional approach focuses on offering numerous recreational pursuits--bicycling, hiking, cross-country skiing, rollerblading, backpacking and horseback riding. The corridor also provides access to canoeing the Little Miami River. Three staging areas (Loveland, Morrow and Corwin) have been located along the developed portion of the park. These include parking lots, restrooms, public phones and trail access points.

STONELICK STATE PARK

Edenton - *2895 Lake Drive (1 mile South of Edenton off State Route 727), 45162. Phone: (513) 625-7544. Web: www.dnr.state.oh.us/parks/parks/stonelck.htm.* An interesting feature of the Stonelick landscape is the significance of sweet gum trees. Normally, sweet gum is a subordinate tree but co-dominates the woodlands of Stonelick with beech and maple. Also, colonies of dense flying star, purple fringeless orchid and Virginia mountain mint - all uncommon wildflowers in Ohio - can be found in the park. 5+ miles of hiking trails provide opportunities for exercise and nature study. Hiking trails are also open to mountain bikes. 1,258 acres of camping, hiking trails, boating, fishing, swimming & winter sports.

GLASS REFACTORY

Georgetown - *9262 Mt. Orab Pike, 45121. Phone: (888) 291-5690. Web: www.glassrefactory.com. Admission: FREE. Tours: By appointment, Tuesday-Friday 9:00am-5:00pm. Minimum group size is 8, maximum is 75. Must be at least 6 years old.* Recycling with a twist...recycling bottles into pieces of art. First collect used glass, melt it and form it into suncatchers. Custom designed molds and some whimsical. Some of their items are sold in the gift shop at places like the National Underground Railroad Freedom Center. Plan to bring $6.00-$10.00 to purchase one at the shop.

GRANT BOYHOOD HOME & SCHOOLHOUSE

Georgetown - *219 East Grant Avenue (one block west of SR 125), 45121. Web: www.ohiohistory.org/places/grantsh. Phone: (937) 378-4222. Hours: Wednesday-Sunday Noon-5:00pm (summer). Weekends only (September, October). Admission: $1.00-$3.00 per adult or student.* The Grant Boyhood Home in Georgetown was the home of Ulysses S. Grant, 18th president of the United States, from 1823, when Grant was one year old, until 1839, when he left to attend West Point. Ulysses Grant lived in this home longer than any other during his lifetime. Ulysses worked in his father's tannery and, from the ages of about six to thirteen, he attended classes in the little schoolhouse on Water Street. The home was restored and furnished, with one room which is dedicated to Grant and Georgetown memorabilia.

PYRAMID HILL SCULPTURE PARK

Hamilton - *1763 Hamilton-Cleves Road (I-275 to SR 27 to SR 128), 45011. Phone: (513) 868-8336. Web: www.pyramidhill.org Hours: Tuesday-Sunday 10:00am-6:00pm (April-October). Weekends only (winter). Admission: $1.50-$4.00 (age 5+).* Pyramid Hill is an outdoor museum focusing on monumental pieces of sculpture in an environment of meadows, forests, and various gardens. Their mission includes the eventual establishment of a collection which will demonstrate the complete history of sculpture, making Pyramid Hill the only art park in the world working on the accomplishment. This park currently has 50 titled sculptures. Especially noticeable is "Abracadabra" by internationally famous sculptor, Alexander Liberman. Many passengers flying into Cincinnati can see the 2 ½ story high, bright red contemporary walk-thru sculpture from above. Isn't Rockababy Moon sweet? The Baroque Trajectory arrived the summer of 2002. This piece survived the September 11 attack - it stood just 3 blocks away in New York City!

FORT HILL STATE MEMORIAL

Hillsboro - *13614 Fort Hill Road (Rte. 23 south to Rte. 50 west to Rte. 41 south), 45133. Phone: (937) 588-3221 or (800) 283-8905. Web: www.ohiohistory.org. Hours: Museum closed. Park open* *summertime daylight hours only. Admission: FREE.* Atop one of the only flat hills in the area, the Hopewell Indians built a walled structure that enclosed almost 50 acres. Inside, they built two large covered structures. The original mound (obscured by trees) still stands at 40 feet wide and up to 15 feet tall. The Museum at Fort Ancient contains 9000 sq. ft. of exhibits, including many interactive units, focusing on 15,000 years of American Indian history in the Ohio Valley. There is a two 2-4 mile trails, a picnic area and restrooms on the premises.

ROCKY FORK STATE PARK

Hillsboro - *9800 North Shore Drive (6 miles Southeast of Hillsboro off State Route 124), 45133. Phone: (937) 393-4284. Web: www.dnr.state.oh.us/parks/parks/rockyfrk.htm.* Unlimited horsepower boating allows for excellent skiing on the lake which also provides catches of bass, muskellunge and walleye. A scenic gorge, dolomite caves and natural wetlands add to the popularity of this recreation area. A 1.5 mile hiking trail takes visitors through cool woodlands, scenic gorges and moist wetlands. A short trail near the campground takes nature lovers to an observation station where excellent birdwatching can be pursued. A two-mile mountain bike trail is also popular with park visitors. 3,464 acres of camping, hiking, boating rentals, and swimming.

WARREN COUNTY HISTORICAL SOCIETY MUSEUM & AREA

Lebanon - *105 South Broadway, 45036. Phone: (937) 932-1817. Web: www.wchsmuseum.com. Hours: Tuesday-Saturday 9:00am-4:00pm, Sunday Noon-4:00pm. Admission: $2.00-$4.00.* The Museum contains artifacts from prehistoric eras to the 1830s and mid-20th century periods. In its Village Green exhibit, antiques are displayed in re-created store fronts. They have the largest collection of Shaker furniture. The Golden Lamb (Ohio's oldest inn) is open for lunch/dinner. Many Presidents have spent the night here. Historical rooms.

LOVELAND CASTLE

12025 Shore Dr. (2 miles South of Kings Island), **Loveland** 45140

❑   Phone: (513) 683-4686, **Web: www.lovelandcastle.com**

❑   Hours: Daily 11:00am-5:00pm (April-September). Weekends only (October – March).

❑   Admission: $3.00 adult, $2.00 child (under 12). Self-guided tour. Higher fee for special events.

❑   Tours: Guided tours are weekdays, by appointment (warm weather season). Groups must have 20+ people. 35-40 minute tours.

❑   Miscellaneous: Only authentically built medieval castle in the United States. Call for directions, or for a map that you can print, **www.kidslovepublications.com/lovelandcastlemapscan.jpg**

This is a real hidden castle and a huge family favorite! Chateau LaRoche was the vision of Harry D. Andrews and construction spanned some 50 years beginning in 1929. He actually did 99% of the work himself! The castle is authentic in its rugged structure with battlement towers, a princess chamber, a dungeon, narrow passageways, tower staircases, a "king's" dining room, and tower bedrooms. Over 32,000 hand-made (cast in milk cartons donated by neighbors) bricks were used to build parts of the structure (ask to see a sample). Learn a lot about castle building and why the front door has over 2500 nails in it. A real Knight of the Golden Trail (or Lady) will greet you and answer any questions throughout your visit. If you have time, plan to bring a picnic, they have many tables scattered near the garden or the water below. If you're brainy, try some of the challenging games and puzzles that Harry and his Knights designed. Curious about Harry and his Knights? Look for the 10 Commandments Creed in the Chapel and the video interviews with Harry playing continuously upstairs. Don't miss this real adventure that your children and you will love (maybe even play pretend - bring along dress up clothes)!

BEACH, (THE)

2590 Waterpark Dr. (I-71 Exit 25B-20 miles N. of Cincinnati)
Mason 45040

❑   Phone: (513) 398-SWIM, (800) 886-SWIM, **thebeachwaterpark.com**

- Hours: Daily opens 10:00am-Closing varies (usually at dark). (Memorial Weekend to mid-September).
- Admission: $11.00-$27.00 Children – Senior – Adult. Discounts after 3:00pm. Group of 4 under $50.00. Parking fee $6.50.
- Miscellaneous: Food Service. No outside food or drink allowed into the park. Bags are checked.

Over 40,000 square feet of beach and two million gallons of water and waves await you! Favorites include the Pearl leisure heated tropical spa pool, Aztec Adventure watercoaster, Thunder Beach Wave Pool and the Lazy Miami River inner tube ride. The young children's water area has Splash Mountain with warm water and Jolly Mon non-water areas!

PARAMOUNT'S KINGS ISLAND

I-71 to Exit 25A or 24 (24 miles North of Cincinnati)

Mason (Kings Mills) 45034

- Phone: (513) 754-5700 or (800) 288-0808, **Web: www.pki.com**
- Hours: Daily 9:00am-Dark (Memorial Day-Late August). Weekends Only (April, May, September, October).
- Admission: ~$45.00 general, ~$25.00 child (3-6) and senior (60+). Discounts available at area hotels, online and at local stores. Check local tourism site. Parking Fee $9.00.
- Miscellaneous: Three restaurants plus 60 fast food areas. Local favorites like LaRosa's Pizza, Graeter's Ice Cream, Montgomery Inn Ribs and Skyline Chili. Kings Island is now smoke-free (except in designated areas).

Some of the 80+ featured attractions at King's Island are: Crocodile Dundee's Boomerang Bay Water Park Resort - The Aussie-themed resort area has more than 50 water activities, including 30 water slides, tropical lagoons, rushing rivers, surfable waves, three family activity areas and careening waterfalls. ACTION ZONE – The Beast (longest wooden coaster), The Outer Limits (1st indoor coaster to catapult in the dark at high velocity), Days of Thunder (racing car simulator of high speed stock car racing). TOMB RAIDER: THE RIDE - journey into ancient temples, proceed thru chambers and strap into a vehicle to make a daring escape. STUNT TRACK

RIDE. Paramount's Kings Island has the greatest variety of children's attractions, including four kids' coasters (more than any park in the world), a collection of 20 rides and the fun, live stage shows including: HANNA BARBERA LAND – Scooby Doo's, Cartoon characters. NICK UNIVERSE includes a total of 18 rides and attractions bringing to life Nickelodeon's most popular character celebrities and adventures – Nick Parade (daily, summers) and Slime Time Area (water spray, pipe work maze, Mess-A-Mania). Most popular with school age kids. Family rides of all types. Favorite Nick Jr. Characters might visit (i.e. Dora or Jimmy Neutron). Amusement Today readers awarded Paramount's Kings Island with the prestigious Golden Ticket Award for Best Kid's Area in the world. Live shows throughout the park, too.

CINCINNATI NATURE CENTER

Milford - *4949 Tealtown Road, 45150. Phone: (513) 831-1711.* **Web: www.cincynature.org.** *Hours: Open all year, dawn to dusk. Admission: FREE.* This original Cincinnati Nature Center site boasts 18 miles of hiking trails for visitors to explore and enjoy. Educational programs for people of all ages take place in this outdoor classroom. Hike a trail through pristine natural habitat at Rowe Woods, Milford or Long Branch in Goshen. Or, explore the children's garden and farmyard at Gorman Heritage Farm, Evendale.

DUDE RANCH, (THE)

Morrow - *3205 Waynesville Road (I-71 to exit 32, SR 123 southeast), 45152.* **Web: www.theduderanch.com.** *Phone: (513) 956-8099. Hours: Open year round. Daytime and evening programs. Admission: $5.00 - $35.00 per person, depending on activities. Cattle Drive is best for ages 7 and up. Miscellaneous: Just 10 minutes from Kings Island. Camps and birthday programs. Paddleboats and petting zoo, too.* Re-live an adventure of the Old West. During your trail ride, we'll go out and round up some Texas Longhorns and have you to actually drive them just like in the movie "City Slickers." Here's an opportunity to do something really unique and feel like a real cowboy or cowgirl. Horseback riding thru woods and meadows, authentic cattle drives, hayrides, pony rides and party/picnic facilities. Learn to rope like a real cowboy or cowgirl or fish awhile. Ask about Dinner Rides (eat out on the trail around a campfire), Western Family Fun Night or the Campfire Hayride (marshmallow roasts, wiener roasts).

GOVERNOR BEBB PRESERVE

Okeana - *1979 Bebb Park Lane (follow SR 129 (Hamilton-Scipio Road) about 8 miles. Turn left on California Road then right on Cincinnati-Brookville Road), 45053. Phone: (513) 867-5835 or (877) PARK-FUN.   www.butlercountyohio.org/countyparks/governor.htm. Hours: Saturday and Sunday 1:00-5:00pm (May-September).* Visit the small 1812 village with the restored log cabin (birthplace of William Bebb - born in 1802). He was the governor of Ohio from 1846 - 48 and a trial lawyer noted for his emotional zeal. There is an 1850's covered bridge, picnic sites, a group picnic shelter, playgrounds, nature trails, restrooms and an on-site park ranger. Rustic family campsites, youth group campsites and a reservable cabin are also available. Good to visit during special events.

FORT ANCIENT STATE MEMORIAL

6123 State Route 350 and Middleboro Road (I-71 to Rt. 123 to State Route 350), **Oregonia** 45054

❑   Phone: (513) 932-4421 or (800) 283-8904
    Web: www.ohiohistory.org/places/ftancien
❑   Hours: Wednesday-Saturday 10:00am-5:00pm (summer). Weekends only (March, April, October, November).
❑   Admission: $7.00 adult, $3.00 student (all ages).

The Museum at Fort Ancient contains 9000 sq. ft. of exhibits, including many interactive units, focusing on 15,000 years of American Indian history in the Ohio Valley. Ohio's entire Indian heritage is displayed from prehistoric to modern times. The 100 acre field is where graves and artifacts were found and is also home to the second largest earthwork in the nation (constructed by Hopewell Indians between 300 BC - 600 AD). Great to visit during Indian Celebration weekends, Children's Day (games and chores) or Night Hiker evenings. Hiking trails.

MCGUFFEY MUSEUM

Spring and Oak Streets (Miami University campus area)

Oxford 45056

❑ Phone: (513) 529-2232 or (513) 529-1809 campus tours
  Web: www.units.muohio.edu/mcguffeymuseum/
❑ Hours: Tuesday-Sunday 1:00-5:00pm (Except Campus holidays and breaks). Campus tours are at your leisure during University hours of operation.
❑ Admission: FREE
❑ Miscellaneous: Points of interest around campus are: Gardens, Anthropology & Zoology Museums (Upham Hall), Geology Museum (Shideler Hall on Patterson), the Library & the Chapel.

See an original collection of McGuffey Readers (lesson books on the three R's and morality, i.e. brotherly love, honesty and hard work). The First Eclectic Readers, published in 1836, started the series of books that was to educate five generations of Americans by 1920. They are still in print and still used today. The home, (built in the early 1830's) is where William Holmes McGuffey wrote his readers while preparing class work for children. On display is Professor McGuffey's lectern and traveling 3-part secretary/bookcase. Check out his eight-sided desk!

HUESTON WOODS STATE PARK

6301 Park Office Road (5 miles North of Oxford off SR 732)

Oxford (College Corner) 45003

❑ Phone: (513) 523-6381 or (800) 282-7275 reservations
  Web: www.huestonwoodsresort.com

A big feature of this park is the Nature Center with programs including their nature crafts, movies, fossils, and fabulous animals (like bobcat, cougar, bunny, snakes, turtles). The Raptor Rehab Center is where they care for injured animals, nursing them back to health (hawks, owls, etc). At the park is also a Rent-a-Camp, biking and rentals, camping, hiking/bridle trails and rentals, boating and rentals, fishing, swimming and winter sports. Kids/Family activities include swimming pool games, candy crafts, guided hikes (fossil hunts) and the ever popular, Bingo games. Evening hikes and bonfire/marshmallow roasts, too. There are cute, cozy, newly remodeled family cottages and a lodge with overnight rooms, indoor / outdoor pools, sauna and fitness areas.

GRANT BIRTHPLACE MUSEUM

Point Pleasant - *219 East Grant Avenue (off US 52), 45157. Web: www.ohiohistory.org/places/grantbir. Phone: (513) 553-4911 or (800) 283-8932. Admission: $1.00-$2.00 per adult or student. Tours: Wednesday – Saturday 9:30am – 5:00pm, Sunday Noon-5pm (April-October). Closed for lunch each day. 5th grade and above.* Civil War General and 18th President's birthplace cottage with period furniture. This restored one-story, three-room cottage, which was built in 1817, was next to the tannery where Grant's father worked. At one time the birthplace made an extensive tour of the United States on a railroad flatcar and was also temporarily displayed on the Ohio State fairgrounds. The small white home has no heat and is sparsely lit – daytime in comfortable weather is best.

RANKIN HOUSE STATE MEMORIAL

Ripley - *6152 Rankin Road, Rankin Hill (Northeast off US 52, Race Street or Rankin Road), 45167. Phone: (937) 392-1627 or (800) 752-2705. Web: www.ohiohistory.org/places/rankin. Hours: Wednesday-Saturday 10:00am-5:00pm, Sunday Noon-5:00pm (early May - mid-December). Admission: $1.00-$3.00 per adult or student.* This restored home of Reverend John Rankin (early Ohio abolitionist) was part of the Underground Railroad and home to Eliza, a character in "Uncle Tom's Cabin", who found refuge off the Ohio River. They sheltered (along with neighbors) more than 2,000 slaves escaping to freedom. In this modest home, there were as many as 12 escapees hidden at one time. Winding roads lead to the remote cabin hidden in a clearing in the woods.

CAESAR CREEK STATE PARK

Waynesville - *8570 East State Route 73 (State Route 73, 6 miles West of I-71, near Waynesville), 45068. Phone: (513) 897-3055. Web: www.dnr.state.oh.us/parks/parks/caesarck.htm.* The park's excellent fossil finds give testimony to the life of this long vanished body of water. The Caesar Creek area was named for a black slave captured by the Shawnee on a raid along the Ohio River. The Shawnee adopted Caesar and gave him this valley as his hunting ground. Caesar lived in this area during the time Blue Jacket was war chief and was said to have gone on many raids with him. Caesar Creek's clear waters and 1,300-foot beach offer excellent swimming opportunities. A five-mile mountain bike trail is located between Harveysburg Road and Center Road. The park's nature center houses interesting displays of the cultural and natural history of the area. Naturalist programs are offered year round. The pioneer village (open seasonally for special events) features 15 historic buildings depicting life in the early 1800s. Bridle trails. 10,771 acres of camping, hiking trails, boating, fishing and winter sports.

COWAN LAKE STATE PARK

Wilmington - *1750 Osborn Road (5 miles South of Wilmington off US 68), 45177. www.dnr.state.oh.us/parks/parks/cowanlk.htm. Phone: (937) 289-2105.* The limestone near Cowan and other parts of the exposed arch are some of the most famous fossil hunting fields in the world. (Collection of fossils requires a permit from the Chief). American Lotus, a brilliant water lily, is abundant in the lake's shallow areas. It is unusual to find such a large colony of lotus on an inland lake. The plant's leaves grow up to two feet in diameter supporting large yellow flowers. Swimming, fishing, sailing and canoeing are popular on the lake. Meandering trails through mature woodlands compliment the natural features of this scenic park. Nature programs. Bike Rental. 1,775 acres of camping, boating and rentals, winter sports and family cabins.

SUGGESTED LODGING AND DINING

HOMEWOOD SUITES BY HILTON – 2670 E. Kemper Road (I-275 exit 44, Mosteller Rd.). **Cincinnati**-North (866) 613-9330. Full breakfast, all suites (w/kitchenette), pool, whirlpool, sport courts, and Family Fun Packages.

Chapter 9

Seasonal &
Special Events

JANUARY

NE – MARTIN LUTHER KING PROGRAM - Cleveland. (216) 231-1111. In observance of the Martin Luther King Jr. Day holiday, many museums and attractions in University Circle will offer free or discounted admission on that day…plus, Orchestra Concert. (Martin Luther King Day-January)

NE – SLED DOG CLASSIC - Newbury, Punderson Resort State Park. (440) 564-2279. Dog sled racing in Ohio? Yes! See sled dog racers mush their teams through challenging race courses. Fee for racers. Spectators are admitted FREE. (one weekend in January, depending on weather)

FEBRUARY

CW – BLACK HISTORY MONTH - Wilberforce, National Afro-American Museum. (937) 376-4944. Events/exhibits month-long.

NE – ICE FESTIVAL - Medina, Uptown Square. (800) 463-3462. Cash prizes and medals for an ice carving competition. Sculpting demos and a "parade" of ice sculptures in front of uptown merchants' businesses. FREE. (mid-February long weekend)

NE – PRESIDENTS DAY AT THE GARFIELD NATIONAL HISTORIC SITE - Mentor, Lawnfield. www.wrhs.org/lawnfield/home.htm. (440) 255-8722. Join their annual President's Day program and take part in a new game, Presidential Squares. Join Presidents Lincoln and Garfield, along with several other presidents and their first ladies, in an interactive game of trivia tic-tac-toe for all ages. Crafts and activities in the afternoon. Small fee for each craft and discounted tickets for tours of the Garfield Home will be sold in honor of the event. (President's Day in February)

MARCH

NE – BUZZARD DAY - Hinckley, Cleveland Metroparks Reservation. (440) 351-6300. Annual migration of the buzzard with breakfast watch. Admission. (March)

MAPLE SYRUP FESTIVALS

Syrup making demos. Pancake dinners/breakfasts. Sugarbush tours by foot or by wagon or by train. (weekends in March)

- ❏ **C - Delaware**. Camp Lazarus. (740) 548-5502.
- ❏ **C - Newark**. Dawes Arboretum. (740) 323-2355 or (800) 44-DAWES.
- ❏ **CW – Dayton**. Aullwood Audubon Center/Farm. (937) 890-7360

- ❑ **NC - Mansfield**. Malabar Farm. (419) 892-2784
- ❑ **NE – Kirtland**. Lake Farmpark. (800) 366-FARM. Admission.
- ❑ **NE – Peninsula**. Cuyahoga Valley National Park/ Hale Farm & Scenic RR. **www.cvsr.com**
- ❑ **S – Hocking Hills**. Old Man's Cave Naturalist Cabin behind Visitor Center, (740) 385-6841. (second weekend in March)
- ❑ **SW – Oxford (College Corner)**. Hueston Woods State Park Resort. (513) 523-6347. (first two weekends in March)

ST. PATRICK'S DAY PARADES & CELEBRATIONS

Cincinnati, Cleveland, Dublin (Columbus), and Toledo - Downtown.

APRIL

EASTER EGG HUNTS

Easter Bunny appearance, treat stations, egg hunts, and kids' entertainment and crafts. Usually held the Saturday before Easter.

- ❑ **C - Ashville**. Slate Run Farm. Egg decorating & egg rolling contests. Admission.
- ❑ **C – Columbus (Powell)**. Eggs, Paws & Claws. Columbus Zoo, (614) 645-3550, ages 2-12. Admission.
- ❑ **C – Hebron**. Buckeye Central Scenic Railroad. (800) 579-7521. **www.buckeyecentralrailroad.org**. Train ride with the Easter Bunny.
- ❑ **CE – Frazeysburg**. Longaberger Homestead. (740) 322-5588.
- ❑ **CW – Yellow Springs**. Young's Dairy. Over 4000 colored Easter eggs. Free. (937) 325-0629
- ❑ **NC – Sandusky**. Great Wolf Lodge. (888) 779-2327 or **www.greatwolflodge.com**.
- ❑ **NE – Cleveland**. Nautica Queen boat ride. **www.nauticaqueen.com**
- ❑ **NE - Peninsula**. Easter Bunny Express, Cuyahoga Valley Railroad, (800) 468-2000 or **www.cvsr.com**.
- ❑ **S – Nelsonville**. Hocking Valley Scenic RR, **www.hvsry.com**.
- ❑ **SW – Cincinnati**. Easter Celebration, Cincinnati Zoo, (513) 281-4700 or **www.cincyzoo.org**. Zoo Blooms, Animal enrichment.
- ❑ **SW – Lebanon**. Cincinnati Railways, **www.cincinnatirailway.com/lebanon.htm**.

April *(cont.)*

NE - GEAUGA COUNTY MAPLE FESTIVAL - Chardon Square.
(440) 286-3007 or **www.maplefestival.com**. Sap Run contest, midway, parades, bathtub races and maple syrup production and sales. (long third weekend in April)

NE – I-X CENTER INDOOR AMUSEMENT PARK - Cleveland (Brookpark) - 6200 Riverside Drive, next to airport. (800) 897-3942 or **www.ixamusementpark.com**. Hours vary daily (Call for details). Admission: $13.00-$16.00 (age 3+), Seniors (60+) FREE. Food service. After riding the World's Tallest Indoor Ferris Wheel (10 stories high) you can SCREAM through 150 rides! Also features a video arcade, miniature golf, laser karaoke, Kidzville, and live entertainment. (month-long most of April)

MAY

C – ASIAN FESTIVAL - Columbus, Franklin Park. (614) 292-0613 or **www.asian-festival.org**.   Entertainment, children's activities, cultural demos, food demos. FREE. (Memorial Day weekend)

C – ICE CREAM FESTIVAL - Utica, Ye Old Mill. (800) 589-5000. **www.velvet-icecream.com**. Velvet Ice Cream hosts a tribute to our national dessert, ice cream, with family entertainment and lots of food made from ice cream. Kids can watch sheep herding with border collies, catch the kiddie tractor pull and wheelbarrow races, or watch the parade or magic circus. Admission. (Memorial Day Weekend)

CE - RAILROAD FESTIVAL - Dennison. (877) 278-8020. Enjoy the heritage and history of the famous World War II Dennison Depot with food, games, contests, rides and parade. Train rides. (week – mid. May)

NE – DAY OUT WITH THOMAS THE TANK ENGINE - Cleveland (Peninsula), Cuyahoga Valley Railroad, Boston Mills Ski Resort, 7100 Riverview Road. (800) 468-4070 or **www.cvsr.com**. Four day event offering 20 minute rides onboard coaches pulled by a real-live 55 ton steam engine Thomas. Play games, watch Thomas videos, interact with exhibits, clowns, magic shows, food and Sir Topham Hatt. Admission, reservations suggested. (last two long weekends in May)

S – FEAST OF THE FLOWERING MOON - Chillicothe, Yoctangee City Park. (800) 413-4118. This three-day themed event features Native-American dancing, crafts and village as well as a mountain-man encampment depicting pioneer life in the early 1800's. Extensive quality arts and crafts displays, food, entertainment, and a variety of activities to see and do. Free. (Memorial Day Weekend – Friday thru Sunday)

SW – **CIVIL WAR DAYS** - Cincinnati **(Sharonville)**. Heritage Village, Sharon Woods Park. **www.heritagevillagecincinnati.org**. Heritage Village Museum becomes the ideal backdrop for the public to experience the fascinating civil war adventures in an authentic 19th-Century setting. Demonstrations of military and civilian activities, military drills, inspections, Calvary units and general camp life will open up a forgotten world for visitors, with many hands-on activities for all ages. Admission. (second weekend in May)

JUNE

C - **CRANBERRY BOG ANNUAL OPEN HOUSE** - Buckeye Lake, Cranberry Bog State Nature Preserve. (800) 589-8224. Take a tour of the island's rare and fascinating plants by pontoon boat. Admission. (last Saturday in June)

C – **FESTIVAL LATINO** - **Columbus**, Downtown Riverfront. (614) 645-7995. **www.musicintheair.org**. Celebrate Latin culture, food (contemporary and traditional) and music (Mambo, Salsa, Conjunto, Flamenco). Children's workshops. FREE (third weekend in June)

CE – **HOT AIR BALLOON FESTIVAL** - Coshocton, County Fairgrounds, 707 Kenilworth Avenue,. (740) 622-5411. Balloon launches at dawn and dusk, Nightglow (Saturday), entertainment and rides. FREE. (second weekend in June)

CE - **TRI-STATE POTTERY FESTIVAL** - East Liverpool, 43920. (330) 385-0845. Celebration of pottery heritage featuring pottery olympics, industry displays, potters at work, ceramic museum, international doorknob tossing championships, factory tours (local companies like Hall China or Pioneer Pottery), art show, rose show, window displays, amusement rides and daily entertainment. (June)

CE - **ORRVILLE DEPOT DAYS** - Orrville. Orrville Depot Museum. 145 South Depot Street. (330) 683-2426 or **www.orrvillerailroad.com**. Mostly railroad-related festival, with both model trains and real trains. Tour Orrville Museums and take rides on trains & track cars. Most activities by donations. (early June weekend)

CE – **FORT STEUBEN FESTIVAL** - Steubenville, Old Fort Steuben Site. (740) 283-1787 or **www.oldfortsteuben.com**. This first American Regiment was built to protect government surveyors from hostile Indians. Next to the fort site is the first Federal Land Office built in the U.S. in 1801. Watch mountain men reenactment groups, storytellers and craftspeople. Admission. (third weekend in June)

June (cont.)

CW – **KIDS FEST** - **Kettering**, Lincoln Park Commons, 675 Lincoln Park Blvd. (937) 296-2587. Designed for young children and their parents to participate in activities ranging from hands-on crafts to face painting. FREE. (third Saturday in June)

CW - **STRAWBERRY FESTIVAL** - **Troy**, the Strawberry Capital of the Midwest. (937) 339-7714. The first full weekend in June the fountain on Town Square runs pink water! Loads of fresh-picked berries and strawberry foods (donuts, pizza, fudge) are sold. Parade, entertainment and hot-air balloons. Free. (first weekend in June)

CW – **KEEPING THE TRADITIONS NATIVE AMERICAN POWWOW** - **Xenia**, Blue Jacket grounds.. (937) 275-8599 or **www.tmvcna.org**. Native American dancing, singing, foods. One of the largest powwows in Ohio. Admission (age 13+). (last weekend in June)

NC – **PRAIRIE PEDDLER** - **Butler**, Bunker Hill Woods, State Route 97. (419) 663-1818. **www.prairietown.com**. Almost 200 costumed craftspeople offer their items made with frontier style tools, foods cooked over open fires and bluegrass music. Horse drawn wagon rides. Stop by the Medicine Show and buy a bottle of elixir. Admission. (last 2 weekends of June)

NC – **INTERNATIONAL FESTIVAL** - **Lorain**, Downtown Veterans Park. Dance, music and authentically prepared foods from many different countries throughout the world. **www.loraininternational.com**. FREE. (last full weekend in June)

NC – **FESTIVAL OF FISH** - **Vermilion**, Victory Park. (440) 967-4477. Walleye and perch sandwiches, "crazy" craft race, entertainment, crafts and a lighted boat parade. FREE. (Fathers Day Weekend)

NE – **GRAND PRIX OF CLEVELAND** - **Cleveland**, Burke Lakefront Airport, Downtown. (800) 498-RACE. The world's top Indy Car drivers compete on the 213 miles of racing. Also a Grand Prix Parade on Friday. Admission. (last weekend in June)

NE - **OHIO IRISH FESTIVAL** - **Cleveland**, West Side Irish-American Club (sponsor), Nautica Complex, Flats, downtown. (888) OH-IRISH. **www.ohioirishfestival.com**. Celebrating the best of Ireland with lively Irish dance reels and lots of Irish food like tasty scones. Admission. (last weekend in June)

NW – **TRAINS, PLANES & AUTOMOBILES FEST** - **Bluffton**, Airport, 1080 Navajo Drive. (419) 358-5675. Airplane rides, tandem skydiving, antique cars & model trains. FREE. Saturday only. Fees for air rides. (June)

NW – **LATINOFEST** - Toledo, Promenade Park. **www.voceslatinas.com**. Folkloric dancing, ethnic foods, mariachi bands, arts and crafts and gifts . Admission. (second weekend in June)

NW – **BLACK SWAMP STEAM & GAS SHOW** - Defiance, Auglaize Village. (419) 784-0107. Working gas tractors and over 30 operating steam engines on the sawmill, threshing wheat and plowing machines. Admission. (second weekend in June)

S – **WASHBOARD MUSIC & ARTS FESTIVAL** - Logan, Town Center (Main, Market, Spring Streets). (740) 390-3828. Fun filled weekend event for the whole family. Free tours of the Columbus Washboard Company, the only washboard factory left in the United States. Continuous music, factory tours, quilt show and food. FREE. (third weekend in June)

SW- **BANANA SPLIT FESTIVAL** - Wilmington, Memorial Park. **www.bananasplitfestival.com**. (877) 428-4748. Celebrate the birthplace of the banana split (first made at Hazzard's Drug Store in 1907). Also tribute to Elvis era. (second weekend in June)

JULY

JULY 4TH CELEBRATIONS - All cities listed (by area, alphabetically) include a full day of parades, rides, entertainment and fireworks.

- ❏ **C – Ashville.** (740) 983-8122. Visit Ohio's Small Town Museum.
- ❏ **C - Columbus** (614) 421-BOOM or **www.redwhiteandboom.org**. Red, White & Boom! July 3rd. Largest fireworks display synchronized to music and lights in the Midwest.
- ❏ **C - Dublin** (614) 761-6500. Top name oldies entertainment.
- ❏ **CE – Carrollton**, Atwood Lake. (800) 362-6406.
- ❏ **CE – Gnadenhutten.** (740) 254-4143.
- ❏ **CE - Zanesville** (740) 743-2303. Stars & Stripes on the River.
- ❏ **CW – Dayton**, US Air Force Museum. (937) 255-0776. Balloon Festival.
- ❏ **CW - Lakeview**, Indian Lake. (937) 843-5392. Decorated boat parade.
- ❏ **NC - Mansfield** (419) 756-6839. Freedom Festival. Airport air show.
- ❏ **NC – Port Clinton** (800) 441-1271.
- ❏ **NC - Put-in-Bay** (419) 285-2804 Perry's Victory Mem'l. 3 days.

July 4th Celebrations (*cont.*)

- ❏ **NE - Cleveland** (216) 664-2484. Festival of Freedom, Edgewater Park.
- ❏ **S – Nelsonville**, Hocking College. Thunder in the Valley. (614) 563-3434.
- ❏ **S - Marietta** (800) 331-9336. Red, White & Blues.
- ❏ **SW - Cincinnati** (513) 621-9326. All American Birthday Party.

C – FRANKLIN COUNTY FAIR - Columbus (Hilliard), County Fairgrounds. Open during the fair is Northwest Village including the church, 1850's log cabin, outhouse, caboose, train station, granary, barn and museum with vintage household equipment. (mid-July for 7 days)

C – MARION COUNTY FAIR - Marion, County Fairgrounds. (740) 382-2558. Huber Machinery Museum open (steam & gas tractors, threshers and road-building equipment, plus Marion steam shovel #6). (first week of July)

C – KNOX COUNTY FAIR - Mt. Vernon, Fairgrounds (SR 3). (740) 397-0484 or **www.visitknoxohio.org**. Check out the traditional favorites plus rodeo, bull-riding, tractor pulls, and Safety Day. The Agricultural Museum that houses hundreds of old-fashioned pieces of equipment and tools is open. (last week of July)

CE – ITALIAN AMERICAN FESTIVAL - Canton, Stark County Fairgrounds, 305 Wertz Avenue. **www.cantonitalianfesta.org**. (330) 494-0886 or Italy in Ohio with entertainment, foods, dancing, exhibits, rides and a bocci tournament. Thursday - Sunday. Admission. (long weekend after July 4th)

CE – CIVIL WAR RE-ENACTMENT - Coshocton, Roscoe Village. **www.roscoevillage.com**. (800) 877-1830. The village transforms into a battlefield. Stroll thru camps, talk with living historians, listen to music of the era, share a campfire and watch a soldier prepare for battle. Children's activities. Admission. (third weekend in July)

CW – CITYFOLK FESTIVAL - Dayton, Downtown. (937) 223-3655. **www.cityfolk.org/festival/festival.html**. Hundreds of the country's best folk performers and artists entertain you with shows, activities, games, crafts and food. (first weekend in July)

CW – **DAYTON AIR SHOW** - **Dayton (Vandalia),** Dayton International Airport. (937) 898-5901. **www.usafc.org**. This is the leading event of its kind highlighted by the outstanding civilian and military air show performances. The event includes ground flight simulators, aerobatics, barnstormers, air races, pyrotechnics and sky divers. Parade, entertainment and Kids Hanger. Admission ($16-19.00, age 6+). (third weekend in July)

NC - **ASHLAND BALLOONFEST** - **Ashland,** Main Street. (877) 581-2345. **www.ashlandoh.com/cvb**. Hot air balloon races and twilight balloon glow. Ashland is a top balloon manufacturer – factory tours available. (long weekend after 4th of July)

NC – **EASTERN WOODLANDS GATHERING** - **Lexington,** SR 42. (419)362-1600. A Native American gathering of all nations. Friendly Voices will be the host drum and there will be a guest drum. Plus dancers, Native vendors, food, auction, children's candy dance. FREE. (last weekend in July)

NC – **GREAT MOHICAN INDIAN POW-WOW** - **Loudonville,** Mohican Reservation Campgrounds & Canoeing. (800) 766-CAMP. **www.mohicanpowwow.com**. Nine different tribes gather to a pow-wow featuring foods, music, crafts, hoop dancers and storytellers. Learn the proper throwing of a tomahawk or a new Native American custom. Admission. (second weekend in July and third weekend in September)

NE – **ALL AMERICAN SOAP BOX DERBY** - **Akron,** Derby Downs, 1-77 & State Route 244 East. (330) 733-8723 or **www.aasbd.org**. The annual gravity "grand prix" of soap box derby racing is still run the same way since 1934. Youths from over 100 local competitions participate and learn workmanship, completing a project and competing. Parade at 10:00am. Admission. (late July weekend)

NE – **IRISH FESTIVAL** - **Berea,** Cuyahoga County Fairgrounds, 164 Eastland Blvd. (440) 251-0711 or **www.clevelandirish.org**. Irish culture at its best with dancing, music, arts & crafts, storytelling and workshops. Admission. (third weekend in July)

NE – **KIDSFEST** - **Cleveland,** Nautica Entertainment Complex. (216) 247-2722 or **www.cleveland.com/kidsfest/**. Playground World Pavilion, Treasure Island, sand castle building, Edible Art, animal acts, kid-friendly music and great kids' entertainment. Admission. (second or third weekend in July)

July (*cont.*)

NE – GREAT LAKES MEDIEVAL FAIRE - **Geneva**, 3033 State Route 534. **www.medievalfaire.com**. (888) 633-4382. The recreation of a 13th century English village with jugglers, jesters, musicians, crafts, full-armored knights and sumptuous foods. Admission. (weekends July to mid-August)

NW – GLASS & HERITAGE FESTIVAL - **Fostoria**, Main Street. (419) 435-1995. Celebrating glass manufacturing heritage with entertainment, food and glass-making demos. Free. (second weekend in July)

NW – LAGRANGE STREET POLISH FESTIVAL - **Toledo**, Lagrange Street between Central & Mettler Sts. (419) 255-8406 or **www.polishfestival.org**. All kinds of Polish foods, polish bands, dancers, a polka contest, rides and craft area. Free. (first full weekend in July, after the 4th)

AUGUST

OHIO'S AGRICULTURAL FAIRS **www.ohioagriculture.gov**. (614) 728-6200. Schedules available through the Ohio Department of Agriculture.

C – OHIO STATE FAIR - **Columbus**, Ohio Expo Center, I-71 & 17th Avenue. (614) 644-4000. **www.ohiostatefair.com**. Includes the largest junior fair in the nation, puppet shows, laser light shows, petting zoo, rodeo, tractor pulls, horse shows, fishing and lumberjack shows, exhibitors from agriculture to the arts, rides and big name entertainment. Favorite family areas include: the Natural Resources area (live wildlife, log cabin, butterfly house); the Nursery; and the Butter Cow sculpture and ice cream. Admission. Family Value Days on Mondays. (twelve days beginning the middle of the first week of August)

C – IRISH FESTIVAL - **Dublin**, Coffman Park, 6665 Coffman Road. (614) 410-4545 or (877) 67-GREEN or **www.dublinirishfestival.org**. A weekend of all things Irish, from entertainment, dance competitions and sports demos to the very best in Irish foods. Admission. (first weekend each August)

C – ZUCCHINI FESTIVAL - **Obetz**, Lancaster Park. (614) 497-2518. Try some yummy zucchini fudge or burgers while seeing a parade, riding amusement rides, listening to music or looking over crafts. FREE. (weekend prior to Labor Day in August)

CE – OLDE CANAL DAYS - **Canal Fulton**. (330) 854-6295. Along the Ohio/Erie canal see a water float parade, fireworks, music contests, saw carving and concerts. (last weekend in August)

CE - PROFESSIONAL FOOTBALL HALL OF FAME FESTIVAL
- **Canton**. (800) 533-4302. Check out the 9 days of celebrating football greats including a parade, hot air balloon show, enshrinement ceremony and a televised professional game. Some fees. (first week of August)

CE - CANAL FESTIVAL - Coshocton. Historic Roscoe Village. (800) 877-1830. www.roscoevillage.com. Canal boat rides highlight the celebration of the canal boat era. Parade and crafts show, entertainment, kiddie tractor pull, and fiddle contests. Admission. (third weekend in August)

CE – PIONEER DAYS - Gnadenhutten, Historical Park & Museum, 352 Cherry Street,. (740) 254-4143. An 1840's pioneer encampment, entertainment, parade, arts and crafts. FREE. (first weekend in August)

CE– TUSCARAWAS COUNTY ITALIAN-AMERICAN FESTIVAL
- **New Philadelphia,** downtown. (330) 339-6405. Italian foods, pizza eating contests, bocci and morri tournaments, music and dance. FREE. (second weekend in August)

CE – INDIAN FESTIVAL - Powhatan Point. (740) 795-4440. An authentic Native American event including crafts, dancing, an historic reenactment, storytelling, archery & more. FREE. (last weekend in August)

CW – ANNIE OAKLEY DAYS - Greenville, Darke County Fairgrounds, 752 Sweitzer Road. (800) 504-2995. Annie Oakley's hometown celebrates with a parade, live entertainment, a sharpshooter's contest and a contest to name Miss Annie Oakley. (first weekend in August)

NC - BUCYRUS BRATWURST FESTIVAL - Bucyrus, Sandusky Avenue. (419) 562-2728 or **www.bratfest.org**. "Ohio's eatingest festival". German foods, live entertainment, rides, kids' activities during the day. (mid-August weekend)

NC – GREAT LAKES WOODEN SAILBOAT REGATTA -
Sandusky, Battery Park Marina. (440) 871-8174. Wooden sailboats large and small are raced for special awards in many categories. Free. (second weekend in August)

NC – LORAIN COUNTY FAIR & SCENIC RAILWAY - Wellington, County Fairgrounds. **www.loraincountyfair.com**. (440) 647-2781. Rides, livestock, horse races, entertainment & Lakeshore Railroad rides. (August)

NE – ASHTABULA COUNTY FAIR - Jefferson, Corner of Poplar & Walnut Sts. (440) 576-0755 or **www.ashtabulafair.com**. The first fair in Ohio features an octagon barn, log cabin home to Camp Gidding (Civil War encampment). Family rides, entertainment, livestock shows and harness racing. (first week of August)

August (*cont.*)

NE – TWINS DAYS FESTIVAL - **Twinsburg**, I-80/90 to SR-91, follow signs. (330) 425-3652. The largest gathering of twins in the world (usually over 2500) includes twins contests, entertainment, fireworks and the nationally televised "Double Take" parade. Small fee for non-twins. Twinsburg was originally named by the Wilcox twins in the early 1800s. Admission.(first weekend in August)

SW – OHIO RENAISSANCE FESTIVAL - **Harveysburg**, 5 miles East of Waynesville on SR-73. (513) 897-7000 or **www.renfestival.com**. The recreation of a 16th century English Village complete with costumed performers, strolling minstrels, may pole dances, full-armored jousting, sword play or feast on giant turkey legs and hearty bread bowls. Two Student Days (Wednesdays) are open special each year: (This is the recommended time to attend with families) Interview Sessions with Queen Elizabeth, Puppet Theatre, Experiment with Historical Games & Rides, Pirate Invasions on the 65-foot Pirate Ship, Combat Demonstrations, Knighthood & Chivalry Discussions, Scottish Dance & Bagpipe Demonstrations, Music Workshops. Admission avg. $8-15.00 (age 5+). (weekends beginning end of August through mid-October)

SEPTEMBER

C – GREEK FESTIVAL - **Columbus**, Greek Orthodox Cathedral, Short North Area. (614) 224-9020 or **www.greekcathedral.com**. Gyros, baklava, music, dance, tours of the church, cooking demos and videos about Greece. Admission. (Labor Day Weekend)

C – FAMILY FUNFEST - **Columbus**, Downtown Riverfront. (614) 645-3800. **www.musicintheair.org**. Cruise the River, roving performers, games & prizes, hands-on crafts, rides, obstacle course, rock climbing and a fish pond. FREE. (second or third weekend in September)

C – LITTLE BROWN JUG & ALL HORSE PARADE - **Delaware**, County Fairgrounds, 236 Pennsylvania Avenue. (800) 335-3247 or **www.littlebrownjug.com**. The most coveted horse race for three-year old pacers held on the fastest half-mile track in the world. Kick off parade with the largest all-horse, mule and donkey parade east of the Mississippi. Admission. (mid-September - Saturday only)

C – POPCORN FESTIVAL - **Marion**. (740) 387-FEST or **www.popcornfestival.com**. Highlights include a parade, tours of the Popcorn Museum, popcorn sculptures and nationally known entertainment nightly. Free. (weekend after Labor Day)

C – **BUCKEYE FLINT FESTIVAL** - Newark, Courthouse Square,. (740) 345-1282. Ohio's gemstone is flint rock and you'll learn everything you could want to know about flint through displays, entertainment, crafts and food preparation. FREE. (last weekend in September)

C – **TOMATO FESTIVAL** - Reynoldsburg, Civic Park, 6800 Daugherty Drive. (614) 866-2861. www.reynoldsburgtomatofestival.org. Ohio's tomato harvest is celebrated with things like free tomato juice, fried green tomatoes, tomato pies, tomato fudge, tomato cakes & cookies, Tiny Tim Tomatoland, crafts, parade and The Largest Tomato Contest ($100 per pound). Fee for parking. (September - Wednesday through Sunday)

CE – **BARNESVILLE PUMPKIN FESTIVAL** - Barnesville. (740) 695-4359. www.barnesvillepumpkinfestival.com. All kinds of pumpkin contests (largest pumpkin, pumpkin rolling and pie eating), parade, foods, fiddle contest, rides, crafts and entertainment. Free. (Thursday – Sunday - last full weekend of September)

CE – **OHIO SWISS FESTIVAL** - Sugarcreek. (888) 609-7592. Experience the best of Switzerland from Polka bands, dancing, tons of Swiss cheese, Steinstossen (stone throwing) and Schwingfest (Swiss wrestling). FREE (last Friday & Saturday of September)

CW – **POPCORN FESTIVAL** - Beavercreek. (937) 426-5486. A balloon rally, live entertainment and most of all, "popcorn showers". FREE. (September)

CW – **OHIO FISH AND SHRIMP FESTIVAL** - Urbana, downtown. (937) 652-1161. Food, music, kids games (old time crawfish races, trout grabs, frog-jumping contest, water battles, sand castle building, and radio-controlled boat races). (second Saturday in September)

CW – **RASPBERRY FESTIVAL** - Urbana, Rothschild Berry Farm, 3143 East SR-36. (800) 356-8933. www.robertrothschild.com. Celebrate the raspberry harvest with entertainment, foods and children's activities. (Weekend after Labor Day). Pick your own and café, too.

NC – **MELON FESTIVAL** - Milan, SR 113. (419) 499-2766. www.accnorwalk.com. Melons in baskets, by the slice, muskmelon ice cream and watermelon sherbet. Melon eating contests. Parade, rides, crafts and a kiddie pedal tractor pull. Free. (Labor Day Weekend)

NC - **HISTORICAL WEEKEND** - Put-In-Bay. Perry's Monument. www.lake-erie.com. or (800) 441-1271. Military living history camps with displays of Indian wars to the present. Boy Scout camporee. Parade, live entertainment. (second long weekend in September).

September (*cont.*)

NC – TIFFIN-SENECA HERITAGE FESTIVAL - **Tiffin**, Hedges Boyer Park. (888) SENECA1. Living history village and entertainment, food, fireworks. Tours of area glass factory (888-298-7236). (third weekend in September)

NE - CANFIELD FAIR - **Canfield** Fairgrounds. **www.canfieldfair.com** or (330) 533-4107. Grandstand headliners, the World's Largest Demolition Derby, Truck and Tractor Pull, agricultural displays, milk a cow, pet pigs, Elephant Encounter. Admission. (Wednesday - Sunday-Labor Day week)

NE – CLEVELAND NATIONAL AIR SHOW - **Cleveland**, Burke Lakefront Airport, downtown. **www.clevelandairshow.com**. (216) 781-7747. One of the nation's top air shows featuring the best in military jet demonstrations and civilian aerobatics performers. Thunderbirds and Blue Angels Flybys. Tour the International Women's Air & Space Museum on premises. Admission. (Labor Day weekend)

NE – GRAPE JAMBOREE - **Geneva**, downtown. (440)466-JAMB. The local grape harvest is celebrated with parades, fresh-picked grapes, grape stomping contests, grape products, ethnic foods, rides and entertainment. FREE. (last weekend in September)

NW – TRACKS TO THE PAST - **Findlay**, NW Ohio Railroad. **www.nworrp.org**. Gas engines, tractors, steam engines, operating sawmill, antique cars, firetrucks, quarter-scale live steam Train Rides, B&O caboose tours, HO Model Trains, Wood carvers, Alpacas, Birds of Prey, Callipes, Infantry Reenactments, Blacksmithing, Kiddie tractor pull and all-you-can-eat breakfasts. Small admission. (weekend after Labor Day)

NW – RIVERFEST - **Toledo**, Promenade Park, downtown. (419) 243-8024. Festival and parade. Free. (Labor Day Weekend)

S – RIVER DAYS - **Portsmouth**. (740) 354-6419. Parade, rides, crafts, entertainment and children's events. Free. (Labor Day Weekend)

S – OHIO RIVER STERNWHEEL FESTIVAL - **Marietta**, Ohio River Levee. (800) 288-2577. Thirty plus sternwheelers dock for the weekend, some for commercial and some for residential use. Continuous musical entertainment, fireworks and grand finale sternwheeler races. FREE. (weekend after Labor Day)

SW – HARVEST FEST - **Cincinnati (Sharonville)**. The weekend will be full of heritage games, crafts, activities, entertainment, demonstrations and refreshments. **www.heritagevillagecincinnati.org**. Included in the bountiful Harvest Fest will be "pioneer chores", candle dipping, sack races, tug-o-war, scarecrow making, hearth cooking and many other activities. In addition, the Village will host guided tours of its 19th-century buildings. Admission. (last weekend in September)

SW – **OKTOBERFEST-ZINZINNATI** - **Cincinnati**. Fifth Street, downtown (513) 579-3187 or **www.oktoberfest-zinzinnati.com**. The nation's largest authentic Oktoberfest featuring seven areas of live entertainment, food and a children's area. FREE. (third weekend in September)

SW - **THUNDER IN THE HILLS HYDROPLANE RACE** - **Hillsboro** - Rocky Fork Lake State Park. (937) 393-4284. Hydroplane boat racing, 2nd largest race in the country. FREE. (September)

SW – **SCARECROW FESTIVAL** - **Washington Court House**. (740) 636-2340. A street fair, parade, live entertainment and a living scarecrow contest. FREE. (mid-September long weekend)

SEPTEMBER / OCTOBER

APPLE FESTIVALS - Apples & cider. Apple pie eating contests. Apple peeling contests. Apple butter. Candy apples. Wagon/hayrides. Apple Dumplings, Fritters, Donuts, etc. Parades. Pioneer crafts. Petting Zoo. For contact info, see listings. Participating Areas:

❑   **CE** – **Big Prairie**, Whispering Hills Campground (8248 State Route 514). (330) 567-2137 or **www.whisperinghillsrvpark.com**. (first weekend in October)

❑   **CE** – **Coshocton**, Roscoe Village. **www.roscoevillage.com**. Apple Butter Stirrin' living history tours. Soap carving, pumpkin carving, and hog calling. (third weekend in October)

❑   **CE - Gnadenhutten Village** (second weekend in October)

❑   **CE** – **Millersburg**, Yoders Amish Home. (330) 893-2541. (last 2 Saturdays in September & first 3 Saturdays in October)

❑   **CE - Zoar Village** (first weekend in October)

❑   **CW – Dayton**, Aullwood Audubon Farm (end of September)

❑   **NC – Rittman**, Bauman Orchards. **www.baumanorchards.com** (first Saturday in October)

❑   **NE – Brunswick**, Mapleside Farms, 294 Pearl Road, US 42. (330) 225-5577 or **www.mapleside.com**. (mid-September weekend)

❑   **NE – Burton**, Century Village. (440) 834-1492. Admission. (second weekend in October)

September / October - Apple Festivals (*cont.*)

- ❏ **NW – Archbold**, Sauder Farm Village. **www.saudervillage.com**.
- ❏ **NW – Lima**, Allen City Farm Park,1582 Slabtown Road. (419) 221-1232 or **www.jampd.com** (first weekend in October)
- ❏ **S – Belpre**, Washington Blvd. (740) 423-5233. (first weekend in October)
- ❏ **S – Vincent**, Sweetapple Farm, CR805. (740) 678-7447 or **www.sweetapplefarm.com**
- ❏ **SW - Lebanon**, Irons Fruit Farm, 1650 Stubbs Mills Road. (513) 932-2853.

PIONEER / PEDDLER FESTIVALS - Early 1800's frontier life & Indian village. Re-enactors, craft demonstrations, authentic open fire, wood cooked food and folk entertainment.

- ❏ **CW – Zanesfield**, Marmon Valley Farm. **www.marmonvalley.com** (first or second Saturday in October) Rodeo, archery, barn dance, wagon rides.
- ❏ **CE – Columbiana**, Shaker Woods (Rte. 11). (800) 447-8201 or **www.shakerwoods.com**. (3 weekends in August)
- ❏ **CE – Dellroy**, Atwood Lake Area. (330) 343-6780. Wagon rides and Revolutionary War encampment. (first weekend in October)
- ❏ **CW – Springfield**, George Rogers Clark Park. (937) 882-9216 or **www.grcha.org**. Area where Gen. Clark defeated Shawnee to open NW Territory. Admission. (Labor Day Weekend)
- ❏ **NC - Bellevue**, Historic Lyme Village. (419) 483-6052. (mid-September weekend)
- ❏ **NC – Butler**, SR 97. **www.prairietown.com**. Admission. (first two weekends in October)
- ❏ **NC – Milan** Historical Museum. (419) 499-2968 or **www.milanhist.org**. (October weekend)
- ❏ **NE – Jefferson**, Buccaneer Lake, Rte. 307, I-90 exit 223. (440) 466-8414 or **www.yankeepeddlerfestival.com**. Admission. (first & second weekend in September)
- ❏ **NE – Kirtland**, Lake Farmpark Village Prairie Festival. **www.lakemetroparks.com**. or (440) 256-2122. Includes corn maze, pumpkin patch & pony rides. Admission. (third weekend in September)

☐ **NE - Medina** , Buckeye Woods Park, (Part of the Medina County Fall Foliage Tour). (330) 722-9364. (second weekend in Oct.)

☐ **NW – Attica**, Oak Ridge Festival. (419) 426-2715 or **www.oakridgefestival.com**. (mid-October weekend)

☐ **SW – Morgan Township**, Governor Bebb Preserve. (877) PARKFUN. **www.butlercountymetroparks.org**.

HARVEST FESTIVALS - Press cider. Apple butter making. Veggie harvest. Living history demos. Lumberjacks. Butter churning. Grainthreshing. Open-fire cooking. Participating Areas:

☐ **C – Centerburg**, Memorial Park, US 36/SR 3. Old Time Farming Festival. (second weekend in September)

☐ **C – Utica**, Ye Olde Mill. (800) 589-5000. (Sundays in October)

☐ **CE – Carrollton**, Algonquin Mill, SR 332. (330) 627-5910. (first full weekend in October)

☐ **NC – Mansfield**, Malabar Farm. (419) 892-2784 or **www.malabarfarm.org**. (last Saturday in September)

☐ **NC – Marblehead**, Lighthouse. (419) 797-4530. (second Saturday in October)

☐ **S – West Portsmouth**. Sorghum Makin Festival, Pond Creek (off Rte. 73). (740) 259-6337. FREE. (first weekend in October)

☐ **NE – Bath**, Hale Farm and Village. 330-666-3711. Admission. (first weekend in October)

☐ **NW – Archbold**. Sauder Village, St. Rt. 2, Archbold. 800-590-9755 or **www.saudervillage.org**. Admission. (second Saturday in October)

☐ **SW – Madison Township**, Chrisholm Historic Farmstead. **www.butlercountyohio.org/countyparks/chrisholm.htm**. (877) Park Fun.

OCTOBER

PUMPKIN PATCHES/ HAYRIDES/ CORN MAZES/ FALL PLAYLANDS - All sites charge admission (avg. $5.00). Plan on at least two hours playtime. all are open weekends, some open weekdays (by appointment) and weeknights (late September - late October).

☐ **C - Grove City**. Circle S Farms. 2 mazes, entertainment on weekends, snack bar & autumn treats. (614) 878-7980 or **www.circlesfarm.com**.

Pumpkin Patches/ Hayrides/ Corn Mazes/ Fall Playlands (*cont.*)

- ❑ **C – Hilliard**. Kuhlwein's Gardens, 1859 Walker Road (west of Alton Darby Road). (614) 876-2833. Pony rides and live entertainment on weekends.
- ❑ **C – Milford Center**. The Maize at Little Darby Creek, 8657 Axe Handle Rd. (937) 349-4781 or **www.cornfieldmaze.com**.
- ❑ **C – Newark**. Pigeon Roost Farm, (I-70 exit 122 to Rte. 40). (740) 928-4925.
- ❑ **C - Pataskala**. Lynd Fruit Farm. (I-270 exit Morse Rd. east). (740) 927-7013 or **www.lyndfruitfarm.com**. Flashlight nights.
- ❑ **C – Sugar Grove**. Sharp Farms, (off US 33). (614) 519-2368 or **www.sharpfarms.com**.
- ❑ **CE - Columbiana**. Detwiler Farm. (330) 482-2276.
- ❑ **CE – Wooster**. Ramseyer Farms. (330) 264-0264 or **www.ramseyerfarms.com**. Closed Sunday and Monday.
- ❑ **CW – Centerville**. Bonneybrook Farms. (9400 Clyo Road). **www.bonneybrookfarms.com**
- ❑ **CW - Yellow Springs**. Young's Jersey Dairy. (937) 325-0629.
- ❑ **NC – Ashland**. Honey Haven Farm Family Corn Maze. 1327 CR 1475. (877) 581-2345. Usually an Ohio themed or OSU maze.
- ❑ **NC – Elmore**. Klickman's Farms. (800) 441-1271
- ❑ **NE – Peninsula**. Heritage Farms. (330) 657-2330 or **www.heritagefarms.com**. (October weekends)
- ❑ **NE – Amherst**. Hillcrest Orchard. (440) 965-8884 or **www.hillcrestfunfarm.com**.
- ❑ **NE - Brunswick**. Mapleside Farms. (330) 225-5576.
- ❑ **NE - Canfield**. Lanterman's Corn Maize. (8807 Akron Canfield Rd). 330-533-7189.
- ❑ **NE – Geneva**. Spring Hill Farm. 6062 South Ridge Road West. (800) 793-4299 or **www.shopspringhill.com**.
- ❑ **NE - Hartville**. Maize Valley Farm Market, 6193 Edison St. NE. **www.maizevalley.com**. (daily, September –October).
- ❑ **NE – Kirtland**. Lake Farmpark. **www.lakemetroparks.com**.
- ❑ **NE – Middlefield**. Ridgeview Farm (SR 87, west of SR 45), (440) 693-4000.
- ❑ **SW – Lebanon**. Schappacher Farms. (513) 398-0904.

❑ **SW - Milford.** Shaw Farm. (513) 575-2022 or
   www.shawfarms.com.

❑ **SW – Trenton.** Barn N Bunk Farm Market, State Rt. 73 &
   Wayne-Madison Road. **www.barnnbunk.com.**

C – PUMPKIN SHOW - Circleville. www.pumpkinshow.com. (740)
474-7000. Ohio's largest and oldest harvest celebration has seven parades,
lots of pumpkin, squash and gourds, pumpkin foods (cotton candy,
burgers, chips and ice cream), rides and entertainment. See some of the
largest pumpkins and the world's largest pumpkin pie (approx. 350 lbs.
and 5 feet in diameter). Contests galore like hog calling, egg toss, pie
eating and carved pumpkins. FREE. (mid-October, Wednesday-Saturday)

C – ALL AMERICAN QUARTER HORSE CONGRESS - Columbus,
Ohio Expo Center, I-71 & 17th Avenue. (614) 943-2346 before October,
(614) 294-7469 (during show). The world's largest single breed horse
show with seven acres of commercial exhibits and demos. Fee per
vehicle. (two weeks long during mid-to-late October)

C – OKTOBERFEST - Columbus, German Village. (614) 221-8888.
www.germanvillage.com. German music, dancing, food (potato salad,
brats), crafts, games and rides. Kinderplatz area for kids. Admission. (first
weekend in October)

C – WORLD'S LARGEST GOURD SHOW - Mount Gilead,
Morrow County Fairgrounds, US 42 & State Route 61 South.
http://Americangourdsociety.org/ohiochapter. Gourd crafts, fresh gourds,
gourd cleaning and carving demos, and the gourd show parade. Even make
music from a gourd! Admission. (first full weekend in October)

CE – FOX CREEK OUTDOOR EXPERIENCE - Canal Fulton,
Clays Park. **www.foxcreekoutdoors.com.** (330) 854-9083. The first
outdoors show that is really held in the great outdoors. Bring the whole
family and spend the day or all three days playing: archery, fishing, kids
motorcycle training, climbing wall, canoeing, Frisbee golf, butterfly tent,
low ropes course, crafts, bicycle test rides, air gun range, boomerang
throwing, fly-fishing and bird identification. Demos include: water ski
shows, retriever dogs, extreme bikes, hovercrafts, chainsaw carving,
watercross-snowmobiles, sled dogs, Clydesdales horses, kite flying, R/C
vehicles and motorcycle stunts. Admission per day (avg. $5.00-$10.00 per
person). (second full weekend in October)

October (*cont.*)

CE – FOREST HERITAGE FESTIVAL - **Dover**, Tuscarawas County Fairgrounds. (330) 339-2205 or **www.forestheritagefestival.com**. Pro lumberjack show, chainsaw carvers, barbecue, crafts, logging and wood-processing equipment and local artisans all make this a fun experience to learn how wood products make their way "from the woods to Wal-Mart." FREE. (second Friday & Saturday in October)

NC – WOOLLYBEAR FESTIVAL - **Vermilion**. (440) 967-4477. An annual tribute to the weather "forecasting" woollybear caterpillar with a huge parade, caterpillar races, woollybear contests for kids, crafts and entertainment. FREE. (first Sunday in October)

NE – ASHTABULA COUNTY COVERED BRIDGE FESTIVAL -**Jefferson**, Ashtabula County Fairgrounds. (440) 576-3769 or **www.coveredbridgefestival.org**. Ashtabula is known as the working covered bridge capital of the Western Reserve. Enjoy a tour of 16 covered bridges during the beautiful fall season, plus entertainment, crafts, and draft horse contests. Admission. (second weekend in October)

NW – JOHNNY APPLESEED FESTIVAL - **Defiance**, AuGlaize Village, off US-24, west of town. (419) 784-0107. The historic village is busy with crafts, apple butter, cider and molasses making, and harvest demonstrations. Admission. (first weekend in October)

PUMPKIN TRAIN - Take your little ones on a delightful train ride to the Pumpkin Patch where they can choose their special pumpkin to be transported back to the station on the flatbed car attached to the train. Small admission fee for ride and for pumpkin. (October weekends)

❑ **C – Hebron**, Buckeye Central Scenic Railroad. **www.buckeyecentralrailroad.com**.

❑ **NW – Findlay**, NW Ohio Railroad. 11600 County Road 99. (419) 423-2995 or **www.nworrp.org**.

❑ **SW – Lebanon**, Cincinnati Railway, Lebanon Railroad. (513) 933-8022 or **www.cincinnatirailway.com/lebanon.htm**. Ride the train to Schappacher Farm where you can pet animals, select a pumpkin and play in the hay before heading back.

S – HOCKING FALL COLOR TOUR - **Rockbridge**, Hocking State Forest. (740) 385-4402. Enjoy a guided tour at Cedar Falls and a hayride through the fall colors, along with a bean dinner. FREE. (October)

S – **PAUL BUNYAN SHOW** - **Nelsonville**, Hocking College Campus. (740) 753-3591. Ohio's largest forestry exposition features lumberjack competitions, forestry displays, guitar pickers championship and chainsaw sculpting. Admission. (first weekend in October)

S – **FARM FESTIVAL** - **Rio Grande**, Bob Evans Farm, State Route 588. (800) 994-3276 or **www.bobevans.com**. Down on the farm feeling with over 100 craftspeople, country music, square dancers, homestyle foods and contests such as apple peeling, cornshelling, cow chip throwing and hog calling. Admission. (mid-October)

SW – **MIDDFEST INTERNATIONAL** - **Middletown**, Donham Plaza. **www.middfestinternational.org**. (513) 425-7707. Exhibits, music, authentic ethnic dances & menus from many countries. Youth Park. International sports and games, ethnic craft demos, food prep and customs. (October weekend)

SW – **OHIO SAUERKRAUT FESTIVAL** - **Waynesville**. (937) 897-8855. All kinds of sauerkraut foods like cabbage rolls, sauerkraut candy, pizza, and desserts, fair food, crafts and live entertainment. Prizes are awarded for the greenest cabbage, the largest and the most pathetic cabbage! Fee for parking. (second weekend in October)

NOVEMBER

C – **COLUMBUS INTERNATIONAL FESTIVAL** - **Columbus**, Veterans Memorial, 300 West Broad Street. (614) 228-4010. More than 60 nationalities and cultures will participate in a mix of dance, music, foods and crafts. Educational interactive activities for kids. Admission. (first weekend in November)

NE – **CLEVELAND CHRISTMAS CONNECTION** - **Cleveland (Brookpark)**, I X Center, near Hopkins Airport. (216) 676-6000. Gifts, arts and crafts, regional entertainment, Santa, train rides, giant indoor ferris wheel rides, nice free gift craft area for kids, variety of ethnic food. Admission. (long weekend before Thanksgiving weekend)

THANKSGIVING WEEKEND PARADES - Downtown Cleveland, Columbus, Cincinnati, Dayton, and downtown Toledo (**www.citifest.org**).

DECEMBER

CHRISTMAS DECORATIONS / OPEN HOUSES - Buildings decorated for holidays, Santa visit, entertainment and light refreshments served. Great way to expose younger ones to historical homes that might be boring otherwise. Admission. (mostly first weekend of December)

❑ **C – Columbus.** Ohio Village. **www.ohiohistory.org/places/ohvillage/.** Celebrate a traditional 19th century holiday. Admission. (second and third weekend in December)

❑ **C – Columbus (Worthington).** Orange Johnson House, (614) 885-1247. Open house is free. Programs have fee. (weekends in Dec.)

❑ **C – Marion.** Harding Home, **www.ohiohistory.org/calendar.** (800) 600-6894 or (first and second weekend)

❑ **CE – Berlin.** Schrocks Amish Farm, (330) 893-3232. Sleigh rides, buggy rides, hayrides and crafts.

❑ **CE – Canton, North.** Hoover Historical, (330) 499-0287.

❑ **CE –** J.E. Reeves Victorian Home, Dover. (800) 815-2794 or **www.doverhistory.org.** (begins Thanksgiving weekend for 1 month)

❑ **CE – Frazeysburg.** Longaberger Homestead, (740) 322-5588 or **www.longaberger.com.** Lights, lunch and teas.(first three weekends in December)

❑ **CE – Millersburg.** The Mansion, **www.victorianhouse.org.**

❑ **CE – Zoar** Village. (800) 874-4336 or **www.ohiohistory.org/calendar.**

❑ **CW – Dayton.** Dunbar House. (800) 860-0148 or **www.ohiohistory.org/calendar.**

❑ **CW – Piqua** Historical Area. (800) 752-2619 or **www.ohiohistory.org/calendar.**

❑ **CW - West Liberty.** Mac-O-Cheek Castle. **www.piattcastles.org**

❑ **NC - Bellevue.** Lyme Village. (419) 483-4949. (mid/late Dec.)

❑ **NC – Elyria.** Hickories Museum, **www.lchs.org.** (second Saturday in December)

❑ **NC – Fremont.** Hayes Presidential Center (800) 998-7737 or Special hands-on mini-train display and carriage rides. **www.rbhayes.org.** (month long)

❑ **NC - Lucas.** Malabar Farm.

❑ **NC - Mansfield.** Kingwood Center & Greenhouses.

- ❏ **NC – Oberlin.** Jewett House, (440) 774-1700. Gingerbread house contest display.
- ❏ **NE – Akron** Zoo. **www.akronzoo.org.** Snack with Santa. (second & third weekend in December)
- ❏ **NE - Akron.** Stan Hywet Hall & Gardens. **www.stanhywet.org.**
- ❏ **NE - Brunswick.** Mapleside Farms Santa Fest. **www.mapleside.com.** (breakfast, crafts, face painting & sleigh/wagon rides)
- ❏ **NE – Mentor.** Lawnfield, (440) 255-8722. (Winter Break @ 2:00pm)
- ❏ **NE - Youngstown.** Lanterman's Mill, Mill Creek Park,
- ❏ **NW – Archbold.** Sauder Village, (419) 446-2541 or **www.saudervillage.org.**
- ❏ **NW - Maumee.** Wolcott Museum Complex, (419) 893-9602.
- ❏ **NW – Perrysburg.** Fort Meigs, (800) 283-8916 or **www.ohiohistory.org/calendar.** (third Sunday)
- ❏ **S – Gallipolis.** Our House,
- ❏ **S – Marietta.** The Castle, (740) 374-4461.
- ❏ **SW – Cincinnati.** Krohn Conservatory, (513) 421-4086.
- ❏ **SW - Lebanon.** Glendower State Memorial, (513) 932-1100 or **www.ohiohistory.org/calendar.**
- ❏ **SW – Cincinnati (Sharonville).** Heritage Village Holly Days, Sharon Woods Park, **www.heritagevillagecincinnati.org.**

NUTCRACKER BALLET - Both young and old will enjoy the magic of the season with this holiday favorite for family and friends. A great way to kick off your holiday season with The Arts. Music accompaniment by the local symphonies. Admission. (log on to websites for dates – December)

- ❏ **C – Columbus** Balletmet. (614) 229-4860 or **www.balletmet.org.**
- ❏ **CE – Canton** Ballet. (330) 455-7220 or **www.cantonballet.com/ballet1.php.** Palace Theatre.
- ❏ **CW – Dayton** Ballet. (937) 449-5060 or **www.daytonballet.org.**
- ❏ **NW – Toledo** Ballet. **www.toledoballet.net.** Stranahan Theater. (second weekend)
- ❏ **SW – Cincinnati** Ballet. **www.cincinnatiballet.com.** (513) 621-5219. The Nutcracker is performed each holiday season at Music Hall. Often limited backstage tours can be arranged.

FESTIVALS OF LIGHTS - All include hundreds of thousands of lights & holiday / storybook characters. Daily, evenings (unless noted). Admission. (Thanksgiving - January 1)

❑ **C – Columbus (Powell).** Wildlight Wonderland. Columbus Zoo. (614) 645-3550 or **www.columbuszoo.org.** Ice skating, carolers, delicious treats and wagon/train rides.

❑ **C - Delaware.** Alum Creek Holiday Fantasy of Lights. (740) 548-6056. Entrance is on Hollenback Road, at Alum Creek Marina. Drive thru. Free cookies and cocoa with Santa.

❑ **C – Marion.** Christmas by Candlelight. Marion County Fairgrounds. (740) 382-2558. Drive thru.

❑ **CE – Carrollton.** Holiday Lights. County Fairgrounds, SR 9. (877) 727-0103. (Thursday-Sunday)

❑ **CE – Gnadenhutten.** Christian Indian Christmas. Gnadenhutten Historical Park. (740) 254-4143. Drive through display depicting Christian Indians celebrating Christmas.

❑ **CW – Clifton.** Clifton Mill Legendary Light Display. (937) 767-5501. Miniature village, Santa' s workshop and 1802 log cabin. 3.2 million lights. Promptly lit at 6:00pm.

❑ **CW – Ludlow Falls.** The Lights at Ludlow Falls. SR 48. (937) 698-3318. (during Winter Break)

❑ **CW - Zanesfield.** A Country Christmas - Marmon Valley Farm. (937) 593-8000. Costumed characters, carolers, live animals in a presentation of the nativity story. Hayride wagons take guests to different scenes around the barns and fields. Hot chocolate, goodies, singing, Christmas crafts. By reservation. (First two weekends in December).

❑ **NC – Mansfield.** Christmas Wunderland. (419) 747-3717 or **www.richlandcountyfair.com.**

❑ **NE – Canfield** . Holiday of Lights. Canfield Fairgrounds. (330) 392-6527.

❑ **NE – Cleveland.** December Days, Cleveland Metroparks Zoo. Walk into the Welcome Plaza (Ice Carving or model railroad display), fun activities / entertainment, seasonal greenhouse, Pachyderm Bldg. w/ Santa, and ride the complimentary Sleighbell Express past the monkeys and polar bear with a stop at the Wolf

Cabin (can you spot the wolf in the woods?). Top the visit off with a warm hot chocolate and snack. Admission (ages 2+), FREE for zoo members. www.clemetzoo.com. (December, daytime).

❑ NE - Kirtland. Country Lights Lake Farmpark, www.lakemetroparks.com. Horse-drawn sleighbell rides through the light show; live entertainment; baby calves, chicks and pigs; miniature railroad displays; delightful holiday horse shows; and, best of all, the life-like Toy Workshop where elves help kids make an old-fashioned wooden toy to take home. Your kids hammer, drill and paint their own creations. Holiday food served at the Visitor's Center, too. By reservation only! $1.00 extra admission over normal prices.

❑ NE – Kirkland. Halle's Winter Wonderland. Penitentiary Glen Nature Center. (440) 256-1404 or www.lakemetroparks.com. exhibit featuring scenes from everyone's favorite childhood board game, Candy Land. Play with the family on a life-sized game board as you pass through Peppermint Stick Forest, cross over Gumdrop Pass, travel through Lollipop Woods and wind your way down the colorful trail to Home Sweet Home. Celebrate memories and re-live Cleveland shopping days in the Halle tradition and help keep alive the memory of Mr. Jingeling. Commemorative key. Ginger Bread Man craft (Suggested donation: $1). Refreshments. Be sure to visit the Kevin P. Clinton Wildlife Center. (afternoon vs. evening hours)

❑ NE – Youngstown. Festival of Lights. Yellow Duck Park. (330) 533-3773. Ohio's largest display.

❑ NW – Bluffton. Bluffton Blaze of Lights. (419) 358-5675 or www.blufftonohio.org. Wagon rides.

❑ NW – Toledo. Lights Before Christmas. Toledo Zoo. (419) 385-5721 or www.toledozoo.org. (begins second weekend of Nov.)

❑ SW – Cincinnati Zoo. (513) 281-4700 or Ice skating, decorated villages, and Santa. www.cincinnatizoo.org.

❑ SW - Hamilton. Holiday Lights on the Hill. Pyramid Hill Sculpture Park. (513) 868-8336.

❑ SW – Sharonville. Holiday in Lights. Sharon Woods, (513) 381-2397.

TRAIN RIDES WITH SANTA - Train trip in decorated coaches with Santa. Songs & treats. Dress warmly. Weekends only. Admission.

❑ **C – Hebron**. Buckeye Central Scenic Railroad. (740) 366-2029.

❑ **CE – Dennison** Depot. **www.dennisondepot.org** or (740) 922-6776. Polar Express

❑ **CE – Orrville** Railroad. (330) 683-2426 or Christmas in the Depot. **www.orrvillerailroad.com**. (last Nov. weekend only)

❑ **NE – Cleveland**. Lolly the Trolley. **www.lollytrolley.com**

❑ **NE – Jefferson**. AC & J RR. (440) 576-6346, **www.acjscenic.net**.

❑ **NE – Peninsula**. Cuyahoga Valley Scenic Railroad. (800) 468-4070 or **www.cvsr.com**. Christmas Tree Adventure (pick own tree) or Polar Express (ride in pajamas). (Some weekdays, too)

❑ **NW – Findlay**. Northwest Ohio Railroad. **www.nworrp.org**. (long weekends day after Thanksgiving through Christmas)

❑ **S - Nelsonville**. Hocking Valley Scenic Railroad. (800) HOCKING

❑ **SW – Lebanon and Riverfront**. Cincinnati Railway Company. Lebanon and Riverfront locations. (513) 933-8022.

C – LIVING CHRISTMAS TREE CONCERTS - Columbus (Worthington/Westerville), Grace Brethren Church, 8225 Worthington-Galena Road. (614) 431-8223. 150-voice choir fills the branches of two large trees as they sing along with a themed story and live animals. Admission. (December weekends)

CE – CHRISTMAS CANDLELIGHTINGS - Coshocton, Historic Roscoe Village, State Route 16/83. **www.roscoevillage.com**. (800) 877-1830 or Shop all day for holiday gifts in a 19th century holiday setting and then stay for the candlelighting ceremony each night at 6:00pm. Strolling carolers, visits with Santa, live arctic reindeer, chestnuts roasting over open fire, free hot-mulled cider & cookies, and carriage rides. Also see display of decorated trees and gingerbread houses on Main Street, downtown. Parking fee. (first three Saturdays in December)

CW – BETHLEHEM EXPERIENCE - Eaton, Preble County Fairgrounds, SR 122 south (Franklin St.). **www.bethlehemexperience.org**. (937) 456-5507 or Follow the Star to the Bethlehem Experience. You will enter the crowded streets of the small town of Bethlehem as it might have been the night Jesus Christ was born. Wander the streets of Bethlehem at your own pace; visit the shops and talk with the local craftsmen. They will direct you to the live nativity. FREE. Heated building. (first long weekend in December)

NE – UNDERLINE UNIVERSITY CIRCLEFEST - **Cleveland**, University Circle area. (216) 791-3900. FREE admission to University Circle museums plus holiday carolers and Santa. FREE. (first Sunday in December)

NW – CHILDREN'S WONDERLAND - **Maumee**, Lucas County Recreation Center, 2901 Key Street. (419) 213-2200. Children's Wonderland has received national recognition as the only display of its kind in the nation. The entire 22,000 square feet is turned into a fantasyland filled with animated displays, colorful lighting, and holiday music. Children can ride the North Pole train, visit with Talking Tree, and see over 40 holiday displays. Small Admission. (entire month of December)

SW – HOLIDAY JUNCTION - **Cincinnati**, Museum Center at Union Terminal, 1301 Western Avenue. www.cincymuseum.org. (513) 287-7000 or Annual celebration of model trains. Enjoy the four-level, multi-train layout highlighted by theatrical backgrounds. See vintage trains traveling through one-of-a-kind towns, through hills and mountains, and across bridges. Children will enjoy special activities designed just for them, including a journey by train through a winter wonderland and crafts in the Kids Corner. Museum Admission. (Thanksgiving weekend - New Years Day)

SW – CHRISTMAS FESTIVAL - **Lebanon**. (513) 932-1100. Holiday characters, musicians strolling the streets, a candlelit parade of sixty horse-drawn carriages, a train display and warm food. Free. (first Sunday of December)

SW – HOLIDAY FEST - **Mason**, The Beach Waterpark. (513) 398-7946. (800) 886-7946 or www.thebeachwaterpark.com. A festive holiday paradise featuring the largest outdoor ice skating rink under the stars, old fashion carriage rides, the area's largest outdoor miniature train display, and twinkling holiday lights. The little ones will have lots to see and do with the North Pole Petting Corral, Santa Stable pony rides, and the Candy Cane Maze. This holiday display is complete with a live Nativity and the chance to visit with Santa. Admission. (Thanksgiving weekend thru New Years Eve)

SW – CHRISTMAS IN THE VILLAGE - **Waynesville**. (513) 897-8855. www.waynesvilleohio.com. Carriage rides, Victorian street strollers, 1300 luminaries, carolers and a live nativity depict a traditional Dickens holiday. FREE. (Two long weekends in early December)

NEW YEARS EVE CELEBRATIONS

A family oriented non-alcoholic event with indoor and outdoor activities such as kid's/parent's food, entertainment and crafts, and a countdown to midnight. Admission.

- ❑ **C – Columbus**. First Night Columbus, Ohio Statehouse Square, downtown. (614) 481-0020. **www.firstnightcols.com**.
- ❑ **NC – Port Clinton**. Walleye Madness at Midnight, downtown. (800) 441-1271.
- ❑ **NE - Akron**. First Night, downtown. (330) 762-8555
- ❑ **NE – Youngstown**. First Night. (330) 742-0445

Master Index

7 Caves Nature Preserve, 171
A.W. Marion State Park, 4
AC & J Scenic Railroad, 143
Adena State Memorial, 174
African Safari Wildlife
    Park, 104
Akron Aeros, 122
Akron Art Museum, 122
Akron Civic Theatre, 122
Akron Symphony Orchestra,
    122
Akron Zoo, 121
All American Quarter Horse
    Congress, 235
All American Soap Box
    Derby, 225
Allen County Museum, 161
Alpine Hills Museum, 56
Al's Delicious Popcorn, 12
Alum Creek State Park, 18
American Whistle
    Corporation, 17
Amish Door Dinner Theatre, 57
Annie Oakley Days, 227
Anthony Thomas Candy
    Company, 13
Apple Festivals, 231
Aquatic Visitors Center, 107
Armstrong Air And Space
    Museum, 82
Ashland Balloonfest, 225
Ashtabula County Covered
    Bridge Festival, 236
Ashtabula County Fair, 227
Ashtabula Marine Museum, 125
Asian Festival, 220
Atwood Lake Resort, 61
Auglaize Village Farm
    Museum, 158
Aullwood Audubon Center
    And Farm, 70
Balletmet, 8
Banana Split Festival, 223
Barkcamp State Park, 31

Barn, The, 188
Barnesville Pumpkin
    Festival, 229
BB Riverboats, 204
Beach, (The), 210
Bear's Mill, 75
Beaver Creek State Park, 46
Behalt, 32
Bethlehem Experience, 242
Biblewalk, 95
Bicycle Museum Of
    America, 78
Black History Month, 218
Black Swamp Steam & Gas
    Show, 223
Blue Jacket, 85
Blue Rock State Forest, 34
Blue Rock State Park, 59
Bluebird Farm Toy Museum
    And Restaurant, 41
Bluebird Passenger Train, 162
Bob Evan's Farm, 187
Bookmasters, 97
Boonshoft Museum Of
    Discovery, 71
Boyd's Crystal Art Glass
    Company, 35
Broad Run Cheesehouse, 44
Brukner Nature Center, 81
Brush Creek State Forest, 190
Buck Creek State Park, 79
Buckeye Central Scenic
    Railroad, 21
Buckeye Flint Festival, 229
Buckeye Furnace Museum, 188
Buckeye Lake State Park, 24
Bucyrus Bratwurst Festival, 227
Buggy Haus, 57
Burr Oak State Park, 178
Butler Institute Of American
    Art, 152
Butterfly House, 107
Buzzard Day, 218
Caesar Creek State Park, 215

Campus Martius: Museum Of
    Northwest Territory, 181
Canal Experience, 160
Canal Festival, 227
Canfield Fair, 230
Canton Classic Car Museum, 37
Canton Symphony Orchestra, 37
Carew Tower, 195
Carousel Magic! Factory &
    Richland Carousel Park, 93
Carriage Hill Farm And
    Museum, 74
Castaway Bay, 112
Castle, (The), 182
Catawba Island State Park, 106
Cedar Bog And Nature
    Preserve, 81
Cedar Point & Soak City, 112
Celeryville, Buurma Vegetable
    Farms, 117
Central Ohio Fire Museum &
    Learning Center, 9
Century Village Museum &
    Country Store, 129
Children's Museum Of
    Cleveland, 131
Children's Wonderland, 243
Chocolate Café & Museum, 108
Christmas Candlelightings, 242
Christmas Decorations / Open
    Houses, 238
Christmas Festival, 243
Christmas In The Village, 243
Cincinnati Art Museum, 195
Cincinnati Bengals, 195
Cincinnati Fire Museum, 196
Cincinnati History Museum, 198
Cincinnati Museum Of Natural
    History And Science, 199
Cincinnati Nature Center, 212
Cincinnati Railway
    Company, 205
Cincinnati Reds, 195
Cincinnati Sports, 195

Cincinnati Symphony
    Orchestra, 201
Cincinnati Zoo & Botanical
    Gardens, 202
Cinergy Children's
    Museum, 200
Citizens Motorcar Packard
    Museum, 67
Cityfolk Festival, 224
Civil War Days, 221
Civil War Re-Enactment, 224
Clark State Performing Arts
    Center, 79
Cleveland Botanical
    Garden, 132
Cleveland Browns, 131
Cleveland Cavaliers, 131
Cleveland Center For
    Contemporary Art, 132
Cleveland Christmas
    Connection, 237
Cleveland Indians, 131
Cleveland Lakefront State
    Park, 135
Cleveland Metroparks Zoo &
    Rainforest, 135
Cleveland Museum Of Art, 132
Cleveland Museum Of Natural
    History, 133
Cleveland National Air
    Show, 230
Cleveland Orchestra, 134
Cleveland Playhouse, 134
Cleveland Sports, 131
Clifton Mill, 65
Coblentz Chocolate
    Company, 56
Columbus Blue Jackets
    Hockey, 4
Columbus Children's Theatre, 6
Columbus Clippers Baseball, 4
Columbus Crew Soccer, 4
Columbus International
    Festival, 237

Columbus Motor Speedway, 7
Columbus Museum Of Art, 9
Columbus Sports, 4
Columbus Symphony
   Orchestra, 9
Columbus Zoo & Aquarium, 15
Coney Island, 203
Cooper's Mill Apple Butter &
   Jelly Factory, 92
COSI, 10
COSI Toledo, 164
Covedale Center For The
   Performing Arts, 203
Covered Bridge Pizza, 154
Cowan Lake State Park, 216
Cox Arboretum, 73
Cranberry Bog Annual Open
   House, 221
Crane Creek State Park &
   Magee Marsh Wildlife
   Area, 104
Creegan Company Animation
   Factory, 54
Crystal Cave & Heineman's
   Grape Juice Winery, 108
Cuyahoga Valley National
   Park, 128
Cuyahoga Valley Scenic
   Railroad,149
Davis Discovery Center, 10
Dawes Arboretum, 26
Day Out With Thomas The
   Tank Engine, 220
Dayton Air Show, 225
Dayton Art Institute, 69
Dayton Bombers Hockey, 66
Dayton Dragons Baseball, 66
Dayton History At Carillon
   Park, 69
Dayton Philharmonic
   Orchestra, 68
Dayton Sports, 66
Dean State Forest, 185
Deer Creek State Park, 25

Delaware State Park 18
Dennison Railroad Depot
   Museum & Canteen, 44
Dickson Longhorn Cattle
   Company, 31
Dietsch Brothers, 159
Dillon State Park, 60
Dover Lake Waterpark, 150
Dude Ranch, (The), 212
Dunbar State Memorial, Paul
   Lawrence, 67
East Fork State Park, 195
East Harbor State Park, 99
Eastern Woodlands
   Gathering, 225
Edison Birthplace Museum, 102
Elm Farm - Americas Ice
   Cream & Dairy Museum &
   Parlor, 146
Elson Flouring Mill, 50
Erieview Park, 142
Fairport Harbor Marine
   Museum, 142
Family Funfest, 228
Farm Festival, 237
Feast Of The Flowering
   Moon, 220
Fernwood State Forest, 55
Festival Latino, 221
Festival Of Fish, 222
Festivals Of Lights, 240
Findley State Park, 116
Flint Ridge State Memorial
   Museum, 20
Forest Heritage Festival, 236
Forked Run State Park, 187
Fort Ancient State
   Memorial, 213
Fort Hill State Memorial, 208
Fort Laurens State Memorial
   And Museum, 34
Fort Meigs, 162
Fort Recovery State
   Memorial, 75

Fort Steuben Festival, 221
Fox Creek Outdoor
  Experience, 235
Franklin County Fair, 224
Franklin Park Conservatory
  And Botanical Gardens, 7
Freshwater Farms Of Ohio, 82
Frisch's Commissary, 200
Garst Museum, Darke County
  Historical Society, 76
Geauga County Maple
  Festival, 220
Geauga Lake & Wildwater
  Kingdom, 126
Geneva State Park, 142
Georgian / Sherman House
  Museum, 21
Glamorgan Castle, 31
Glass & Heritage Festival, 226
Glass Axis, 14
Glass Refactory, 207
Gnadenhutten Museum And
  Park, 48
Good Time III, 137
Goodtime I, 113
Goodyear World Of Rubber, 124
Gorant Candies, 153
Governor Bebb Preserve, 213
Graeter's Ice Cream Factory, 12
Grand Lake St. Mary's State
  Park, 80
Grand Prix Of Cleveland, 222
Grandma's Alpine Homestead
  Restaurant & Clock Shop, 56
Grant Birthplace Museum, 215
Grant Boyhood Home &
  Schoolhouse, 208
Grape Jamboree, 230
Great Circle Earthworks, 26
Great Lakes Medieval Faire, 226
Great Lakes Popcorn
  Company, 104
Great Lakes Science Center, 137

Great Lakes Wooden Sailboat
  Regatta, 227
Great Mohican Indian Pow-
  Wow, 225
Great Seal State Park, 175
Great Wolf Lodge Indoor
  Waterpark, 113
Greek Festival, 228
Greene County Historical
  Society Museum, 86
Guggisberg Cheese Factory, 50
Guilford Lake State Park, 49
Hale Farm And Village, 127
Hanby House, 16
Harding Memorial & Home, 22
Harriet Beecher Stowe
  House, 201
Harrison Lake State Park, 159
Harrison State Forest, 35
Harry London Chocolate
  Factory, 40
Hartzler Family Dairy, 57
Harvest Fest, 230
Harvest Festival, 233
Hayes Presidential Center, 92
Headlands Beach State
  Park, 149
Heritage Village Museum, 206
Historical Weekend, 229
Hocking Fall Color Tour, 236
Hocking Hills State Park, 180
Hocking State Forest, 188
Hocking Valley Scenic
  Railway, 185
Holden Arboretum, 144
Holiday Fest, 243
Holiday Junction, 243
Homewood Suites By
  Hilton, 216
Hoover Historical Center, 39
Hopewell Culture National
  Historical Park, 175
Hot Air Balloon Festival, 221

Hubbard House And
    Underground Railroad
    Museum, 125
Hueston Woods State Park, 214
Ice Cream Festival, 220
Ice Festival, 218
Independence Dam State
    Park, 158
Indian Festival, 227
Indian Lake State Park, 77
Indian Mill, 116
Inland Seas Maritime Museum
    & Lighthouse, 116
International Festival, 222
Irish Festivals, 225, 226
Italian American Festival, 224
I-X Center Indoor Amusement
    Park, 220
Jackson Lake State Park, 185
Jefferson Depot, 143
Jefferson Lake State Park, 54
Jet Express, 105
John & Annie Glenn Historic Site
    & Exploration Center, 51
John Bryan State Park, 86
Johnny Appleseed Festival, 236
Johnny Appleseed Heritage
    Center, 97
July 4th Celebrations, 223
Jungle Jim's Int'l Farmers
    Market, 205
Jurassic Journey, 20
Kalahari Resort & Indoor
    Waterpark, 114
Keeping The Traditions Native
    American Powwow, 222
Kelleys Island Ferry Boat
    Lines, 100
Kelley's Island State Park, 106
Kent State University
    Museum, 144
Kids Fest, 222
Kidsfest, 225
Kingwood Center, 96

Kiser Lake State Park, 80
Kitchenaid Experience &
    Factory Tours, 76
Knox County Fair, 224
Knox County Historical
    Society Museum, 24
Krohn Conservatory, 196
Lagoon Deer Park, 115
LaGrange Street Polish
    Festival, 226
Lake Alma State Park, 189
Lake Erie Islands Museum, 109
Lake Erie Islands Regional
    Welcome Center, 105
Lake Erie Islands State
    Park, 106
Lake Farmpark, 145
Lake Hope State Park, 184
Lake Logan State Park, 181
Lake Loramie State Park, 77
Lake Milton State Park, 145
Lake White State Park, 188
Lakeside, 101
Landoll's Mohican Castle, 118
Latinofest, 223
Lawnfield - Garfield National
    Historic Site, James A., 146
Learning Tree Farm, 72
Lee Middleton Original Doll
    Factory, 173
Lithopolis Fine Arts/Wagnalls
    Memorial Library, 22
Little Brown Jug & All Horse
    Parade, 228
Little Miami State Park, 207
Living Christmas Tree
    Concerts, 242
Living Word Passion Play, 35
Lockington Locks State
    Memorial, 77
Lolly The Trolley Tours, 136
Longaberger Museum &
    Factory Tour, 47

Lorain County Fair & Scenic Railway, 227
Lorena Sternwheeler, 59
Loveland Castle, 210
Lucy Hayes Heritage Center, 176
Lyme Village, 91
Mac-O-Chee And Mac-A-Cheek Castles (Piatt Castles), 83
Mad River & NKP Railroad Society Museum, 91
Mad River Theater Works, 83
Madison Lake State Park, 22
Magic Waters Amphitheatre, 172
Magical Farms, 146
Malabar Farm State Park, 98
Malley's Chocolates, 140
Mansfield Symphony Orchestra, 94
Mapleside Farms, 129
Mapleside Farms Restaurant, 154
Mapletree Baskets, 59
Maps Air Museum, 40
Marblehead Lighthouse State Park, 100
Marietta Soda Museum, 182
Marietta Trolley Tours, 182
Marion County Fair, 224
Marmon Valley Farm, 87
Martin Luther King Program, 218
Mary Jane Thurston State Park, 161
Maumee Bay State Park, 166
Maumee State Forest, 163
Mazza Collection Museum, 159
McCook House, 41
McGuffey Museum, 214
McKinley Birthplace Memorial And Museum, 148

McKinley Museum & Discover World, 38
Melon Festival, 229
Memphis Kiddie, Park 141
Merry-Go-Round Museum, 115
Metroducks & Riverscape, 68
Miamisburg Mound, 74
Mid Ohio Sports Car Course, 97
Middfest International, 237
Middlefield Cheese House, 147
Mid-Ohio Historical Doll & Toy Museum, 3
Milan Historical Museum, 102
Mill Creek Park, 151
Miller Boat Line, 92
Mitchellace Shoestring Factory, 186
Mohican State Park Resort, 98
Mohican-Memorial State Forest, 99
Monsoon Lagoon, 107
Mosquito Lake State Park, 141
Mosser Glass, 36
Most Magnificent McDonald's In America, 154
Motorcycle Heritage Museum, 14
Motts Military Museum, 14
Mount Gilead State Park, 24
Museum Of Ceramics, 46
Museum Of Postal History, 158
Muskingum River Parkway State Park, 59
Muskingum Watershed Conservancy District Lakes, 52
Mysterious Revolving Ball, 23
NASA Glenn Research Visitor Center, 140
National Afro-American Museum And Cultural Center, 84
National Inventors Hall Of Fame, 123

National Museum Of The Us
   Air Force, 73
National Packard Museum, 153
National Road Zane Grey
   Museum, 54
National Underground Railroad
   Freedom Center, 197
Nautica Queen, 138
New Years Eve
   Celebrations, 244
Noah's Ark Animal Farm, 179
Noah's Lost Ark Animal
   Sanctuary, 130
Northwest Ohio Railroad
   Preservation Live Steam
   Train Rides, 160
Nutcracker Ballet, 239
Oberlin Heritage Tour, 103
Ohio Agricultural Research &
   Development Center, 58
Ohio Bird Sanctuary, 94
Ohio Caverns, 84
Ohio Fish & Shrimp Festival, 229
Ohio Historical Center, 7
Ohio Irish Festival, 222
Ohio Railway Museum, 17
Ohio Renaissance Festival, 228
Ohio River Museum, 183
Ohio River Sternwheel
   Festival, 230
Ohio Sauerkraut Festival, 237
Ohio State Fair, 226
Ohio State Reformatory, 96
Ohio State University
   Buckeyes, 4
Ohio State University
   Museums, 4
Ohio Statehouse, 6
Ohio Swiss Festival, 229
Ohio's Agricultural Fairs, 226
Oktoberfest, 235
Oktoberfest-Zinzinnati, 231
Olde Canal Days, 226
Olentangy Indian Caverns, 19

Orange Johnson House, 17
Orrville Depot Days, 221
Our House Museum, 178
Paint Creek State Park, 172
Paramount's Kings Island, 211
Parky's Farm, 204
Paul Bunyan Show, 237
Perkins Observatory, 19
Perry State Forest, 25
Perry's Cave & Family Fun
   Center, 109
Perry's Victory And
   International Peace
   Memorial, 110
Pike Lake State Park, 172
Pike State Forest, 179
Pioneer / Peddler Festivals, 232
Pioneer Days, 227
Pioneer Waterland And Dry
   Park, 130
Piqua Historical Area Tour, 78
Players Guild Theatre, 38
Popcorn Festival, 228, 229
Portage Lakes State Park, 124
Portsmouth Murals, 187
Prairie Peddler, 222
Prehistoric Forest & Mystery
   Hill, 100
Presidents Day At The Garfield
   National Historic Site, 218
Pro Football Hall Of Fame, 39
Professional Football Hall Of
   Fame Festival, 227
Pump House Center For The
   Arts, 176
Pumpkin Patches/Hayrides/Corn
   Mazes/ Fall Playlands, 233
Pumpkin Show, 235
Pumpkin Train, 236
Punderson Manor House
   Resort, 154
Punderson State Park
   Resort, 148
Put-In-Bay Tour Train, 110

Pymatuning State Park, 125
Pyramid Hill Sculpture
    Park, 208
Quail Hollow State Park, 49
Railroad Festival, 220
Rankin House State
    Memorial, 215
Raspberry Festival, 229
Richland Academy, 94
River Days, 230
Riverfest, 230
Rock And Roll Hall Of Fame
    Museum, 138
Rocky Fork State Park, 209
Rolling Ridge Ranch, 50
Roscoe Village, 42
Ross County Historical Society
    Museums, 176
Rossi Pasta, 183
Salt Fork State Park Resort, 36
Sandpiper Canal Boat, 165
Santa Maria, 11
Sauder Village, 157
Scarecrow Festival, 231
Schrock's Amish Farm And
    Home, 32
Scioto Trail State Park, 177
Seneca Caverns, 91
Serpent Mound State
    Memorial, 186
Shawnee State Forest, 190
Shawnee State Park, 190
Shoenbrunn Village State
    Memorial, 52
Shrum Mound, 13
Slate Run Historical Farm, 3
Sled Dog Classic, 218
Smoke Rise Ranch Resort, 184
Snooks Dream Cars
    Museum, 157
Splash Down, 179
Spruce Hill Inn & Cottages, 117
SS Willis B Boyer Maritime
    Museum, 164

St Helena III, 37
St. Mary's Fish Farm, 80
St. Patrick's Day Parades &
    Celebrations, 219
Stan Hywet Hall, 121
Steubenville City Of Murals, 55
Stone Laboratory, 111
Stonelick State Park, 207
Strawberry Festival, 222
Stroud's Run State Park, 171
Suggested Lodging And Dining
    61,117, 154,167,191,216,
Sumburger Restaurant, 191
Summit County Historical
    Society/John Brown
    Home/Perkins Stone
    Mansion, 124
Sunwatch, 72
Sycamore State Park, 80
Taft Museum Of Art, 198
Taft National Historic Site,
    William Howard, 202
Tar Hollow State Forest, 174
Tar Hollow State Park, 180
Tecumseh!, 177
Telephone Museum, James M.
    Thomas, 178
Thanksgiving Weekend
    Parades, 237
Thunder In The Hills
    Hydroplane Race, 231
Thurber House, 11
Tiffin-Seneca Heritage
    Festival, 230
Tinker's Creek State Park, 150
Toledo Botanical Gardens, 166
Toledo Firefighters
    Museum, 166
Toledo Mud Hens Baseball, 163
Toledo Museum Of Art, 166
Toledo Sports, 163
Toledo Storm Hockey, 163
Toledo Symphony
    Orchestra, 164

Toledo Zoo, 165
Tomato Festival, 229
Tony Packo's Café, 167
Topiary Garden, 12
Tower City Center Observation
    Deck, 137
Tracks To The Past, 230
Train - O – Rama, 101
Train Rides With Santa, 242
Trains, Planes & Automobiles
    Fest, 222
Tri-State Pottery Festival, 221
Trumpet In The Land, 53
Tuscarawas County Italian-
    American Festival, 227
Tuscora Park, 53
Twins Days Festival, 228
U.S.S. Cod, 139
United Dairy Farmers, 201
University Circlefest, 243
Valley Gem Sternwheeler, 184
Van Buren Lake State Park, 167
Veggie U Education Center, 103
Velvet Ice Cream: Ye Olde Mill
    Ice Cream Museum, 27
Victorian Perambulator
    Museum, 144
Wagon Trails Animal Park, 153
Wahkeena Nature Preserve, 21
Warren County Hist'l Society
    Museum & Area, 209
Warther Carvings Tour, 45
Washboard Music & Arts
    Festival, 223
Wayne County Historical
    Society Museum, 58
Weathervane Playhouse, 123
Wendall August Forged Gift
    Tour, 33
West Branch State Park, 150
Western Reserve History
    Museum, 134
Westwoods Park, 148
Wilds, (The), 43

William G. Mather Museum, 139
Wolcott House Museum
    Complex, 163
Woollybear Festival, 236
Works, (The) - Ohio Center
    Of History, Art &
    Technology, 26
World's Largest Gourd
    Show, 235
Wright B. Flyer, 75
Wright Cycle Company, 69
Wyandot Lake Adventure
    Park, 16
Wyandot Popcorn Museum, 23
Yellow Duck Park, 130
Yoder's Amish Home, 51
Young's Jersey Dairy Farm, 86
Youngstown Historical Center
    Of Industry & Labor, 152
Youngstown Symphony, 152
Zaleski State Forest, 191
Zane Shawnee Caverns, 65
Zoar Village, 60
Zucchini Festival, 226

Activity Index

PROUDLY

MADE IN THE USA

AMUSEMENTS

C - Columbus (Powell), *Wyandot Lake Adventure Park*, 16
C - Heath, *Jurassic Journey*, 20
CE - New Philadelphia, *Tuscora Park*, 53
CE - Wilmot, *Grandma's Alpine Homestead Restaurant And Clock Shop*, 56
NC - Marblehead, *Prehistoric Forest & Mystery Hill*, 100
NC - Port Clinton, *Monsoon Lagoon*, 107
NC - Sandusky, *Castaway Bay*, 112
NC - Sandusky, *Cedar Point & Soak City*, 112
NC - Sandusky, *Great Wolf Lodge Indoor Waterpark*, 113
NC - Sandusky, *Kalahari Resort And Indoor Waterpark*, 114
NE - Aurora, *Geauga Lake & Wildwater Kingdom*, 126
NE - Canfield, *Yellow Duck Park*, 130
NE - Chardon, *Pioneer Waterland And Dry Park*, 130
NE - Cleveland, *Memphis Kiddie Park*, 141
NE - Geneva-on-the-Lake, *Erieview Park*, 142
NE - Peninsula (Sagamore Hills), *Dover Lake Waterpark*, 150
NE - Youngstown (Warren), *Most Magnificent McDonald's In America*, 154
S - Jackson, *Splash Down*, 179
SW - Cincinnati, *Coney Island*, 203
SW - Cincinnati (Fairfield), *Jungle Jim's International Farmers Market*, 205
SW - Mason, *Beach, The*, 210
SW - Mason (Kings Mills), *Paramount's Kings Island*, 211

ANIMALS & FARMS

C - Columbus (Powell), *Columbus Zoo And Aquarium*, 15
CE - Barnesville, *Dickson Longhorn Cattle Company*, 31
CE - Cumberland, *Wilds, The*, 43

CE - Millersburg, *Rolling Ridge Ranch*, 50
CW - Dayton, *Learning Tree Farm*, 72
CW - Yellow Springs, *Young's Jersey Dairy Farm*, 86
CW - Zanesfield, *Marmon Valley Farm*, 87
NC - Mansfield, *Ohio Bird Sanctuary*, 94
NC - Port Clinton, *African Safari Wildlife Park*, 104
NC - Sandusky, *Lagoon Deer Park*, 115
NC - Willard, *Celeryville, Buurma Vegetable Farms*, 117
NE - Akron, *Akron Zoo*, 121
NE - Brunswick, *Mapleside Farms*, 129
NE - Canfield (Berlin Center), *Noah's Lost Ark Animal Sanctuary*, 179
NE - Cleveland, *Cleveland Metroparks Zoo & Rainforest*, 135
NE - Kirtland, *Lake Farmpark*, 145
NE - Media (Litchfield), *Magical Farms*, 146
NE - Youngstown (Vienna), *Wagon Trails Animal Park*,
NW - Toledo, *Toledo Zoo*, 165
S - Jackson, *Noah's Ark Animal Farm*, 179
S - Murray City, *Smoke Rise Ranch Resort*, 184
S - Rio Grande, *Bob Evan's Farm*, 187
SW - Cincinnati, *Cincinnati Zoo And Botanical Gardens*, 202
SW - Cincinnati, *Parky's Farm*, 204

HISTORY

C - Ashville, *Slate Run Historical Farm*, 3
C - Columbus, *Ohio Statehouse*, 6
C - Columbus, *Ohio Historical Center*, 7
C - Columbus, *Santa Maria*, 11
C - Columbus, *Shrum Mound*, 13
C - Columbus (Westerville), *Hanby House*, 16

HISTORY (cont.)

C - Columbus (Worthington), *Orange Johnson House*, 17
C - Delaware, *Olentangy Indian Caverns*, 19
C - Glenford, *Flint Ridge State Memorial Museum*, 20
C - Lancaster, *Georgian / Sherman House Museum*, 21
C - Marion, *Harding Memorial And Home*, 22
C - Mount Vernon, *Knox County Historical Society Museum*, 24
C - Newark, *Great Circle Earthworks*, 26
CE - Bolivar, *Fort Laurens State Memorial And Museum*, 34
CE - Canal Fulton, *St Helena III*, 37
CE - Carrollton, *McCook House*, 41
CE - Coshocton, *Roscoe Village*, 42
CE - Dennison, *Dennison Railroad Depot Museum & Canteen*, 44
CE - East Liverpool, *Museum Of Ceramics*, 46
CE - Gnadenhutten, *Gnadenhutten Museum And Park*, 48
CE - New Concord, *John & Annie Glenn Historic Site & Exploration Center*, 51
CE - New Philadelphia, *Shoenbrunn Village State Memorial*, 52
CE - New Philadelphia, *Trumpet In The Land*, 53
CE - Norwich, *National Road Zane Grey Museum*, 54
CE - Sugarcreek, *Alpine Hills Museum*, 56
CE - Wooster, *Wayne County Historical Society Museum*, 58
CE - Zoar, *Zoar Village*, 60
CW- Bellefontaine, *Zane Shawnee Caverns*, 65
CW- Clifton, *Clifton Mill*, 65
CW- Dayton, *Dunbar State Memorial, Paul Lawrence*, 67
CW- Dayton, *Wright Cycle Company*, 69
CW- Dayton, *Dayton History At Carillon Park*, 69

CW- Dayton, *Sunwatch*, 72
CW- Dayton (Huber Heights), *Carriage Hill Farm And Museum*, 74
CW- Dayton (Miamisburg), *Miamisburg Mound*, 74
CW- Fort Recovery, *Fort Recovery State Memorial*, 75
CW- Greenville, *Garst Museum, Darke County Historical Society*, 76
CW- Lockington, *Lockington Locks State Memorial*, 77
CW- Piqua, *Piqua Historical Area Tour*, 78
CW- West Liberty, *Ohio Caverns*, 84
CW- Wilberforce, *National Afro-American Museum And Cultural Center*, 84
CW- Xenia, *Blue Jacket*, 85
CW- Xenia, *Greene County Historical Society Museum*, 86
NC - Bellevue, *Lyme Village*, 91
NC - Fremont, *Hayes Presidential Center*, 92
NC - Mansfield (Ashland), *Johnny Appleseed Heritage Center*, 97
NC - Mansfield (Lucas), *Malabar Farm State Park*, 98
NC - Marblehead, *Marblehead Lighthouse State Park*, 100
NC - Milan, *Edison Birthplace Museum*, 102
NC - Milan, *Milan Historical Museum*, 102
NC - Oberlin, *Oberlin Heritage Tour*, 103
NC - Put-in-Bay, *Lake Erie Islands Museum*, 109
NC - Put-In-Bay, *Perry's Victory And International Peace Memorial*, 110
NC - Upper Sandusky, *Indian Mill*, 116
NC - Vermillion, *Inland Seas Maritime Museum & Lighthouse*, 116
NE - Akron, *Summit County Historical Society/John Brown Home /Perkins Stone Mansion*, 124
NE - Ashtabula, *Hubbard House And Underground Railroad Museum*, 125

HISTORY (cont.)

NE - Bath, *Hale Farm & Village*, 127
NE - Burton, *Century Village Museum And Country Store*, 129
NE - Cleveland, *Western Reserve History Museum*, 134
NE - Fairport Harbor, *Fairport Harbor Marine Museum*, 142
NE - Jefferson, *Jefferson Depot*, 143
NE - Mentor, *Lawnfield-Garfield National Historic Site, James A.*, 146
NE - Niles, *McKinley Birthplace Memorial And Museum*, 148
NW- Archbold, *Sauder Village*, 157
NW- Defiance, *Auglaize Village Farm Museum*, 158
NW- Lima, *Allen County Museum*, 161
NW- Perrysburg, *Fort Meigs*, 162
NW- Toledo, *Wolcott House Museum Complex*, 163
S - Chillicothe, *Adena State Memorial*, 174
S - Chillicothe, *Hopewell Culture National Historical Park*, 175
S - Chillicothe, *Lucy Hayes Heritage Center*, 176
S - Chillicothe, *Ross County Historical Society Museums*, 176
S - Chillicothe, *Tecumseh*, 177
S - Gallipolis, *Our House Museum*, 178
S - Marietta, *Campus Martius: Museum of Northwest Territory*, 181
S - Marietta, *Castle, The*, 182
S - Peebles, *Serpent Mound State Memorial*, 186
S - Wellston, *Buckeye Furnace Museum*, 188
SW- Cincinnati, *National Underground Railroad Freedom Center*, 197
SW- Cincinnati, *Cincinnati History Museum*, 198
SW- Cincinnati, *Harriet Beecher Stowe House*, 201
SW- Cincinnati, *Taft National Historic Site, William Howard*, 202
SW- Cincinnati (Sharonville), *Heritage Village Museum*, 206

SW- Georgetown, *Grant Boyhood Home & Schoolhouse*, 208
SW- Hillsboro, *Fort Hill State Memorial*, 208
SW- Lebanon, *Warren County Historical Society Museum & Area*, 209
SW- Okeana, *Governor Bebb Preserve*, 213
SW- Oregonia, *Fort Ancient State Memorial*, 213
SW- Point Pleasant, *Grant Birthplace Museum*, 215
SW- Ripley, *Rankin House State Memorial*, 215

MUSEUMS

C - Canal Winchester, *Mid-Ohio Historical Doll And Toy Museum*, 3
C - Columbus, *Central Ohio Fire Museum & Learning Center*, 9
C - Columbus, *Thurber House*, 11
C - Columbus (Groveport), *Motts Military Museum*, 14
C - Columbus (Pickerington), *Motorcycle Heritage Museum*, 14
C - Columbus (Worthington), *Ohio Railway Museum*, 17
C - Marion, *Wyandot Popcorn Museum*, 23
C - Newark, *Works, The - Ohio Center Of History, Art & Technology*, 26
C - Utica, *Velvet Ice Cream: Ye Olde Mill Ice Cream Museum*, 27
CE - Canton, *Canton Classic Car Museum*, 37
CE - Canton, *McKinley Museum & Discover World*, 38
CE - Canton, *Pro Football Hall Of Fame*, 39
CE - Canton, *Hoover Historical Center*, 39
CE - Canton, North, *Maps Air Museum*, 40
CE - Carrollton, *Bluebird Farm Toy Museum And Restaurant*, 41

MUSEUMS (cont.)

CW- Dayton, *Citizens Motorcar Packard Museum*, 67
CW- Dayton, *Boonshoft Museum Of Discovery*, 71
CW- Dayton (Fairborn), *National Museum of the US Air Force*, 73
CW- Dayton (Miamisburg), *Wright B. Flyer*, 75
CW- New Bremen, *Bicycle Museum Of America*, 78
NC - Bellevue, *Mad River & NKP Railroad Society Museum*, 91
NC - Mansfield, *Biblewalk*, 95
NC - Marblehead, *Train-O-Rama*, 101
NC - Port Clinton, *Lake Erie Islands Regional Welcome Center*, 105
NC - Put-in-Bay, *Chocolate Café & Museum*, 108
NC - Sandusky, *Merry-Go-Round Museum*, 115
NE - Akron, *Stan Hywet Hall*, 121
NE - Ashtabula, *Ashtabula Marine Museum*, 125
NE - Cleveland, *Children's Museum Of Cleveland*, 131
NE - Cleveland, *Rock And Roll Hall Of Fame Museum*, 138
NE - Cleveland, *U.S.S. Cod*, 139
NE - Cleveland, *William G. Mather Museum*, 139
NE - Jefferson, *Victorian Perambulator Museum*, 144
NE - Medina, *Elm Farm - Americas Ice Cream & Dairy Museum & Parlor*, 146
NE - Youngstown, *Youngstown Historical Center Of Industry & Labor*, 152
NE - Youngstown (Warren), *National Packard Museum*, 153
NW- Bowling Green, *Snooks Dream Cars Museum*, 157
NW- Delphos, *Museum Of Postal History*, 158
NW- Toledo, *SS Willis B Boyer Maritime Museum*, 164
NW- Toledo, *Toledo Firefighters Museum*, 166

S - Chillicothe, *Telephone Museum, James M. Thomas*, 178
S - Marietta, *Marietta Soda Museum*, 182
S - Marietta, *Ohio River Museum*, 183
SW- Cincinnati, *Cincinnati Fire Museum*, 196
SW- Cincinnati, *Cinergy Children's Museum*, 200
SW- Oxford, *McGuffey Museum*, 214

OUTDOOR EXPLORING

C - Circleville, *A.W. Marion State Park*, 4
C - Columbus, *Topiary Garden*, 12
C - Delaware, *Alum Creek State Park*, 18
C - Delaware, *Delaware State Park*, 18
C - Lancaster, *Wahkeena Nature Preserve*, 21
C - London, *Madison Lake State Park*, 22
C - Marion, *Mysterious Revolving Ball*, 23
C - Millersport, *Buckeye Lake State Park*, 24
C - Mt. Gilead, *Mount Gilead State Park*, 24
C - Mt. Sterling, *Deer Creek State Park*, 25
C - New Lexington, *Perry State Forest*, 25
C - Newark, *Dawes Arboretum*, 26
CE - Belmont, *Barkcamp State Park*, 31
CE - Blue Rock, *Blue Rock State Forest*, 59
CE - Cadiz, *Harrison State Forest*, 35
CE - Cambridge, *Salt Fork State Park Resort*, 36
CE - East Liverpool, *Beaver Creek State Park*, 46
CE - Hartville, *Quail Hollow State Park*, 49
CE - Lisbon, *Guilford Lake State Park*, 49
CE - New Philadelphia, *Muskingum Watershed Conservancy District Lakes*, 52

OUTDOOR EXPLORING (cont.)

CE - Steubenville, *Jefferson Lake State Park*, 54

CE - Steubenville, *Fernwood State Forest*, 55

CE - Zanesville (Blue Rock), *Blue Rock State Park*, 59

CE - Zanesville (Blue Rock), *Muskingum River Parkway State Park*, 59

CE - Zanesville (Nashport), *Dillon State Park*, 60

CW- Dayton, *Aullwood Audubon Center And Farm*, 70

CW- Dayton, *Cox Arboretum*, 73

CW- Lakeview, *Indian Lake State Park*, 77

CW- Minster, *Lake Loramie State Park*, 77

CW- Springfield, *Buck Creek State Park*, 79

CW- St. Mary's, *Grand Lake St. Mary's State Park*, 80

CW- St. Paris, *Kiser Lake State Park*, 80

CW- Trotwood, *Sycamore State Park*, 80

CW- Troy, *Brukner Nature Center*, 81

CW- Urbana, *Cedar Bog And Nature Preserve*,

CW- Yellow Springs, *John Bryan State Park*, 86

NC - Mansfield, *Kingwood Center*, 96

NC - Mansfield (Loudonville), *Mohican State Park Resort*, 98

NC - Mansfield (Perrysville), *Mohican-Memorial State Forest*, 99

NC - Marblehead, *East Harbor State Park*, 99

NC - Port Clinton, *Crane Creek State Park & Magee Marsh Wildlife Area*, 104

NC - Put-in-Bay, *Perry's Cave & Family Fun Center*, 109

NC - Wellington, *Findley State Park*, 116

NE - Akron, *Portage Lakes State Park*, 124

NE - Ashtabula (Andover), *Pymatuning State Park*, 125

NE - Brecksville, *Cuyahoga Valley National Park*, 128

NE - Cleveland, *Cleveland Botanical Garden*, 132

NE - Cleveland, *Cleveland Lakefront State Park*, 135

NE - Cleveland, *Tower City Center Observation Deck*, 137

NE - Cortland, *Mosquito Lake State Park*, 141

NE - Geneva-on-the-Lake, *Geneva State Park*, 142

NE - Kirtland, *Holden Arboretum*, 144

NE - Lake Milton, *Lake Milton State Park*, 145

NE - Newbury, *Punderson State Park Resort*, 148

NE - Painesville, *Headlands Beach State Park*, 149

NE - Portage, *Tinker's Creek State Park*, 150

NE - Ravenna, *West Branch State Park*, 150

NE - Youngstown, *Mill Creek Park*, 151

NW- Defiance, *Independence Dam State Park*, 158

NW- Fayette, *Harrison Lake State Park*, 159

NW- Grand Rapids, *Mary Jane Thurston State Park*, 161

NW- Swanton, *Maumee State Forest*, 163

NW- Toledo, *Toledo Botanical Gardens*, 166

NW- Toledo (Oregon), *Maumee Bay State Park*, 166

NW- Van Buren, *Van Buren Lake State Park*, 167

S - Athens, *Stroud's Run State Park*, 171

S - Bainbridge, *7 Caves Nature Preserve*, 171

S - Bainbridge, *Paint Creek State Park*, 172

S - Bainbridge, *Pike Lake State Park*, 172

S - Chillicothe, *Tar Hollow State Forest*, 174

S - Chillicothe, *Great Seal State Park*, 175

OUTDOOR EXPLORING (cont.)

S - Chillicothe, *Scioto Trail State Park*, 177
S - Glouster, *Burr Oak State Park*, 178
S - Latham, *Pike State Forest*, 179
S - Laurelville, *Tar Hollow State Park*, 180
S - Logan, *Hocking Hills State Park*, 180
S - Logan, *Lake Logan State Park*, 181
S - McArthur, *Lake Hope State Park*, 184
S - Oak Hill, *Jackson Lake State Park*, 185
S - Pedro, *Dean State Forest*, 185
S - Reedsville, *Forked Run State Park*, 187
S - Rockbridge, *Hocking State Forest*, 188
S - Waverly, *Lake White State Park*, 188
S - Wellston, *Lake Alma State Park*, 189
S - West Portsmouth, *Brush Creek State Forest*, 190
S - West Portsmouth, *Shawnee State Forest*, 190
S - West Portsmouth, *Shawnee State Park*, 190
S - Zaleski, *Zaleski State Forest*, 191
SW- Amelia, *East Fork State Park*, 195
SW- Cincinnati, *Carew Tower*, 195
SW- Corwin, *Little Miami State Park*, 207
SW- Edenton, *Stonelick State Park*, 207
SW- Hillsboro, *Rocky Fork State Park*, 209
SW- Milford, *Cincinnati Nature Center*, 212
SW- Morrow, *Dude Ranch, The*, 212
SW- Waynesville, *Caesar Creek State Park*, 215
SW- Wilmington, *Cowan Lake State Park*, 216

SCIENCE

C - Columbus, *Franklin Park Conservatory And Botanical Gardens*, 7
C - Columbus, *COSI*, 10
C - Delaware, *Perkins Observatory*, 19
CW- Urbana, *Freshwater Farms Of Ohio*, 82
CW- Wapakoneta, *Armstrong Air And Space Museum*, 82
NC - Bellevue (Flat Rock), *Seneca Caverns*, 91
NC - Milan, *Veggie U Education Center*, 103
NC - Port Clinton, *Lake Erie Islands State Park*, 106
NC - Put-in-Bay, *Aquatic Visitors Center*, 107
NC - Put-in-Bay, *Butterfly House*, 107
NC - Put-in-Bay, *Stone Laboratory*, 111
NE - Akron, *National Inventors Hall Of Fame*, 123
NE - Cleveland, *Cleveland Museum Of Natural History*, 133
NE - Cleveland, *Great Lakes Science Center*, 137
NE - Cleveland, *NASA Glenn Research Visitor Center*, 140
NE - Newbury, *Westwoods Park*, 148
NW- Toledo, *COSI Toledo*, 164
SW- Cincinnati, *Krohn Conservatory*, 196
SW- Cincinnati, *Cincinnati Museum of Natural History & Science*, 199
SW- Oxford (College Corner), *Hueston Woods State Park*, 214

SPORTS

C - Columbus, *Columbus Sports*, 4
C - Columbus, *Columbus Motor Speedway*, 7
CW- Dayton, *Dayton Sports*, 66
NC - Mansfield (Lexington), *Mid Ohio Sports Car Course*, 97
NE - Akron, *Akron Aeros*, 122
NE - Cleveland, *Cleveland Sports*, 131
NW- Toledo, *Toledo Sports*, 163
SW- Cincinnati, *Cincinnati Sports*, 195

THE ARTS

C - Columbus, *Columbus Children's Theatre*, 6
C - Columbus, *Balletmet*, 8
C - Columbus, *Columbus Museum Of Art*, 9
C - Columbus, *Columbus Symphony Orchestra*, 9
C - Columbus, *Davis Discovery Center*, 10
C - Columbus (Grandview), *Glass Axis*, 14
C - Lithopolis, *Lithopolis Fine Arts/ Wagnalls Memorial Library*, 22
CE - Berlin, *Behalt*, 32
CE - Cambridge, *Living Word Passion Play*, 35
CE - Canton, *Canton Symphony Orchestra*, 37
CE - Canton, *Players Guild Theatre*, 38
CE - Steubenville, *Steubenville City Of Murals*, 55
CE - Wilmot, *Amish Door Dinner Theatre*, 57
CW- Dayton, *Dayton Philharmonic Orchestra*, 68
CW- Dayton, *Dayton Art Institute*, 69
CW- Springfield, *Clark State Performing Arts Center*, 79
CW- West Liberty, *Mad River Theater Works*, 83
NC - Mansfield, *Mansfield Symphony Orchestra*, 94
NC - Mansfield, *Richland Academy*, 94
NC - Marblehead (Lakeside), *Lakeside*, 101
NE - Akron, *Akron Art Museum*, 122
NE - Akron, *Akron Civic Theatre*, 122
NE - Akron, *Akron Symphony Orchestra*, 122
NE - Akron, *Weathervane Playhouse*, 123
NE - Cleveland, *Cleveland Center For Contemporary Art*, 132
NE - Cleveland, *Cleveland Museum Of Art*, 132
NE - Cleveland, *Cleveland Orchestra*, 134
NE - Cleveland, *Cleveland Playhouse*, 134

NE - Kent, *Kent State University Museum*, 144
NE - Youngstown, *Butler Institute Of American Art*, 152
NE - Youngstown, *Youngstown Symphony*, 152
NW- Findlay, *Mazza Collection Museum*, 159
NW- Toledo, *Toledo Symphony Orchestra*, 164
NW- Toledo, *Toledo Museum of Art*, 166
S - Bainbridge, *Magic Waters Amphitheatre*, 172
S - Chillicothe, *Pump House Center For The Arts*, 176
S - Portsmouth, *Portsmouth Murals*, 187
S - Stockport, *Barn, The*, 188
SW- Cincinnati, *Cincinnati Art Museum*, 195
SW- Cincinnati, *Taft Museum of Art*, 198
SW- Cincinnati, *Cincinnati Symphony Orchestra*, 201
SW- Cincinnati, *Covedale Center For The Performing Arts*, 203
SW- Hamilton, *Pyramid Hill Sculpture Park*, 208

TOURS

C - Columbus, *Ohio State University Museums*, 4
C - Columbus, *Graeter's Ice Cream Factory*, 12
C - Columbus, *Al's Delicious Popcorn*, 12
C - Columbus, *Anthony Thomas Candy Company*, 13
C - Columbus (Worthington), *American Whistle Corporation*, 17
C - Hebron, *Buckeye Central Scenic Railroad*, 21
CE - Alliance, *Glamorgan Castle*, 31
CE - Berlin, *Schrock's Amish Farm And Home*, 32
CE - Berlin, *Wendall August Forged Gift Tour*, 33

TOURS (cont.)

CE - Cambridge, *Boyd's Crystal Art Glass Company*, 35
CE - Cambridge, *Mosser Glass*, 36
CE - Canton, North, *Harry London Chocolate Factory*, 40
CE - Dover, *Broad Run Cheesehouse*, 44
CE - Dover, *Warther Carvings*, 45
CE - Frazeysburg, *Longaberger Museum And Factory Tour*, 47
CE - Magnolia, *Elson Flouring Mill*, 50
CE - Millersburg, *Guggisberg Cheese Factory*, 50
CE - Millersburg, *Yoder's Amish Home*, 51
CE - Steubenville, *Creegan Company Animation Factory*, 54
CE - Walnut Creek, *Coblentz Chocolate Company*, 56
CE - Winesburg, *Buggy Haus*, 57
CE - Wooster, *Hartzler Dairy*, 57
CE - Wooster, *Ohio Agricultural Research/Development Center*, 58
CE - Zanesville, *Lorena Sternwheeler*, 59
CE - Zanesville, *Mapletree Baskets*, 59
CW- Dayton, *Metroducks & Riverscape*, 68
CW- Greenville, *Bear's Mill*, 75
CW- Greenville, *KitchenAid Experience & Factory Tours*, 76
CW- West Liberty, *Mac-O-Chee And Mac-A-Cheek Castles (Piatt Castles)*, 83
NC - Bucyrus, *Cooper's Mill Apple Butter & Jelly Factory*, 92
NC - Catawba, *Miller Boat Line*, 92
NC - Mansfield, *Carousel Magic! Factory & Richland Carousel Park*, 93
NC - Mansfield, *Ohio State Reformatory*, 96
NC - Mansfield (Ashland), *Bookmasters*, 97
NC - Marblehead, *Kelley's Island Ferry Boat Lines*, 100
NC - Port Clinton, *Great Lakes Popcorn Company*, 104
NC - Port Clinton, *Jet Express*, 105

NC - Put-in-Bay, *Crystal Cave & Heineman's Grape Juice Winery*, 108
NC - Put-In-Bay, *Put-In-Bay Tour Train*, 110
NC - Sandusky, *Goodtime I*, 113
NE - Akron, *Goodyear World Of Rubber*, 124
NE - Cleveland, *Lolly The Trolley Tours*, 136
NE - Cleveland, *Good Time III*, 137
NE - Cleveland, *Nautica Queen*, 138
NE - Cleveland, *Malley's Chocolates*, 140
NE - Jefferson, *AC & J Scenic Railroad*, 143
NE - Middlefield, *Middlefield Cheese House*, 147
NE - Peninsula, *Cuyahoga Valley Scenic Railroad*, 149
NE - Youngstown, *Gorant Candies*, 153
NW- Findlay, *Dietsch Brothers*, 159
NW- Findlay, *NW Ohio RR Preservation Live Steam Train Rides*, 160
NW- Grand Rapids, *Canal Experience*, 160
NW- Maumee (Waterville), *Bluebird Passenger Train*, 162
NW- Toledo, *Sandpiper Canal Boat*, 165
S - Belpre, *Lee Middleton Original Doll Factory*, 173
S - Marietta, *Marietta Trolley*, 182
S - Marietta, *Rossi Pasta*, 183
S - Marietta, *Valley Gem Sternwheeler*, 184
S - Nelsonville, *Hocking Valley Scenic Railway*, 185
S - Portsmouth, *Mitchellace Shoestring Factory*, 186
SW- Cincinnati, *Frisch's Commissary*, 200
SW- Cincinnati, *United Dairy Farmers*, 201
SW- Cincinnati (Covington, KY), *BB Riverboats*, 204
SW- Cincinnati (Lebanon), *Cincinnati Railway Company*, 205
SW- Georgetown, *Glass Refactory*, 207
SW- Loveland, *Loveland Castle*, 210

Travel Journal & Notes:

Travel Journal & Notes:

GROUP DISCOUNTS & FUNDRAISING OPPORTUNITIES!

We're excited to introduce our books to your group! These guides for parents, grandparents, teachers and visitors are great tools to help you discover hundreds of fun places to visit. Our titles are great resources for all the wonderful places to travel either locally or across the region.

We are two parents who have researched, written and published these books. We have spent thousands of hours collecting information and *personally traveled over 250,000 miles* visiting all of the most unique places listed in our guides. The books are kid-tested and the descriptions include great hints on what kids like best!

Please consider the following Group Purchase options: *For the latest information, visit our website:* **www.KidsLoveTravel.com**

❑ **Group Discount/Fundraising** – Purchase books at the discount price of $2.95 off the suggested retail price for members/friends. <u>Minimum order is ten books.</u> You may mix titles to reach the minimum order. Greater discounts (~35%) are available for fundraisers. <u>Minimum order is thirty books.</u> Call for details.

❑ **Available for Interview/Speaking** – The authors have a treasure bag full of souvenirs from favorite places. We'd love to share ideas on planning fun trips to take children while exploring your home state. The authors are available, by appointment, *(based on availability)* at (614) 792-6451 or **michele@kidslovetravel.com**. A modest honorarium or minimum group sale purchase will apply. Call or visit our website for details.

<u>**Call us soon at (614) 792-6451 to make arrangements!**</u>
Happy Exploring!

☐ **KIDS LOVE GEORGIA** - Explore hidden islands, humbling habitats, and historic gold mines. See playful puppets, dancing dolphins, and comical kangaroos. "Watch out" for cowboys, Indians, and swamp creatures. Over 500 listings in one book about Georgia travel. 6 geographical zones, 272 pages.

☐ **KIDS LOVE ILLINOIS** – Explore places from Deere to Dinos, discover Giant Cities and the Mighty Mississippi, or cross the prairie to the Lands of Lincoln and Superman . Over 600 listings in one book about Illinois travel. 7 geographical zones, 288 pages.

☐ **KIDS LOVE INDIANA** - Discover places where you can "co-star" in a cartoon or climb a giant sand dune. Over 500 listings in one book about Indiana travel. 8 geographical zones, 280 pages.

☐ **KIDS LOVE KENTUCKY** - Discover places from Boone to Burgoo, from Caves to Corvettes, and from Lincoln to the Lands of Horses. Nearly 500 listings in one book about Kentucky travel. 5 geographic zones. 186 pages.

☐ **KIDS LOVE MICHIGAN** - Discover places where you can "race" over giant sand dunes, climb aboard a lighthouse "ship", eat at the world's largest breakfast table, or watch yummy foods being made. Almost 600 listings in one book about Michigan travel. 8 geographical zones, 264 pages.

☐ **KIDS LOVE NORTH CAROLINA** - Explore places where you can "discover" gold and pirate history, explore castles and strange houses, or learn of the "lost colony" and Mayberry. Over 500 listings in one book about travel. 6 geographical zones, 288 pages.

☐ **KIDS LOVE OHIO** - Discover places like hidden castles and caves, puppet and whistle factories, and workshops of great inventors. Over 700 listings in one book about Ohio travel. 8 geographical zones, 288 pages.

☐ **KIDS LOVE PENNSYLVANIA** - Explore places where you can "discover" oil and coal, meet Ben Franklin, or watch your favorite toys and delicious, fresh snacks being made. Over 900 listings in one book about Pennsylvania travel. 9 geographical zones, 268 pages.

☐ **KIDS LOVE TENNESSEE** – Explore places where you can "discover" pearls, ride the rails, "meet" Three Kings (of Rights, Rock & Soul). Be inspired to sing listening to the rich traditions of Country music fame. Over 500 listings in one book about Tennessee travel. 6 geographical zones, 235 pages.

☐ **KIDS LOVE VIRGINIA** – Discover where ponies swim and dolphins dance, dig into archaeology and living history, or be dazzled by world-class caverns and a natural bridge. Nearly 600 listings in one book about Virginia travel. 6 geographical zones. Includes Washington DC activities. 288 pages.

☐ **KIDS LOVE FLORIDA** - coming in late 2006. See website for details!

ORDER FORM

KIDS LOVE PUBLICATIONS

1985 Dina Court, Powell, Ohio 43065, (614) 792-6451

For the latest titles, visit our website: **www.KidsLoveTravel.com**

#	Title		Price	Total
	Kids Love Georgia		$14.95	
	Kids Love Illinois		$14.95	
	Kids Love Indiana		$14.95	
	Kids Love Kentucky		$14.95	
	Kids Love Michigan		$14.95	
	Kids Love North Carolina		$14.95	
	Kids Love Ohio		$14.95	
	Kids Love Pennsylvania		$14.95	
	Kids Love Tennessee		$14.95	
	Kids Love Virginia		$14.95	
	Kids Love Travel Memories!		$14.95	
	Combo Discount Pricing			
	Combo #2 - Any 2 Books		$26.95	
	Combo #3 - Any 3 Books		$37.95	
	Combo #4 - Any 4 Books		$47.95	

(Please make check or money order payable to: KIDS LOVE PUBLICATIONS)	*(Ohio Residents Only – Your local rate)*	**Subtotal**	
		Local/State Sales Tax	
☐ Master Card ☐ Visa	*$2.00 first book $1.00 each additional*	Shipping	
		TOTAL	

Account Number ☐☐☐☐-☐☐☐☐-☐☐☐☐-☐☐☐☐

Exp Date: ☐☐/☐☐ (Month/Year)

Cardholder's Name _____

Signature *(required)* _____

Name: _____

Address:_____

City:_____ State:_____

Zip:_____ Telephone:_____

All orders are generally shipped within 2 business days of receipt by US Mail. If you wish to have your books autographed, please include a <u>legible</u> note with the message you'd like written in your book. Your satisfaction is 100% guaranteed or simply return your order for a prompt refund. Thanks for your order. Happy Exploring!

"Where to go?, What to do?, and How much will it cost?", are all questions that they have heard throughout the years from friends and family. These questions became the inspiration that motivated them to research, write and publish the "Kids Love" travel series.

This adventure of writing and publishing family travel books has taken them on a journey of experiences that they never could have imagined. They have appeared as guests on hundreds of radio and television shows, had featured articles in statewide newspapers and magazines, spoken to thousands of people at schools and conventions, and write monthly columns in many publications talking about "family friendly" places to travel.

George Zavatsky and Michele (Darrall) Zavatsky were raised in the Midwest and have lived in many different cities. They currently reside in a suburb of Columbus, Ohio. They feel very blessed to be able to create their own career that allows them to research, write and publish a series of best-selling kids' travel books. Besides the wonderful adventure of marriage, they place great importance on being loving parents to Jenny & Daniel.